PEOPLES OF WASHINGTON

PEOPLES OF WASHINGTON

Perspectives on Cultural Diversity

Edited by Sid White and S. E. Solberg

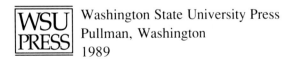
Washington State University Press
Pullman, Washington
1989

This work was written, prepared, and published with support and assistance from the 1989 Washington Centennial Commission

Copyright 1989 by Washington State University Press, Pullman, Washington 99164-5910

Peoples of Washington was published with support from The Evergreen State College
Book design by Terri Nakamura

99 98 97 96 95 94 93 92 91 90 1 2 3 4 5 6 7 8 9 10

Library of Congress Cataloging-in-Publication Data
Peoples of Washington : perspectives on cultural diversity / edited by Sid White and S.E. Solberg
p. cm.
Includes bibliographical references
ISBN 0-87422-067-X : $24.95. — ISBN 0-87422-062-9 (pbk.) : $14.95
      1. Ethnology—Washington (State) 2. Washington (State)—History. 3. Washington (State)—
Biography. 4. Ethnology–Washington (State)–Bibliography. I. White, Sid, 1924- . II. Solberg, S. E.
(Sammy Edward), 1930- .
F900.A1P46 1989
979.7—dc20   98-22556
                 CIP

Cover photograph: Mill workers, Bay City Lumber Company, South Aberdeen, circa 1919.
Courtesy of Bronco's Liberty Tavern Historical Museum.

Photograph facing title page: Chehalis Tribe basketmaker Hazel Pete with daughter Yvonne and grandaughter Billie, Chehalis, 1982. Photo by Eduardo Calderón.

CONTENTS

LIST OF ILLUSTRATIONS

ACKNOWLEDGMENTS

This book is a major outcome of *Peoples of Washington,* a comprehensive research, exhibition and publication project that was carried out on the occasion of the 1989 Washington State Centennial. Starting in January of 1988, a multicultural team of scholars and museum professionals completed research on Washington State ethnic community histories and cultures, shared information, and provided consultation in the planning and development of the Peoples of Washington touring exhibition and *A Guide to Ethnic Washington,* an accompanying interpretive brochure. The authors of this book were among the consultants, from all parts of the state, whose experience and expertise were essential in developing a project of this magnitude. Other consultants for the *Peoples of Washington* project were: *Vivian Adams*, former Curator, Yakima Nation Cultural Center, *Doug Chin*, Historian, Seattle Chinese Community, *Dorothy Cordova*, Director, Demonstration Project for Asian Americans, *Marianne Forssblad*, Director, Nordic Heritage Museum, *Dr. Erasmo Gamboa*, Director, Chicano Studies, University of Washington, *Angela Torres-Henrick*, Audience Relations Coordinator, Celebrate the Differences, KING-TV, *Bettie Sing Luke*, Program Director, Project Reach, Reach Center, *Dr. Jens Lund*, Folklorist, Washington State Folklife Council, *David L. Nicandri*, Director, Washington State Historical Society, *Maria Petrish*, Director, Vela Luka Croatian Dancers, Anacortes, *Charles Sigo*, Tribal Curator, Suquamish Museum, *Dr. Hulme Siwundhla*, Black Studies, University of Washington, *Sheryl K. Stiefel*, Chief Curator, Museum of History and Industry, and *Dr. Stephen H. Sumida*, Department of Comparative American Cultures and Department of English, Washington State University.

Drawing on this rich source of information, the authors of *Peoples of Washington: Perspectives on Cultural Diversity* carried out further extensive research as they wrote their essays, with additional information provided by: Gordon Assink, Doris Balholm, Sharon Dunn, Kenneth M. Gorshkow, Allen Hagen, Ellen S. Hagen, May Hill, Richard D. Johnson, Kara Kondo, Diane Lloyd, Robert Lloyd, Julie Lust, Ben Mulder, Maria Pascualy, Erma Hagen Schotten, Dagny Shervheim, Sharon Storment, and Julie Tammivaara. We wish to thank the individuals who carefully read manuscripts and offered critique that was of much benefit to the authors and editors. Manuscript readers included: Marilyn Benz, David

Buerge, Ricardo Castillo-Griswold, Ken Dolbeare, Russell Endo, Karen Kamara Gose, Michael Gose, Pila Laronal, Gary Okihiro, David Stratton, and Mayumi Tsutakawa.

Permission to use the photographs in this book came from many public and private collections as well from leading professional photographers. These sources are credited throughout the book. Special recognition must be made to Rachel Anderson who performed many important roles at all stages of the project. Ms. Anderson served as project administrative assistant while also maintaining archival records and assisting in bibliographic research.

Appreciation is expressed to the various sources of funding support for the *Peoples of Washington* project and for this book. Primary funding for the first phase of the *Peoples* project was from the 1989 Washington Centennial Commission as a Project of Statewide Significance. Additional support was provided by the Washington Commission for the Humanities and Great American Bank. The *Peoples* project was sponsored by The Evergreen State College in cooperation with the Washington State Folklife Council, the Ethnic Heritage Council of the Pacific Northwest and the Washington Museum Association with Sid White serving as project director and Pat Matheny-White as research coordinator.

Finally, the authors and editors wish to express their appreciation to the Ethnic Heritage Committee of the 1989 Washington Centennial Commission and to the 1989 Washington Centennial Commission itself for underwriting the publication of *Peoples of Washington: Perspectives on Cultural Diversity.*

Sid White
S. E. Solberg

Our roots reach all over the world

Washington is connected to the rest of the world through its ethnically diverse peoples. For the first time a general question on ancestry (ethnicity) was included in the 1980 U.S. Census. Approximately 85% of Washington residents responded to this open-ended question by identifying at least one ancestral relationship, "nationality group, lineage, or country in which they or their parents or their ancestors were born before coming to the United States." *

*Census of Population (1980). *Ancestry of the Population By State: 1980. Supplementary Report.* Washington, D. C.: U. S. Dept. of Commerce, Bureau of the Census, 1983.

The U.S. Census Bureau acknowledges that figures reported in the 1980 census are not entirely accurate. It is anticipated that significantly higher numbers will be reported, especially for Asians and Hispanos, in the 1990 census.

According to the 1980 U. S. Census the following numbers of
Washingtonians identified their ancestral roots to five
geographical areas of the world: Africa and the Middle East
(113,000), Asia and the Pacific Islands (124,000), Europe
(5,013,000), Mexico and Latin America (112,000)and North
America (150,000).

INTRODUCTION

Sid White

This is a first effort at presenting a composite portrait of the culturally diverse peoples of Washington. Written, of necessity, from varying perspectives, it provides historical and contemporary views of Washington communities with origins in North America, Europe, Africa and the Middle East, Asia and the Pacific Islands, and Mexico and other parts of Latin America .

The authors of *Peoples of Washington* are well qualified to tell the stories of these culturally diverse peoples, many of whom have been in our state for generations. Each writer has carried out extensive research and has already published works dealing with one or more of Washington's ethnic groups. Because they are members of the communities about which they write, the authors are able to share perspectives and insights based on personal experience; their voices add fuller dimension to this undertaking.

The perspective I bring as editor is a reflection of my own identity as a person from a multicultural background who, since childhood, has internalized lifeways from a variety of sources. My parents were Rumanian-Jewish immigrants, proud of their dual heritage, and proud to be Americans. Traditional values and practices, and the enjoyment of food and music associated with three distinct cultures, were an integral part of life in our home. My family's five-year residence in Russia, starting when I was five years old, added still another facet to my multiple identity. These childhood experiences prepared me for further appreciation and study of different cultures as I lived, for extended periods of time, in India, Italy, and in different regions of the United States.

This personal fascination with cultural diversity has guided my professional work. During the past ten years I developed a number of exhibition and publication projects featuring regional artists whose works present a broad spectrum of cultural expression. These projects led to close association with artists, scholars, and leaders from a number of ethnic communities. Many are now close friends and mentors, teaching me about their communities and cultures. It was from these associations that *Peoples of Washington* emerged as I learned to shift my focus from art and culture to people and culture.

Four generations, baking for Christmas.
Seattle, 1981.
Photo by Scotty Sapiro.
Published in *Nordic Heritage Northwest*.

Wherever we look around the world, our country, or our state, we see the magnitude and complexity of human inventiveness. We encounter dramatic cultural variations in world views, lifeways, language, religion, customs, and artistic expression. When we get beyond superficial encounters with peoples who are different from us, we are able to see the incredible richness and diversity that is found *within* cultures.

We must exercise care, however, when using labels to identify culturally distinctive communities. People feel invisible, alienated, and resentful when identities they affirm are denied or ignored. Terms like "Hispanic," as applied by governmental bureaucracies, deny and obscure the varying histories and distinctiveness of Mexican and other Latin American communities. In the 1980s, many Croatian, Serbian, and Slovenian Americans are offended when they are labeled Yugoslavians, just as their ancestors were offended when, as immigrants, they were called Austro-Hungarians. These terms deny uniqueness and obscure individual and collective identity. The diversity found in Washington's Asian and Pacific Island communities increases as new peoples arrive. Differences in language and culture distinguish Washington's Ashkenazi and Sephardic Jewish communities. Washington's First Peoples affirm specific identities, seeing their tribes as sovereign nations, struggling to have treaty agreements upheld. There are distinctions to be made between Empire Germans who, over generations, have become assimilated, and Germans from Russia, who have come more recently and continue to maintain traditional lifeways. Washington's peoples of African descent describe themselves in terms of national origin, whether they are American or foreign-born. The need to recognize differences within communities is constant.

Reference to ethnicity in this book implies an identity born within communities, a shared experience of people who are proud of, and who affirm their cultural uniqueness. Our use of the phrase "ethnic community" is not intended to deny variation and individuality; neither is it intended to overlook differences in the nature and degree of a shared identity within a community. Recently-arrived immigrants often form more tightly knit communities than residents of other, older communities who tend to maintain or affirm identities more symbolic in character.

This diversity served as a conceptual framework for the many individuals who contributed directly and indirectly to this book. A team of twenty consulting scholars, associated with ethnic communities across the state, shared the results of their research and collaborated in the development of information and a photographic archive used as a primary resource in creating *Peoples of Washington* and in producing a traveling exhibition by the same name.

Drawing on their own expertise, and the consultant resources available to them, the authors of *Peoples of Washington* have presented stories that help us understand differences and commonalities among Washington's peoples. For the first time, they have placed these stories into a single framework organized around themes of migration, settlement, struggle, accomplishment, and contribution. Each community story is one of struggle and of persistence.

The stories of struggle are seen in discrimination and oppression—the forces of assimilation and exclusion—that have been directed against peoples who are racially or culturally different. This dimension of our national and state history centers on efforts by government, schools, and the dominant society to eliminate these cultural differences. Many exclusionary laws were aimed at preventing racially different people from owning property or enjoying the rights and benefits of citizenship. The pressure exerted on Native Americans and foreign peoples to assimilate was an expression of the melting pot ideology that forced many to deny their cultural heritage. For example, in 1917 Theodore Roosevelt declared that "There is no room for hyphenated Americanism." This assertion was made in the atmosphere of World War I, a time when patriotism and anti-foreign sentiment prevailed. Rooted in ethnocentrism and racism, this attitude has always been part of the social landscape in America, including the state of Washington.

The stories of persistence tell of the survival of ethnic communities continuing to give social, cultural, and spiritual strength to their members. Despite social and political forces that threatened extinction, many Washington indigenous and immigrant communities have flourished as a focus of identity, pride, and hope. Churches, synagogues, mosques, temples, fraternal organizations, and benevolent societies, continue to offer fellowship and assistance to newcomers and to long-time members of these communities. They also provide the means for cultural continuity between old and new ways, elders and youth.

In the 1980s, we feel the growing impact of many thriving cultural programs that serve audiences within and outside community based museums, cultural centers, historical societies, publications, festivals, exhibits, and performances. The emerging cultural consciousness these programs represent is of great significance as we look to Washington's future. There has also been a growing interest in documenting and sharing Washington's ethnic community histories. Most of this work has been done by historians who have based much of their research on oral histories and other direct sources, including photographs and family, community, and government documents. There is a sense of urgency surrounding this work because elders, who are a primary source of information, are passing away and taking community memories to the grave. Much of the written record documenting recent and contemporary life, which includes the concerns and aspirations of communities, is found in the pages of ethnic newspapers including *Northwest Ethnic News*, published by the Ethnic Heritage Council of the Pacific Northwest, the *International Examiner*, Seattle's and King County's journal of Asian communities, and *La Voz: The News Magazine of the Concilio for the Spanish-Speaking*.

A major outcome of the *Peoples of Washington* project was the development of an archive and database of information on Washington ethnic community histories and cultures. Selections were made from this resource in preparing the extensive bibliography that concludes this book. Containing over four hundred entries, the bibliography testifies to the amount of information that is available to the public. It also reveals that a few communities are well documented, while little has been written about many others.

According to the 1980 federal census records, there were over one hundred ethnic communities in Washington. By 1990 the number will increase significantly. At least twelve books, most published on the occasion of the America's bicentennial, are devoted to specific Washington ethnic community histories. *Peoples of Washington* draws on these and other sources of information; it also serves as a resource for further research. Yet to be written is a comprehensive history of Washington giving careful attention to the contributions made by *all* its people to the social, economic, political, and cultural development of the state.

Everything that has been done, and is yet to be done, to develop a fuller historical record is of special importance to teachers and students in Washington's schools, colleges, and universities; this fuller historical record is necessary for the production of curriculum materials and textbooks that accurately reflect long-ignored social and cultural realities.

The Epilogue in *Peoples of Washington* reminds us that the dream of America as a land of freedom and opportunity still lives in the minds of peoples who continue to come to our state. Their motivation is the same as that possessed by earlier immigrants. We are reminded further that immigrants *continue* to bring their cultures with them as their most prized possession, and that loyalty to their "roots" in no way contradicts commitment to their new homeland. The presence of newly arrived peoples in our midst invites us to reflect on the importance of Washington's culturally diverse past, present, and future, as well as the lessons we can learn from it.

We all look at our state, its history, and its peoples, from perspectives formed by our own life experiences—our family backgrounds, where we came from, where we live, where we work, and who we know as friends and associates. These are the vantage points from which we define our own identities and those of others. These are also the sources of perceptions that may be limited or distorted. *Peoples of Washington: Perspectives on Cultural Diversity* aims at helping us to develop a broader and richer view of our state and its peoples.

The first peoples have been here since time immemorial

Over thousands of years the first inhabitants of this region lived in harmony with nature, enjoying a rich cultural and spiritual life. From their close relationship to the land arose distinctive plateau, inland water, and coastal cultures. European intervention greatly disrupted the first peoples' traditional ways of life. With the establishment of permanent white settlements, smallpox and other diseases decimated their numbers; access to fishing, hunting, and gathering sites was reduced. Treaties forced Indian peoples onto reservations and created lasting problems. Despite their struggles, Washington's Native Americans have maintained their cultures and survived the challenges of this century.

Father and son from the
Yallup family.
Lower Yakima Valley, circa
the early 1900s
Kamiakin Research Institute,
Yakima Nation Museum

WASHINGTON'S NATIVE AMERICAN COMMUNITIES

Clifford E. Trafzer

Flying across Washington for the first time more than a decade ago, I surveyed the wonderful landscape below. Through the window of a small, Cascade Airlines commuter plane that had just left Seattle-Tacoma International Airport, I first marveled at the carpet of green that stretched off in all directions below me. Then the outlines of jagged peaks appeared through thick clouds as we flew east toward the Cascades. Over the mountains we continued, and through the now-broken clouds, I viewed for the first time the vast expanse of the Great Columbia Plain. The contrast between the two Washingtons was dramatic; it reminded me of my home in Arizona and the great diversity between its mountains and deserts. I felt sure that, like Arizona, Washington's environments had given rise to specific Indian cultures that had for generations related to the world each in its own way. This proved to be true, and like the Indians I had known all my life, the Native Americans of Washington had a deep, abiding love for the earth, its plants, and its animals. Significantly, however, Washington's first people, from both the interior and coast, shared a common reverence for and reliance on salmon, roots, berries, and game.

In 1977 I had accepted a position as an assistant professor of Native American Studies and History at Washington State University. When I arrived in the heart of the Palouse Country, I began a research project on the history of the Palouse Indians. I learned quickly that it would be a difficult task to separate the various tribes, because for generations Indians had exhibited a high degree of informal unity and cooperation. Families, bands, and tribes were interrelated by blood, environment, culture, and language. Although Indians in the interior of the region we now call the Pacific Northwest spoke many dialects, two major languages were found on the Plateau, and many knew and spoke both Sahaptin and Interior Salish. It seemed to me that Indians were related by these factors, but most importantly, by their ties to the land and by their reverence for the bounty of the earth. (Trafzer and Scheuerman, 1986, xii-xv, 1-2)

As an "urban Indian," living in Pullman, I was the outsider from the Southwest, and my Indian students from Washington, Idaho, and Oregon often reminded me of the fact. Urban Indians who belonged to tribes outside the state resided in Spokane, Seattle, Tacoma, Yakima, Walla Walla, Brewster, and many other towns. Like them, I had to earn the acceptance of Washington's Indians. As Wendell Jim, an Indian educator, once put it: "You have to remember that you're from down South. Northwestern Indians are different from Navajos, Apaches, Pimas and Pueblos. You've got to learn about us, because our ways are different." Wendell was right. I accepted the challenge and noted many other urban Indians following Wendell's advice. They were learning more about Washington's Indians by attending area ceremonies and pow wows; they were learning by joining Title IV Indian Education Programs; they were learning by attending meetings held by Indian organizations, health centers, and tribes.

Like other urban Indians, I learned that Washington's first people have much to teach everyone who resides in the state. One of the best ways to learn is to listen to the elders; this is the old Indian way—the traditional manner of Indian education. Long before the arrival of white explorers, Indians shared their stories while gathered around fires in cedar bark houses, mat covered lodges, or in buffalo-skin tipis. They shared their history, religion, morals, and culture by means of a sophisticated oral tradition. Grandmothers and grandfathers told their tales, instructing children to learn their lessons well. In this fashion, Washington's Indians preserved the past, telling about the first days after creation when the animal people ruled the earth and all things—animate and inanimate—communicated with one another.

The story of the Chinook Wind teaches us about the endurance of Washington's Indian people. According to an old Wishram storyteller, there was a time when the Wolf, Salmon, and the Arctic Wind People were very powerful. These ancient ones could not agree whether to allow the warm winds off the ocean to continue coming inland or to allow the cold winter winds to continue to blow indefinitely. The Salmon People favored the warm winds of spring that came up the rivers with them each year during spawning time. The Arctic Wind, Wolf and Coyote People favored perpetual winter. The Animal People divided over the question and both sides prepared for war.

The five Arctic Wind Brothers went to the five Wolf Brothers with a plan to challenge Salmon Chief to a wrestling match. Whoever would win the contest would win the war and could have his way about the wind. "When we defeat Salmon Chief," said one of the Arctic Wind Brothers, "we will spread snow, ice and cold throughout this land." The Wolf Brothers liked the idea and said that they would kill all the Salmon People. The Arctic Wind Brothers challenged Salmon Chief to a wrestling match, and the Chief reluctantly accepted. They met on the frozen floor of the Columbia River, where Salmon Chief defeated three of the Arctic Wind Brothers but lost to the fourth. The Arctic Wind Brother threw Salmon Chief onto the ice and killed him.

In a killing frenzy, the allies of the Wolf and Arctic Wind Brothers began destroying the Salmon People and smashing every egg that came forth from the wife of Salmon Chief. The Wolf Brothers popped every salmon egg, except one that became wedged in the crack of a flat rock. Try as they might, they could not get that egg. Meanwhile the weather turned so cold that old Coyote began to wish he had sided with Salmon Chief. Dark, black clouds enveloped the Northwest, and freezing rain flooded the earth. The Creator had seen the wrestling match and had sent the rain to save the last egg of Salmon Chief's wife. For five sacred days it rained, nourishing that egg until it became a tiny salmon. The newborn entered the river and allowed the current to carry it to the Pacific.

The young salmon met his father's mother, who took care of him, nurtured him, and encouraged him to become strong. Grandmother Salmon told the boy about his parents and how they had died. The young boy vowed to "defeat the Arctic Wind Brothers and win back the power they took from the Salmon People." The boy grew strong enough to challenge the Arctic Wind Brothers to another wrestling match. Grandmother was so proud of him she gave him the name Young Chinook Wind. She said he would carry with him the warmth of the ocean's current as he traveled east up the Columbia River. Young Chinook Wind wrestled the Arctic Wind Brothers, defeating all five of them. Tired of perpetual winter, Coyote and the Animal People cheered Young Chinook Wind to victory. The weak sister of the Arctic Wind Brothers escaped, promising to return now and then to blanket the region with snow, cold, and ice; but her brothers had lost their hold on the Northwest. The Wolf Brothers raced away into the Cascade Mountains, and the Animal People proclaimed the warm wind should be named after Chinook Salmon. This then is how the warm, powerful wind got its name[1] (McWhorter, 1918).

Like the Chinook Wind, Indian people have always been a part of what is today the state of Washington. They were the first, and they believe the Creator placed them on the land. Unlike twentieth-century scholars who argue that Native American ancestors migrated from Asia, Indian people maintain they are of the earth—placed in a beautiful land by divine Providence. The Creator placed Indian men, women, and children on the earth to share in nature's bounty. As Chief Owhi of the Yakimas stated, "God looked one way then the other and named our lands for us to take care of." The Creator did not give Indians title to the land like so much property. Rather, Indian people of Washington were instructed to be caretakers of the earth. Thus, "their land was their religion, and their religion was the land." Neither Coastal nor Plateau Indians separate spiritual belief from their intimate ties to the natural world. Religion was and is the heart of Washington's Native American communities. (Walla Walla Council Proceedings, McWhorter, 520A)

Spiritual beliefs among Washington's Indians are threads that bind a wonderful patchwork of people together. This is particularly true among the peoples of the Puget Sound. The Duwamish, Suquamish, Skokomish, Snoqualmie, Snohomish, Nisqually, Muckleshoot, Puyallup and others share common ideas about the sacred. In a poetic manner, Chief Sealth (Seattle) once explained: "Every part of this soil is sacred in the estimation of my people. Every hillside, every valley, every plain and grove, has been hallowed by some sad or happy event in the days long vanished . . . the very dust upon which you now stand responds more lovingly to their footsteps than to yours, because it is rich with the dust of our ancestors and our bare feet are conscious of the sympathetic touch." Such feelings transcend time, and the Indians of Washington still cling to their love of the earth, plants and animals. (American Friends, 1970, 31)

Indians had, and continue to have, a living faith, one centered on more than ceremony, ritual, or love of nature. Plants and animals first inhabited earth, and in stories like that of Chinook Wind, Coastal Indians maintain an oral record of that time in their history. Indian people today have direct links with a time when everything was alive with emotion, thought, and being. According to many Indians from the coast and Puget Sound, there came a time when The Changer brought form and order to an ever-changing environment. The Changer ordered the final composition of the many varieties of fish, mammals, amphibians, trees, and plants. The Changer directed the exact formation of the mountains, rivers, inlets, lakes, sounds, and springs. Each of these took its final form, but retained its own spirit, ability, and intelligence. The last to take shape were humans, and The Changer permitted them to take their place on this earth. Humans had the most to learn, and the Indians believe that only by knowing and understanding the earth can they truly learn, grow, and develop. This is a central point of life for Indians: to learn an appreciation of earth. According to the elders, all humans should set this as one of life's goals. (Suquamish Museum, 1985, 30)

Andrew George, a Plateau Indian of Palouse and Nez Perce descent, once said that our nation's colleges and universities are filled with scientists who claim to understand plants and animals. Zoologists, botanists, and other scholars regularly write, publish, and lecture on plants and animals. They guide graduate students through research projects, producing experts with master's and doctor's degrees. "And yet," Andrew asserted, "they usually do not know the plants and animals." The scholars, he claims, rarely "talk to the plants and animals, and even if they do, they fail to listen. For the plants and animals speak, and I have heard what they say." Andrew George is an Indian doctor and spiritual holy man who lives with his daughter on the Yakima Reservation. He is over ninety years old, born at the village of Palus on the Snake River. He has spent his life ministering to others, and he well understands the power of religion in the lives of Washington's Indians. (George, 1980)

When Andrew was a small boy, a significant event occurred at the village of Palus. The year was 1905 and government agents escorted by a military detachment forced Andrew and his family to leave their ancient home on the Snake River. They were ordered to gather their belongings and board a steamboat bound for Lewiston, Idaho. Soldiers marched them to Lapwai, and an agent of the Bureau of Indian Affairs enrolled them there as Nez Perces. Since the government did not recognize their tribe, these Palouses were forced to live on the Nez Perce reservation. The government considered Andrew's home at Standing Rock to be part of the Public Domain, and hence off limits to Indians but open to white settlement (George, 1980). In similar fashion, government agents forced a Palouse woman, Mary Jim, and her children to leave their ancestral home at Tasawicks on the Snake River. As Mary tells it, "the Law came and got us, made us move from our home and river, made us go to this reservation." Many times Mary has related the story of her forced removal from her family's Indian homestead. Each time the story is the same, and each time she breaks down and cries.

Indians throughout Washington lost their land because government policies or economic expediency forced tribes, bands, and families to move from the earth that held the bones of their loved ones. From the 1840s to the present, Indians lost thousands of acres of land. They lament this loss, but not because they have been deprived of a piece of real estate or an investment. They grieve because they have lost a part of themselves and their people. They have lost a part of their culture, heritage, livelihood, and sense of place. They have lost elements of their religion. The United States government—that undefined entity called The Law—forced Washington's Indians to surrender their land, even in this century. Indeed, the

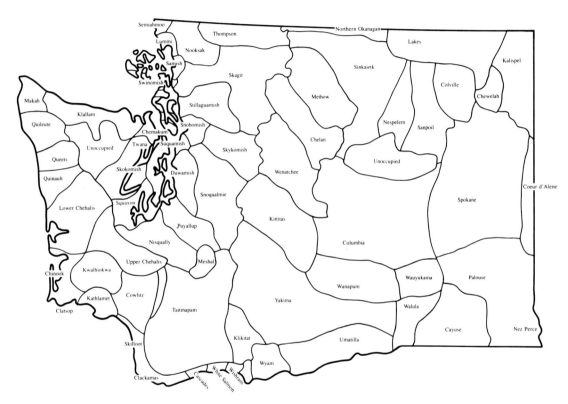

Indian Tribes in what is now known as the State of Washington, circa 1770-1820.

Source: *Historical Atlas of Washington* by James W. Scott and Roland L. DeLorme
University of Oklahoma Press, 1988.

"Law" forced Mary's removal in the 1960s, and the "Law" has never allowed her to return to live next to the beautiful waters that she said "flowed like music to my ears." (George, 1977; 1979; 1980)

The first whites came into the region in the early nineteenth century and were not greatly interested in acquiring Indian lands, removing Indians to designated areas, or making them civilized members of white society. The first whites were traders—generally men intent on earning money for themselves and their companies. But these white men significantly changed Indian society by introducing manufactured goods, deadly diseases, and economies that divorced them from the natural world. White traders had guns, powder, and lead—powerful items desired by Native Americans. The traders offered them pots, pans, tomahawks, knives, fish hooks, and a host of other material items made of metal. In exchange, Indians had to provide the traders with furs, and this changed the way in which Indians saw their environment. Before the coming of whites, Indians had lived with the animals as brothers. After the arrival of whites, some joined in the slaughter of fur-bearing animals in order to acquire the material items offered by traders. Plateau Indians bartered their quality horses for mass-produced trade goods. On the Plateau and Coast, Indian life changed as a result of the trade, and many people became dependent upon whites for trade items.[2]

The issue whether or not to engage in the trade with whites caused factions to develop within tribes and bands. This was particularly true after the first decade of the nineteenth century when the North West Company of Canada, the Hudson's Bay Company of Great Britain, and John Jacob Astor's American Fur Company established trading posts—factories as they were then known, but none of these groups came to the area to wrest the lands from the Indians. They were not interested in making over Indians, creating a "civilized" race in the image of whites. But they were soon followed by those who would uplift and enlighten their red brothers: Christian missionaries—Protestant and Catholic—moved into the region in the 1830s and 1840s to proselytize Indian people. Most famous were the Protestants, Marcus and Narcissa Whitman and Elkanah and Mary Walker, and Catholics, Pierre De Smet. Some Indians gravitated toward Christianity, while others rejected the new religion. Certainly the Catholic fathers had greater success converting Indians, but they added to the schisms within the Indian communities. Pro-and anti-Christian and pro-and anti-Catholic factions emerged to plague the Indians.[3]

In the 1840s, traders, missionaries, and immigrants came into the region by way of the Oregon Trail, bringing their diseases with them to Washington. In some places along the way, among the Blackfeet for instance, whites purposely infested tribes with smallpox. Usually, however, the transmission of disease was unintentional. Yet epidemics killed more Indians than did open warfare. Unlike whites, who had for generations faced the effects of smallpox, chicken pox, influenza, measles, mumps, and numerous other infectious diseases, Indians had never been exposed to them, and thus had developed no natural immunities.

The Indians of the Coast and Puget Sound were particularly devastated by diseases as a result of contact with Pacific traders. Although some diseases traveled up the Columbia River, the Plateau people were not significantly affected until they were struck by a measles epidemic in 1847. The Yakimas, Palouses, Walla Wallas, Umatillas, Wanapums, Cayuses, and others suffered severely from the measles. The Cayuses suffered in silence until November 29, 1847, when a few warriors who could contain themselves no longer killed Marcus and Narcissa Whitman and twelve others who they blamed for the epidemic. (Cook, 306-26; Scott, 1928, 99-107; McWhorter, 149 D, H, M, 520A; Ruby and Brown, 1972: Trafzer and Scheuerman, 1986)

The Whitman killings and the subsequent Cayuse Indian War focused attention on the Pacific Northwest. After successfully negotiating an agreement with Great Britain over the Oregon Country boundary in 1846, the United States government was anxious to establish undisputed control in the region south of the forty-ninth parallel. To that end, the government divided the region into the territories of Washington and Oregon in 1853. When the United States began to establish political, economic, and military control of Washington Territory, it also transplanted its Indian policy to the new territory. This included the liquidation of Indian title to the land and the removal of native people to designated areas, known as reservations, where they would be governed by the Bureau of Indian Affairs.

American Indian policy came to Washington Territory in 1853 and was not welcomed by Indians. At first, rumors circulated among the Coastal and Plateau peoples that they were all to be removed to the Arctic; Indians thus received the first government agents with a good deal of uncertainty and trepidation. The various bills and treaties dealing with Indians enacted into laws by Congress and signed by U. S. presidents were not policies established by Washington Indians. Indians did not ask for treaties, removal, or reservations. They did not ask to be ruled by the Bureau of Indian Affairs nor did they wish to be governed by laws on paper enacted by the House and Senate of the United States Congress. They did not ask for a unique trust relationship with the United States that would set them apart constitutionally from all other Americans. They did not ask to be acculturated, assimilated, or civilized. These were all things forced on

Treaty protest.
Olympia, 1864
Suquamish Museum

them by the treaty process, and like it or not, Indians had to accept the dictates of Isaac I. Stevens, Washington's first territorial governor and Superintendent of Indian Affairs. Indeed, by the 1850s Indians had few options. They could stand and fight or try to accommodate the newcomers. (Trafzer, 1986; Suquamish Museum, 1985, 33-34)

Between Christmas Day, 1854 and January 26, 1855, Stevens met with the Indians of the Puget Sound at Medicine Creek, Point Elliott and Point No Point. During each of the councils, the governor pressed home the points of American Indian policy. The tribes were to surrender their lands to the United States for a specified sum, remove themselves to reservations, and agree to be ruled by the Bureau of Indian Affairs. Further, Governor Stevens asked them to surrender their sovereignty, abstain from using alcohol, and end Indian slavery. In return, Indians secured for themselves the right to fish, hunt, gather, and graze horses on and off their reservations. This action was taken so that the government did not have to feed their new "charges." As an added benefit, the United States promised to educate and provide quality health care to Indians in Washington Territory.

Stevens explained these and other treaty elements, but Indian leaders attending the three councils generally were not enthusiastic about the proposals. In part, misunderstandings arose because the governor had proceedings of the treaty sessions translated for the various attendees in the Northwest Coast trade dialect, commonly called "Chinook Jargon," rather than in the individual languages of the tribes. According to Owen Bush, a pioneer from Olympia who knew the Indians, "it was utterly impossible to explain the treaties." When Chief Leschi of the Nisquallies learned what Stevens proposed, he stood up and announced he would fight rather than submit. He then tore up a copy of the treaty and bolted from the council grounds. Several other headmen also refused to sign and left with Leschi. Mysteriously, Leschi's name, along with that of his brother, appears on the Medicine Creek Treaty. Indians and non-Indians alike claim that Stevens forged Leschi's mark on the document that sent several tribes to reservations.

Between January and March, 1855, Stevens met with numerous coastal groups; the Makahs, Hoh, Clallam, Queets, Quinault, Satsops, Chehalis, Chinook, Cowlitz and others. They listened to proposals similar to those made to the Indians of Puget Sound. Ultimately, some agreed to the Neah Bay and Olympia Treaties, but confusion soon developed over what the words in the documents really meant. Certainly not all Indians on the Olympic Peninsula or the coast understood them. Indeed, not all the coastal people wanted formal agreements with the United States, nor did they want to be removed to reservations. Yet, a sufficient number of leaders signed treaties, thus binding Washington's Indians to agreements with the United States. When ratified by the Senate and signed by the President, these documents became the supreme law of the land in relation to Washington's Coastal Indians. (Trafzer, 1986; Richards, 1979; Lane, 1976; Lane and Lane, 1977; Suquamish Museum, 1985, 36-37)

When Stevens finished dealing with the Indians of the Coast and Puget Sound, he turned his attention to the Plateau. By the time Stevens's secretary, James Doty, arrived in Yakima Country, the Indians already knew about the treaty councils west of the Cascade Mountains. Chief Leschi of the Nisquallies was a cousin of Chief Kamiakin of the Yakimas. When Doty visited Kamiakin's home on Ahtanum Creek to ask his followers to attend an upcoming treaty council at Walla Walla, the chief simply packed up and moved. At first he refused to meet Doty, although Chiefs Owhi and Teias—Kamiakin's own uncles—met the secretary. With some reluctance, even Kamiakin conferred with Doty and agreed to meet Stevens in the Walla Walla Valley in May 1855. Although Kamiakin was cordial to Doty, the chief refused to take tobacco from the secretary, saying "that he had never accepted from the Americans the value of a grain of wheat without paying for it." Kamiakin feared the Americans would then claim that they had paid the chief for selling his land, something the leader would not do.

In May 1855 approximately ten thousand Plateau Indians met with Stevens at the Walla Walla Council, but most of them were Sahaptin-speaking people from the lower half of the old Oregon Country rather than the Salish-speaking Indians from the northern reaches that were within Washington Territory. Nonetheless, Indian positions stated at the Walla Walla Council represented the views of Indians in Washington. The land was sacred, given to the Indian people by the Creator. It could no more be sold than the air or the sky, and this point of view was presented time and again. Chief Stickus stated that Indians thought about the earth as if it was their own Mother. "If your mothers were here in this country who gave you birth, suckled you and while you were sucking some person came and took your mother and left you alone and sold your mother, how would you feel then?"

Chief Owhi pointed out that the earth was the parent and the Creator, elder brother of all mankind. According to the Yakima chief, the Creator looked one way and then the other, naming the Columbia Plateau for the Indian people. Thus, the land belonged to the Creator who had designated to certain tribes and bands which lands they could live on. By telling the Indians to move off their lands and sell them, the whites were asking them to commit a great sin. "Shall I steal this land and sell it? Shall I give the lands that are part of my body. . . .?" Owhi could not, at least at first. Few of the Indians were anxious to sign the three treaties made at Walla Walla. But as they talked among themselves in the tipis, many leaders decided that it would be prudent to sign the agreements. In fact, they had little choice: Governor Stevens would have had his treaties even if a number of the chiefs had bolted the council. At the conclusion of the Walla Walla conference, the government established the Yakima, Umatilla, and Nez Perce Reservations. Yet the major harvest of the treaty councils on the Coast, Plateau, and in the Puget Sound was war. (Walla Walla Council Proceedings; Ruby and Brown, 1972; Trafzer and Scheuerman, 1986; Richards, 1979; Josephy, 1965; Ruby and Brown, 1982; Brown, 1961; Kowrach,)

When Governor Stevens addressed the Indians at Walla Walla, he assured them that it would take years before the United States Senate ratified the treaties. Until then, the governor said, Indians could live peacefully on their own land. Yet, even before Stevens left the area to continue his whirlwind treaty tour into Montana, he wrote dispatches to the major newspapers on the West Coast announcing that eastern Washington was open for white settlement.

Worse still, white miners discovered gold near what is now the town of Colville in northeast Washington, which resulted in a gold-rush stampede across eastern Washington Indian lands. When miners were killed for raping and murdering Indians, Yakima Agent Andrew Jackson Bolon, a man disliked by whites and Indians alike, interceded and was himself murdered by a group of Plateau people. His death was the immediate cause of the Yakima War of 1855-1858, a conflict that had been brewing for years; ultimately it developed into the worst war in Pacific Northwest history. (Trafzer and Scheuerman, 1986, 31-93; Ruby and Brown, 1982, 131-64)

Although the fighting began east of the mountains, it became heated on both sides of the Cascades. Indians and whites engaged in combat on the White and Green Rivers, where the hostiles encouraged friendly whites to remain safe by staying neutral. Chiefs Leschi and Quiemuth of the Nisquallies led Indians in a campaign and were supported by Qualchin, the son of Chief Owhi of the Yakimas. As the conflict intensified, a leader named Muckleshoot Indian Nelson attacked whites living at sites between present-day Auburn and Kent. Other Indians became involved as the conflict spread to the east side of Puget Sound. Klickitats under Chief Kitsap and Kenasket joined the hostile camp, attacking settlers on the White River. Eight whites were killed, and the incident quickly became known as the White River Massacre. Many settlers vowed to avenge these deaths and demanded greater involvement by United States and Territorial forces.

While the fighting became more widespread, so did Chief Leschi's attempts to organize an Indian confederacy. Ultimately, his efforts proved unsuccessful, for many Indians believed that, although their cause was just, the outcome of an armed struggle would be futile. Still, Chief Leschi pulled together a fighting force made up of Nisquallis, Lower Puyallups, Muckleshoots, Duwamishes, and Suquamishes. Their strength was augmented by Snoqualmies under Kitsap and Nelson, Upper Puyallups under Quilquilton, and others loyal to Qualchin and Kenasket. The Indians fought as patriots, defending their lands, cultures, and customs. Soon, the conflict became generalized throughout the region, but the boldest attacks came when Indians tried on two occasions to take Seattle.

On January 26, 1856 pro-white Indians warned townspeople and crew of the Naval sloop Decatur, of an impending attack. So Seattle was prepared. The thirty guns of the ship sprayed the forests around Seattle with grape, canister, and shot. The projectiles had little affect on the outcome of the battle, but in the end the Indians withdrew. A few days later, Leschi returned to make a second assault, but, once again, the battle was short-lived and did little to aid the Indian position.

As the war continued to go badly for the Indians, active supporters began to drift away from the cause. Some went in search of families, many of whom had already been forcefully removed to reservations. Government officials used the war as an excuse to round up and remove peaceful Indians to reservations, despite the fact that the treaties negotiated by Governor Stevens had not yet been ratified by the United States Senate or signed by the president. In short, these documents were not constitutionally the law of the land. Regardless, the removals took place and limited fighting continued around Puget Sound and on the Coast. Indians as far away as Alaska canoed south to fight and, although some victories were won, they ultimately lost the largest conflict between Indians and whites in Pacific Northwest history. The Indians east of the Cascades supported the war west of the mountains, but did not significantly influence the course of events because of their own troubles. (Ruby and Brown, 1982, 150-184; Suquamish Museum, 1985, 38-45)

The war initially went well for the Plateau Indians in 1855, but events quickly turned against them. As fighting continued in the Yakima Country and along the Columbia River, forces under Major Gabriel Rains secured Kamiakin's home, burned St. Joseph's Catholic Mission, and demanded an unconditional surrender of all Indians. "Extermination of the Indians" became "the order of the day, and no efforts on the part of territorial officers were made to check it." As had happened around Puget Sound, the Indians divided into camps, some supporting accommodation with the whites and others favoring war. Inter-tribal and intra-tribal difficulties led Kamiakin to break with Owhi, Teias, and others. Kamiakin soon exiled himself to Palouse Country where he took up residence on the Palouse River. Volunteer soldiers, anxious to engage Kamiakin, ventured into the Walla Walla Valley to find the chief. Troops under Colonel James Kelly killed Peopeo Moxmox (Yellow Bird) of the Walla Walla Tribe, an event that only served to extend the war. Similarly, other volunteer troops stirred up intense hostilities, and the Palouses, Walla Wallas, and Umatillas turned to war.

The United States Army became more deeply involved in the conflict east of the Cascades, building Forts Walla Walla and Simcoe. Soldiers from both military posts operated against Indians, but with little initial success. On May 6, 1858 Colonel Edward Steptoe set out from Fort Walla Walla on a mission to quiet the Palouses and to quell minor Indian disturbances near the Colville gold diggings. At Red Wolf Crossing on the Snake River, near present-day Clarkston, Steptoe hired Chief Timothy and fourteen other Nez Perces to scout for the command. The Indians knew of a large gathering of hostiles north of the Snake River, but did not inform Steptoe of the fact. Not far from the Coeur d'Alene Mission, over one thousand men blocked Steptoe's advance. The two forces ultimately fought a heated running battle that culminated in Steptoe's last stand near present-day Rosalia, Washington. Under the cover of darkness Steptoe escaped. Believing they had made their point, the Indians allowed the troops to return to Fort Walla Walla unmolested.

The victory over Steptoe proved, however, to be short-lived. Outraged military officials ordered Colonel George Wright to march against the hostiles in the late summer of 1858. Wright fought the Indians at Four Lakes and Spokane Plain. In both battles Wright drove the Indians from the field. Indians from many tribes—Yakimas, Palouses, Okanogans, Spokanes, Coeur d'Alenes, Lakes, Palouses, Cayuses, Umatillas and others—had fought the United States Army as patriots, standing defiantly against the enemy. But at the conclusion of the campaigns east and west of the Cascade Mountains, they suffered severe military defeats. No longer were they free, independent, and sovereign peoples. They had become "wards" of the United States, subject to laws enacted by a distant Congress and executed by the Bureau of Indian Affairs. Life would never be the same for Washington's Indians. (Trafzer and Scheuerman, 1986, 31-92)

When the government established reservations in Washington—Makah, Quileute, Quinault, Shoalwater Bay, Chehalis, Skokomish, Squaxin Island, Lummi, Swinomish, Tulalip, Port Madison,

Presently there are 34 active tribes in the State of Washington. Twenty-six of these tribes have reservation land and eight are non-reservation tribes. Through petition to the U.S. Bureau of Indian Affairs, seven of the non-reservation tribes are currently seeking federal recognition and eligibility for health and education services.

Source: *Historical Atlas of Washington* by James W. Scott and Roland L. DeLorme
University of Oklahoma Press, 1988.
Information provided by Pat Clements, Director, Small Tribes of Western Washington.

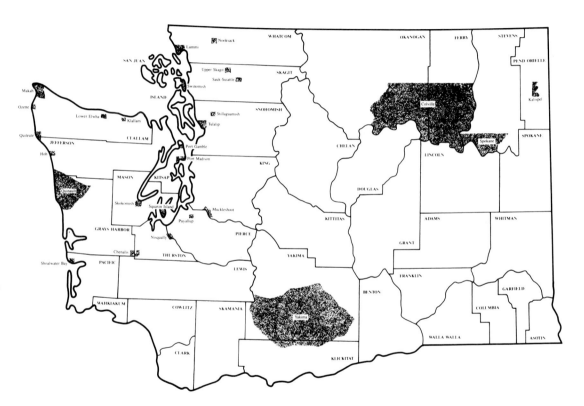

Indian reservations in the State of Washington

Muckleshoot, Puyallup, Nisqually, Yakima, Spokane, Colville and others—it took political and judicial control of these areas. Traditional Indian leaders were pushed aside by the new system of government forced on them. There were no alternatives. If Indian leaders were to have any say in their own governance, they had to deal with agents of the Bureau of Indian Affairs. Some Indians refused to cooperate with the agents, withdrawing into their own world and doing things the old way. Most of Washington's Indians, however, tried to live within the constraints of the new political order, yet maintain as much of the old way as possible. They particularly held onto religious beliefs and economic lifeways. Some Indians criticized those within their communities who appeared to be pro-government, pro-Christian and pro-white. In all fairness, however, Indians had to cope with the Bureau because the Indian office was so powerful.

The Bureau of Indian Affairs dictated policies to reservation Indians, and tried to control the lives of non-reservation Indians, as well. For the most part, policies originated in the nation's capital, but some actions were contrived by local agents who ran their reservations with the power of a big- city boss. In the 1860s and 1870s, the government adopted policies to transform Indians into farmers, a difficult task for Washington's Indians who had lived from fishing, hunting, and gathering. In the course of carrying out their program, the Bureau broke up families and bands, hastening the destruction of the old tribal social system. Indian ways were not permitted to coexist under the new order, as the Bureau—not the elders— decided what was best for everyone. This program was particularly harsh when it applied to Indian children. The Law ordered them to be civilized and Christianized. The government established Indian schools, and literally stole children from their homes, sending them away for months at a time. (Trafzer and Scheuerman, 1986, 92-102; 122-43; Ruby and Brown, 1982, 38-45)

Whites and Indians alike might debate the merits of Indian schools, but no one can argue with the fact that Indians were not permitted to determine for themselves whether or not they would leave the reservation and go to school. Parents were forced to send children away to institutions far from their homes. Carlisle Indian Institute in Pennsylvania, Chemawa Indian School in Oregon, Sherman Indian Institute in California and a host of other schools were established around the United States to handle the "civilization" of the Indian young. Children five years and older were placed in first grade where teachers sought to destroy the part of them that was Indian: tribal ties, language, religion, food, dress, and philosophy. In contemporary terms, teachers tried to "mainstream" the children, teaching them English, math, geography, and history—as it was written by whites in the eastern United States.

Cushman Trade School.
Tacoma, n.d.
Suquamish Museum

17

It is equally significant that Indian boys and girls were trained in vocational education in preparation to work for the dominant society, not as professionals to serve their own people. If parents or grandparents tried to stand in the way of this or any other government policy, agents could call on the Indian police force and a sympathetic court system to jail and punish the so-called "long hairs." Since most Indians were not granted American citizenship until 1924, they had no constitutional guarantees. If an agent ordered his police to round up hostile parents and send them to prison, there was no mechanism in place to prevent it. Indians had no system of redress, except to ask Congress to intervene, which rarely happened.

As a by-product of the reservation system, the government hoped to civilize and Christianize Indians; to this end, agents invited missionaries to live and work among their charges. The Catholics had a long presence on the mission frontier in Washington and continued on after the reservations were created. However, most agents opposed Catholic missionaries and encouraged Protestants to work among the tribes. Factions among the Indians widened; pro- and anti-Christian groups appeared; among the Christians, numerous factions emerged advocating one or another religious denomination. Other individuals gravitated back to the old spiritualism, clinging to ancient ceremonies, songs, and ways. This movement reached a peak during the late nineteenth and early twentieth centuries and, once again, in the middle and late twentieth century. In fact, this spiritual trend continues today.

Government policies of the last century also aimed at destroying the age-old customs, traditions, and practices of tribalism. Agents placed people from numerous groups onto a single reservation, thus pitting Indians of differing, often conflicting cultural backgrounds against one another. As Kamiakin once put it, the United States had "taken us in numbers and thrown us out of our native country into a foreign land among a people who is our enemy, for, between us we are enemies." In other words, American Indian policy called for the placement of many Indian tribes and bands onto reservations, regardless of language, culture, or former relations. Although most Indians on the Coast and in the Puget Sound region traded with one another, there were degrees of friction among many of the groups. The Clallams and Makahs, for instance, did not always agree, and sometimes troubles arose between the two tribes. The same was true on the Plateau, where the Cayuses and Yakimas sometimes were at odds with one another. Such problems were never considered by the Bureau when treaties were enjoined. Indians were indiscriminately lumped together and ordered to a particular reservation. This was the policy of the United States, and Indians had no say in the matter.[19] (Trafzer and Scheuerman (1986), Ruby and Brown (1982)

The government also sought to end the influence of traditional elders—men and women who had long directed the affairs of the tribes and bands. This in turn affected the family, where elders no longer directed affairs as in years past. The basic family structure was altered as the Bureau became the de facto parent of all Indians. Over the years, this policy affected urban Indians, as well as reservation people; Indian communities throughout Washington have long recognized the importance of a greater emphasis on the basic family structure, as well as on the old extended family made up of friends and relatives. In response to this need, many programs have emerged in recent years for child and family services that offer new hope. The result has been a movement toward a renewed emphasis on the family in Washington's Indian community. The revitalization of the old spiritualism and heightened concerns for the family are encouraging signs that the Indians of Washington are weaving a new social fabric that draws on the great strengths of traditional Indian life. The strength and value of Indian spiritual life was given a dramatic illustration in the "Bishops' Apology" of November 21, 1987, a letter in which ten Northwest Christian leaders requested forgiveness for "long-standing participation in the destruction of Native American spiritual practices and pledging support for protecting 'Native spiritual teachings.'" ("A Public Declaration," 1987)

No sooner had the government established the reservation system than politicians, capitalists, and reformers decided to change their minds. In the 1850s, Governor Stevens dictated a harsh settlement, using it to build a new order under which Indians would secure for themselves a small portion of their former lands as reservations. In 1887 Congress passed the Severalty Act or Dawes Act, and the President signed it into law. The act called for the breaking up of reservations into parcels to be eventually owned outright by individual Indians. In this way, the reformers argued, Indians would have a stake in society and work hard to develop their individual allotments. Capitalists in Washington and the other Western territories realized that Indians did not view property ownership like whites and that the Dawes Act would facilitate the purchase of Indian lands by whites. The act did nothing to help Indians become a part of the dominant society; rather, it served to liquidate even more land, and Washington's Indians lost thousands of acres to the name of reform.[4] Under the Indian Reorganization Act of 1934, Native Americans moved to reverse the process by which their land was alienated, but they were able to regain only a small fraction of what had passed out of their hands as a result of allotment (Bentz, 1986).

Indian problems did not end in the 1930s. Actually, they grew as the non-Indian population of Washington expanded dramatically, and as the government in Olympia asserted its rights over those granted

Parker family portrait.
Neah Bay, circa 1896-1903
Photo by Samuel G. Morse
Washington State Historical
Society, Tacoma

to Indians under federal treaties. The state sought to regulate Indian fishing, hunting, gathering, and grazing. It developed hydroelectric power and encouraged the federal government and private firms to build dams that would inundate Indian land. The state also tried to control or manage water, mineral, and forest product resources that belonged to Indians. Great divisions emerged, particularly as Indians asserted treaty rights given them in the nineteenth century. Despite the fact that federal law superseded state law in regard to Indians, the State of Washington worked to influence the course of Indian affairs within its boundaries. Tribal and state officials drew their lines and fought a number of courtroom battles. Indian success in these confrontations—such as the Bolt decision of 1974 and its subsequent approval by the United States Supreme Court—has led to considerable bitterness, the effects of which significantly influence both parties to this day. The struggles continue and the anger can only be abated when all parties achieve a better understanding of the American Indian past in the Evergreen State. (American Friends, 1970; "Boldt Rules...," 1979; "Fishing Regulations...," 1980)

Washington's Indians have influenced and, in turn, have been influenced by the major events of the twentieth century, including the post-World War II growth of the state. In many ways Indians furthered the cause of this growth. Indian men and women labored to preserve the nation during and after the war, working in industry, serving in the military, and helping to develop a dynamic economy. This era has also witnessed another phenomenon as Indians from other parts of the country, Canada, and Mexico have moved to Washington. These "urban Indians," as they are called, came to Washington seeking a better life in Seattle, Tacoma, Spokane, and Walla Walla. From Kansas and Oklahoma came the Kiowas, Comanches, Cherokees and Creeks. From South Dakota, Wyoming, and Montana came the Blackfeet, Lakota and Arapaho. From Arizona and New Mexico came the Zunis, Hopi and Yavapais. From New York came the Senecas, and from California came the Quechans. (McConnell, 1987)

These immigrant Indians came to Washington to work and play in a beautiful environment, to get ahead, and to raise their families. However, they did not come to Washington to forget they were Indians. Throughout Washington's urban areas, Indians maintain contact with their brothers and sisters in other communities. Many participate in pow wows held around the state; indeed, the pow wow serves the Indian community as a link with the past and as a common bond for the future. Urban and reservation Indians commemorate their heritage through the pow wow, a celebration they share with Native Americans throughout Indian Country. But they preserve their heritage in other ways as well, including the practice

Tribal Fisheries lab technician, Charlene Ives. Suquamish, 1983
Suquamish Museum

of Indian ceremonies, coming together at meetings, rituals, and special programs convened every month of the year, on or near reservations. Tribes encourage their youth to participate in Title IV, Indian Education Programs and in Johnson O'Malley workshops. They encourage their youth formally and informally to learn their history, culture, and language. Tribes have established cultural and educational centers, dedicated to the preservation of that which is uniquely Indian. The Suquamish, Makah, Yakimas and others have undertaken programs that serve to educate Indians and non-Indians alike. Washington's colleges and universities have wisely established Indian Studies programs that seek to enlighten students about Washington's first people. (Smith, 1949) Washington's Native American artists, producing both traditional and contemporary works, are visible in regional, national and international exhibits and performances.

National leaders have emerged from within the community of Washington's Indians, and there has been a vital move toward self-improvement among all the Indian communities of Washington State. One example from among the many possible is that offered by the Quinaults, who point with pride to the high value they place on education and to the forty young members of the tribe who are currently studying in institutions of higher learning.

These and other preservation programs help to save some traditions and to make others live again. Much has been lost, but more has been saved. Traditions—like cultures—are not static. They continue to grow and develop on and off reservations. Rural and urban Indians remember the words of Chief Seattle and take heart. When:

the memory of my tribe shall have become a myth among the white man, these shores will swarm with the invisible dead of my tribe, and when your children's children think themselves alone in the field, the store, the shop, upon the highway, or in the silence of the pathless woods, they will not be alone. . . . At night when the streets of your cities and villages are silent and you think them deserted, they will throng with the returning hosts that once filled them and still love their beautiful land. The White Man will never be alone.

Like the Chinook Wind that blows across the state, the influence, power, and promise of Washington's Indians are forever. Like the Chinook Wind, the strength and tenacity of Washington's Indians are undeniable. And like the Chinook Wind, Indians will remain a part of this great land, for they are— above all other people—of this beautiful land we call Washington. (American Friends, 1970, 31)

Makah women drumming,
Makah Days.
Neah Bay, 1984
Photo by Jens Lund
Courtesy of Washington
State Folklife Council

NOTES

1. McWhorter took the story from a Wishram, but it is a story found also among the Klickitat, Cascade, and Wasco Indians. For the only published account, see Nashone (1987) *Grandmother Stories of the Northwest.*

2. Many fine books are available on the fur trade. Some of the most pertinent to Washington include Alexander Ross (1849); Gabriel Franchere (1854); Hiram M. Chittenden (1954); Ross Cox (1831); Frederick Merk, ed (1968).

3. Several works exist discussing missionaries among Washington's Indians, including Frances Norbert Blanchet (1879); Hiram M. Chittenden and A. T. Richardson, eds. (1905); William N. Bischoff (1945); Robert I. Burns (1966); Robert H. Ruby and John A. Brown (1972); Clifford M. Drury (1936) and (1937).

4. For the best overview of the Dawes Act and policies affecting Indians during the post-Civil War era, see Gibson (1980); Prucha (1976) and (1981); Suquamish Museum (1985).

WORKS CITED

American Friends Service Committee. 1970. *Uncommon Controversy: Fishing Rights of the Muckleshoot, Puyallup, and Nisqually Indians.* Seattle: University of Washington Press.

Bentz, Marilyn. 1986. Testimony to the House Committee on Indian Affairs, Jan. 7.

Bischoff, William N. 1945. *The Jesuits in Old Oregon.* Caldwell, Idaho: The Caxton Printers, Ltd.

Blanchet, Francis Norbert. 1879. *Historical Sketches of the Catholic Church of Oregon.* Portland: Catholic Sentinel.

"Boldt Rules Against Five Tribes." 1979. *Wassaja* (7: 4).

Brown, William C. 1961. *The Indian Side of the Story.* Spokane: C.W. Hill Printing Company.

Burns, Robert I. 1966. *The Jesuits and the Indian Wars of the Northwest.* New Haven: Yale University Press.

Chittenden, Hiram M. 1954. *A History of the American Fur Trade of the Far West.* 2 volumes. Stanford, California: Academic Reprints.

Chittenden, Hiram M., and A. T. Richardson., eds. 1905. *Life, Letters and Travels of Father Pierre Jean DeSmet, S. J., 1801-1873.* 4 volumes. New York: Francis P. Harper.

Cook, S. F. 1955. "The Epidemic of 1830-33 in California and Oregon" *University of California Publications in American Archaeology and Ethnology* 43: 303-26.

Cox, Ross. 1831. *Adventures on the Columbia River.* 2 volumes. London: H. Colburn and R. Bentley.

Drury, Clifford M. 1936. *Henry Harmon Spalding.* Caldwell, Idaho: The Caxton Printers, Ltd.

_____. 1937. *Marcus Whitman, M.D.: Pioneer and Martyr.* Caldwell, Idaho: The Caxton Printers, Ltd.

"Fishing Regulations at Chief Joseph Dam Project." 1980. *Tribal Tribune* (6: 9): August, 7.

Franchere, Gabriel. 1854. *Narrative of a Voyage to the Northwest Coast of North America in the Year 1811, 1812, 1813, and 1814, Or the First American Settlement On the Pacific.* New York: Redfield.

George, Andrew. 1977-1980. Multiple interviews by the author and Richard D. Scheuerman.

Gibson, Arrell M. 1980. *The American Indian: Prehistory to Present.* Lexington, Massachusetts: D. C. Heath.

Josephy, Alvin M., Jr. 1965. *The Nez Perce Indians and the Opening of the Northwest.* New Haven: Yale University Press.

Kowrach, Edward J., ed. n.d. *Doty's Journal of Operations.* Yakima.

Lane, Barbara S. 1976. *Background of Treaty Making in Western Washington.* Seattle: Institute for the Development of Indian Law and Cook Christian Training School.

Lane, Robert B., and Barbara. 1977. *Treaties of the Puget Sound.* Seattle: Institute for the Development of Indian Law.

McConnell, Les. 1987. *Economic Contributions Made by Indian Tribes in Washington State.* Washington: Bureau of Indian Affairs.

McWhorter, L. V. 1918. L. V. McWhorter Collection, Manuscripts and Archives, Washington State University Library.

Merk, Frederick., ed. 1968. *Fur Trade and Empire: George Simpson's Journal, 1824-1825.* Cambridge, Massachusetts: Belknap Press.

Nashone. 1987. *Grandmother Stories of the Northwest.* Sacramento, California.

Prucha, Francis P. 1976. *American Indian Policy in Crisis.* Norman: University of Oklahoma Press.

"A Public Declaration to the Tribal Councils and Traditional Spiritual Leaders of the Indian and Eskimo Peoples of the Pacific Northwest." November 21, 1987. In care of Jewell Praying Wolf James, Lummi. Seattle.

Richards, Kent D. 1979. *Isaac I. Stevens: Young Man in a Hurry.* Provo: Brigham Young University Press.

Ross, Alexander. 1849. *Adventures of the First Settlers on the Oregon and Columbia Rivers.* London: Smith, Elder and Company.

Ruby, Robert H., and John A. Brown. 1972. *The Cayuse Indians.* Norman: University of Oklahoma Press.

_____. 1982. *Indians of the Pacific Northwest: A History.* Norman: University of Oklahoma Press.

Scott, Leslie M. 1928. "Indian Disease as Aids to Pacific Northwest Settlement." *Oregon Historical Quarterly* 19: 99-107.

Smith, Marion W., ed. 1949. *Indians of the Urban Northwest.* Columbia University Contributions to Anthropology, Number 36. New York: Columbia University Press.

Suquamish Museum. 1985. *The Eyes of Chief Seattle.* Suquamish, Washington.

Trafzer, Clifford E., ed. 1986. *Indians, Superintendents, and Councils: Northwestern Indian Policy, 1850-1855.* Lanham, Maryland: University Press of America.

Trafzer, Clifford E., and Richard D. Scheuerman. 1986. *Renegade Tribe: The Palouse Indians and the Invasion of the Inland Pacific Northwest.* Pullman: Washington State University Press.

"Walla Walla Council Proceedings." 1855. National Archives. Documents Relating to Negotiations of Ratified and Unratified Treaties. Record Group 75, Microfilm T494, Reel 5.

The major influx of European immigration began in the 1880s.

The fifteenth through the nineteenth centuries were times of unprecedented European exploration throughout the world. Many newly discovered regions like the Pacific Northwest became involved in international trade as fur companies competed to exploit the region's natural wealth. Missionaries, miners, military men, and homesteaders followed the explorers in a progression that ultimately displaced the native tribes and prepared the way for American and European immigrants who began settling across present Washington at the mid-nineteenth century. European immigration followed the national pattern with an initial wave through the 1880s of Northern Europeans who had lived for a time in the Midwest or East. The influx of immigration from Southern and Eastern Europe followed the completion of the Northern Pacific Railroad. More recent arrivals have come to the state in a smaller, third wave that has followed World War II.

WASHINGTON'S EUROPEAN AMERICAN COMMUNITIES

Richard D. Scheuerman

Washington peoples from Europe are as varied and colorful as the Northwest landscapes that attracted so many immigrants because of geographic similarities to their homelands. European immigrant motives for coming have been as complex as the individuals who harbored them: hopes for future prosperity, or eagerness to flee adversity or unfulfillable obligations both played important roles. Many adventurous souls responded to a wanderlust that worked for generations to weave the rich tapestry of European culture. This spirit, combined with idealized visions of life in America, lured many to new homes on this side of the Atlantic. A surprising number found their way across or around the continent to settle in what is now the state of Washington.

The majority of present-day Washingtonians are of European descent; almost one-third of the populace claims a single European ancestry. Diverse ethnic communities situated around the state mirror this: from Finnish loggers in southwestern Washington's Willapa Hills and Dutch farmers in Whatcom County to Ballard's Norwegians and the Russian-Germans of the Big Bend country, European cultural identities are retained and celebrated in Washington. To be sure, historical and geographical factors have led to assimilation and cultural exchange; yet many European American communities retain distinctive social, religious, and occupational patterns that can be traced to eighteenth and nineteenth-century Europe.

These patterns became evident to me as a youth reared in Washington's Palouse Country with grandparents whose homelands were Germany, Russia, and Scandinavia. My brother, sisters, and I would sometimes spend a week with Grandpa and Grandma Peterson at their cabin near Sacheen Lake where we would awaken at dawn to the peculiar sounds of their hushed voices in the rustic kitchen. He would speak to her in Swedish; she would reply in Norwegian. Later, after working in the garden or playing in

Departure from Larsens
Plads.
Copenhagen, 1890
Painting by Edward Petersen
Aarhus Kunst Museum,
Denmark

the countryside, Grandpa would entertain us with stories of his journey to America in 1915, his exploits as a logger in Washington's primeval forests, a worker on the famed Cascade Tunnel, and the adventure of what seemed countless other physically demanding occupations. He did not have to describe the rigors of immigrant labor in great detail, for his iron handshake told us the story of his life, and even in his seventieth year Grandpa could still balance his muscular frame on three fingers. Grandma's favorite stories were of her father, Andrew Sunwold, who had come to the Northwest long before he brought his family from Norway. He had written home describing the region's boundless prairies and of his work supplying wood for steamboats at Fort Benton, Montana Territory. This fort was the eastern terminus of the Mullan Road, the primary immigrant route to Washington Territory before the railroads, and linked the upper Missouri River with Fort Walla Walla, the route he was to follow.

My paternal grandparents, Karl and Mary Scheuerman, were among Washington's Germans from Russia—people of the soil, who for generations had sown their grain and gathered their harvests in a progression that led in the end from the Hessian countryside and Volga steppe to the prairies of the Columbia Plateau. Grandpa knew his land intimately; because of him and my father, we children learned early to see much more than just the fields of grain surrounding our rural home. They taught us to distinguish the benches, swails, draws, and other topographic features and soil conditions of the Palouse Hills meaningful to a farmer. These places grew to hold a special significance as we learned names and locations such as the Huvaluck (Hessian dialect for "Oathole"), "Barley Hill" and "Spud Draw." Grandpa would recount the experiences of the first Russian-German immigrants to the region who had labored for years to turn the tawny, knee-high bunchgrass and plant the "Turkey Red" wheat they had brought from the Old Country. He knew their exploits first hand and was aware that other groups had shared in these pioneering experiences: his neighbors were English, Irish, Scottish, and Norwegian. He also knew that the area's native population had resisted these developments, and he spoke sadly of the Indian removal to reservations as if the forces behind it had been beyond anyone's control.

I was delighted during a 1970 trip to see relatives in Brewster when Grandpa responded enthusiastically to my request to visit the Colville Indian Reservation. The impromptu appearance at the agency headquarters in Nespelem of a kindly old man and his inquisitive grandson met with a cordial response. Through this initial contact I was introduced to a host of new friends who, over the years, have come to share their perspectives on cultural change. One whose words and life story have particularly enriched my life is Isabel Arcasa, a centenarian in Washington's centennial year, who is of European and American Indian background. Her father, J. H. Friedlander, was a German Jew who established a trading post at the foot of Lake Chelan in the 1870s. There he married Elizabeth Slukin, granddaughter of Entiat Chief Shilkohsaskt. This kind of relationship was not uncommon on the Northwest frontier in the nineteenth century. The trappers and traders who were the region's earliest white residents frequently married women of area tribes and forged lasting bonds between the two peoples. Isabel fared less well after her father's unexpected death, however, as this stately woman informed me that her stepfather soon traded her to a local chief for six cows and four horses. Surrounded today by her extended family, she clearly recalls the time nearly a century past when she peered around her father's counter as furs and salmon were exchanged for wool blankets and dried fruit.

The Pacific Northwest's first fur traders were Americans whose appearance in present Washington resulted from Yankee merchant interest in reentering foreign commercial routes disrupted by the Revolutionary War. Although British culture continued to strongly influence American society, citizens of the young nation were forging their own national identity through experiences in democratic government and expansion across the North American frontier. During a Pacific expedition in May, 1792, Robert Gray discovered the Columbia River giving the United States its first firm claim to the region. America's position against the British was strengthened by the overland journey of Lewis and Clark's Corps of Discovery (1804-06). Fort Astoria was founded in 1811 as a strictly commercial venture by New York financier John Jacob Astor's American Fur Company—much to the chagrin of the Canadian North West Company, which had hoped to establish the first fur trading post at this strategic point on the lower Columbia.

The North West Company, organized in 1783 by Montreal merchants of Scottish ancestry, employed many French Canadians. Eager to capitalize on the Pacific Slope's fur trade possibilities, the company dispatched the remarkable explorer-trader David Thompson to find the Columbia's source. He crossed the Continental Divide into present British Columbia in 1807 to successfully complete this mission and he also established Kootenae House, the Nor'Wester's first outpost in the Pacific Northwest. Under his direction Spokane House was founded near the mouth of the Little Spokane River by Finan McDonald and Jacques Finlay in 1810. The American response to Nor'Western activity east of the Cascades was to establish Fort Okanogan in 1811 near the river that also bears this tribal name and Fort

Spokane a year later. During the War of 1812 a British warship threatened Fort Astoria and Donald McKenzie elected to surrender the post with its inventory to their British rivals rather than risk their destruction. Within a year the Astorians sold their entire operation to the North West Company.

But it was the entry of the British Hudson's Bay Company into the Northwest fur trade that marked the genesis of an enduring European American presence in the area north of the Columbia River. From the earliest years of its Pacific Northwest presence, company leadership worked to form "regular establishments" that would serve as more than exchange points for beaver and other peltries. Sir George Simpson, autocratic governor of the company at York Factory on Hudson's Bay, was as interested in barley and growing seasons as in furs and supply routes. In 1824 he directed the construction of Fort Vancouver on a verdant plain north of the Columbia River and appointed Dr. John McLoughlin to serve as chief factor of the fort and supervise company affairs throughout the Columbia Department.

McLoughlin undertook within two years to transform the department from a mismanaged chain of thirteen posts into an expanded and profitable operation of twenty-two, while working to attain Simpson's goal of agricultural self-sufficiency. Fort Vancouver grew into a prosperous settlement by 1840 with approximately 600 whites working on surrounding farms or in other company related occupations (Gibson, 1985).

Fort Colvile replaced Spokane House in 1825 as a center of trading activity on the middle Columbia. Simpson considered the site near scenic Kettle Falls, the highest on the Columbia, a more strategic location for trade and farming. Another Canadian of Scottish descent, Andrew McDonald, was placed in charge of local operations which, by the end of the next decade, had grown to employ twenty men at the 400 acre farm with five sections of pasture, company store, and gristmill. Even languid Fort Nez Perces began to show signs of prosperity under McLoughlin's attentive guidance. Since the drier climate there did not foster agricultural development the post came to specialize in horsebreeding. However, Chief Trader Pierre Pambrum, a native of Vaudreuil, Canada, did raise corn, potatoes, carrots, and other vegetables on fifty acres along the banks of the Walla Walla for consumption by his family and a half-dozen employees.

The company's first penetration of Puget Sound country took place in 1833 when McLoughlin directed the establishment of Fort Nisqually on a broad plain near present DuPont. The venerable Archibald McDonald was appointed Chief Trader and a small fir log enclosure was built as the first step

Dr. John McLoughlin, Chief Factor at Fort Vancouver, 1824-1846. Drawing, San Francisco, 1822 Washington State Historical Society, Tacoma

Europe

Iceland
5,024

Sweden
225,780

Finland
39,496

Norway
286,077

Estonia
931

Latvia
2,560

Lithuania
5,933

Russia
31,191

Scotland
309,596

Denmark
71,026

Poland
70,868

Belorussia
149

Northern Ireland
172

Isle of Man
243

Ukraine
7,885

Ireland
824,994

Wales
54,300

England
1,122,766

Holland
170,992

Germany
1,105,532

Jews
16,542

Belgium
6,673

Luxembourg
975

Czechoslovakia
29,293

Ruthenia
13

Slovak
3,018

Austria
17,308

Hungary
15,885

Rumania
2,613

France
316,012

Switzerland
33,119

Slovenia
919

Yugoslavia

Croatia
3,048

Serbia
797

Gypsy, Romany
248

Bulgaria
790

Italy
106,660

Albania
220

Greece
12,261

Basque
1,134

Portugal
9,895

Spain
364

Malta
136

Shown on the map are the numbers of Washingtonians of European descent who identified their ethnic or national origin (by specific country) in the 1980 U.S. Census.

31

in opening the new area to the fur trade. The post soon shifted emphasis, however, to cultivation of vegetables and stockraising on adjacent meadows. Two retired company employees, French-Canadians Simon Plamondon and Francois Failland, also began farming on Cowlitz Prairie near present Toledo in 1833.

All enclaves of European American settlement in 1840 in the area of present-day Washington were adjacent to the six Hudson's Bay Company forts. The vast majority of settlers served as boatmen, herders, blacksmiths, interpreters, carpenters, clerks or in a variety of other occupations needed to keep the network of diverse company operations running efficiently. Department employees numbered approximately 550 with 450 working at Fort Vancouver, groups of about twenty at Forts Colvile, Okanogan, Nisqually, and Cowlitz Farms, and the remaining fifteen at Fort Nez Perces. Most had been unmarried company *engagés* in Canada who transferred voluntarily to new assignments in the Columbia Department. Most chief factors and officers were of Scottish background and nominal members of the Anglican Church. French-Canadian ancestry predominated among the regular employees; many were Métis, or individuals with European American fathers and Indian mothers, and virtually all were Catholic. Although many did not consider themselves settlers, their labor first tilled Washington's soil and built its earliest frontier outposts, and some remained.

European American Settlement on Puget Sound

With revenues declining in the fur trade due to less demand abroad and a diminishing peltry supply, Simpson and McLoughlin undertook a new venture when the Russian-American Company expressed a need for agricultural provisions in the late 1830s. Simpson viewed the situation as a great opportunity to market the agricultural produce he had worked so diligently to develop in the Columbia Department. Since it was impossible to meet the new demand from existing company farms west of the Cascades, Simpson, McLoughlin, and others incorporated the "Puget Sound Agricultural Company" in 1839 to open new tracts of land to farming near the established operations at Cowlitz and Fort Nisqually. Efforts were undertaken immediately to direct equipment and livestock to the area and arrangements were made to procure colonists from Canada "with the view of gradually forming a European Agricultural Settlement." Leases on 1,000 acres with a house, barn, and livestock were offered to prospective settlers who were encouraged to take land at Cowlitz Prairie where the dark loam was richer than the gravelly soil around Fort Nisqually.

Colonists were recruited from Canada's Red River district (Assiniboia) where the Hudson's Bay Company had developed a flourishing agricultural colony in the 1820s. One important difference, however, distinguished the proposed Puget Sound Colony from the Red River experience. British sovereignty in Canada protected private interests, and settlers there were willing to enter into long term lease arrangements on property. This security did not extend to the jointly occupied Oregon Country. Prospective colonists from Red River were hesitant to risk an arduous journey and the demands of colonist life on leased land with an uncertain future. Twenty-three families, most of whom were Métis, were assembled by Assiniboia Governor Duncan Finlayson in June, 1841 for the three-month overland trek to Fort Vancouver. After a short stay at the post, McLoughlin directed fourteen English families to lands at Fort Nisqually and the remaining French Canadians to Cowlitz Farms (Gibson, 1985).

Complaints over conditions of settlement were immediately voiced: houses were not completed and farm implements were in short supply. The greater problem hindering colonial development, however, was the lure of life across the Columbia in the fertile Willamette Valley where a European American settlement had been prospering for nearly a decade and where rights to patented land were guaranteed. Thus, the families who had been settled on the rocky soil around Fort Nisqually had drifted south of the Columbia by late 1843, although the more favorable conditions at Cowlitz brought an expansion of the colony to sixty-four people by the same date. These thirteen French Canadian families at Cowlitz Farms constituted the first European American settlement in present Washington founded on a principally agricultural base.

Encroachments on Puget Sound Agricultural Company holdings began soon after the terms of the Oregon Treaty of 1846 were announced which finally fixed the U.S.-British North American boundary at the 49th Parallel. Under the circumstances, the Puget Sound Agricultural Company failed to renew its "Russian contract." Nevertheless, the role of the Hudson's Bay Company in fostering European American settlement in present Washington cannot be reduced to the marginal success of its colonists on Puget Sound. To the contrary, the British served as the vanguard of regional development as enunciated by the American explorer Lieutenant Charles Wilkes, who wrote in 1841 that "they had opened the country to safe and secure emigration, and provided it with the means necessary to the success of emigrants."

The network of the company's frontier outposts east of the Cascades provided the nucleus for a series of small settlements. About thirty-two employees were working at the three interior locations in 1846 and many, like Angus McDonald at Fort Colvile and Pierre Pambrum at Fort Walla Walla, chose to remain and continue similar operations among the Indians and growing European American populace. In the late 1840s a settlement appeared about eighteen miles east of Fort Nez Perces where the families of Edouard Beauchemin, Amable Lacourse, and others began raising livestock and farming along the grassy banks of the Walla Walla River. Appropriately, the place became known as Frenchtown. Others like James Birnie, a native of Aberdeen, Scotland, chose to retire from the company and acquire land for themselves in the unspoiled wilderness west of the Cascades as he did in 1845 by moving with his family to present Cathlamet.

With the extension of U.S. sovereignty over the Oregon Country in 1846, renewed interest was expressed by many Americans in the lands north of the Columbia River. The "Great Migration" of 1843 brought nearly 900 immigrants across the Oregon Trail to the sparsely settled Willamette Valley. Like the majority of overland pioneers, they were from America's heartland. This first surge of immigration tapped the states from New York, Pennsylvania, and Virginia across to Iowa and Missouri. Most were descendants of European colonists who had come to America a century or two earlier. They came from rural areas and honored the values of faith, family, and farm. Some of the men also possessed skills as carpenters, livestock raisers, promoters, and businessmen and most tended to be active in church, local politics, and fraternal societies. The women provided stability under frequently primitive conditions and filled the more private roles of mother, wife, physician, and moral guardian. These complimentary functions were joined to create a culture centered on the family which, particularly in the case of those from Iowa, Missouri, and Illinois, could number a half-dozen or more children (Douglas, 1950).

Native-born Americans remained the overwhelming majority of travelers on the Oregon Trail, though there also were Germans, English, Dutch, and French in the wagon trains of the 1840s. Following the ordeal of a journey lasting from four to six months challenged by swollen streams, buffalo herds, mountain passes, and Indians; the immigrants first spied present Washington during their approach to the Whitman Mission. Founded in 1836 by the famed Presbyterian missionaries Marcus and Narcissa Whitman, the site served for ten years as both a center for religious work among the surrounding tribes and as a shelter for travellers on the overland route. A pioneer of 1843 remarked that the area "contained many rich valleys, of considerable extent; and . . . will in the course of time, be inhabited by a civilized people." Although a few immigrant families remained temporarily in the vicinity of the mission, almost all wagons lumbered across the Oregon Cascades into the Willamette Valley which seemed a paradise to the weary pioneers.

Some of the 1,200 immigrants of 1844 found conditions north of the Columbia River more favorable. These included George W. Bush, his wife and six sons, a Black family barred from owning land in the Willamette Valley; a Kentuckian of Irish descent, Michael T. Simmons, his wife and seven children; a fellow Kentuckian with Scottish background, James McAllister, his wife and children; Gabriel Jones, wife and three children; David Kendrick, wife and son; and three single men; Samuel Crockett, Reuben Crowder and Jesse Ferguson.

This group spent the winter of 1844-45 near Fort Vancouver; in the following summer several of the men undertook a series of exploring expeditions to Puget Sound country. They found the two British settlements of Cowlitz and Fort Nisqually where they were treated with diffidence, large numbers of curious but accommodating Indians, and a series of unbroken prairies south of the Sound. The Simmons and Bush families found ideal locations in the lower Deschutes Valley near present Tumwater, originally named New Market, where their farms fostered the first American settlement in present Washington. Others settled elsewhere in the vicinity which became known as Bush Prairie. A new surge of immigration in 1846 brought more Americans south of the Sound and prompted the construction of a gristmill and sawmill at Tumwater and a brick kiln on Simon Plamondon's farm in the Cowlitz Valley. Like many other Canadians who had retired from the Hudson's Bay Company, Plamondon chose to remain on the American side of the boundary.

In a move symbolic of its sovereignty over the newly acquired domain, the United States established Vancouver Barracks near the Hudson's Bay post and Fort Steilacoom on southeast Puget Sound in 1848. While officers at these installations were exclusively native-born Americans, over half the enlisted men (164 out of 292 in 1850) were naturalized citizens from Germany and Ireland. This high incidence of foreign-born military personnel reflected a national phenomenon as European immigrants to America, unable to find employment elsewhere, were welcomed into an army hard-pressed to meet its obligations in the Far West. As was the case with French Canadians and Scots who settled in the area following their years in the fur trade, some of the German and Irish soldiers chose to remain in the scenic   *35* woodlands after fulfilling their terms of enlistment. William O'Leary, a native of Cork County, Ireland, settled on the south shore of Gray's Harbor in 1848 to become the first white in that historic area. O'Leary, a bachelor, was soon followed by the family of William and Martha Ann Medcalf, Irish and English respectively, who became the first white family on the lower Chehalis River. They built their home on a fir lined plain near present Montesano which became known as Medcalf Prairie.

Even though the Northwest experienced a significant depopulation in 1848, due to a short-lived exodus to the California gold strikes, the population of the territory north of the Columbia River in 1849 registered 304 whites. While 189 of these individuals were American citizens, the remaining 115 were aliens principally from Canada, Scotland, England, and Ireland. Most residents were single, only 73 white women were living in the area. Within a year the population tripled to 1,049 with settlements at the future sites of Port Townsend, Steilacoom, and on Elliot Bay. Martin Toftezon, an adventurous young Norwegian from Levanger, became the first of his countrymen in Washington by claiming land at Oak Harbor on Whidbey Island in 1850.

The concentrations of settlers were greatest around Fort Vancouver, Fort Nisqually, and the head of Budd's Inlet where the tiny hamlet of Olympia also appeared at mid-century. The number of foreign-born residents increased to 417 by the time of the 1850 dicennial census. However, relative to the total population their proportion declined from 60% to 40% as latecomers to the Willamette Valley from midwestern and eastern states were being diverted to the newly formed counties of Lewis and Clark north of the Columbia River.

Immigrants were attracted to the Pacific Northwest in unprecedented numbers during the 1850s on a quest for land, gold, and business opportunities. As early as 1850 disgruntled miners who had headed for the California gold strikes a year or two earlier were moving north again in their search for the precious metal. In the summer of 1850 Henry Spalding, the former missionary to the Nez Perce, wrote from the Willamette Valley that "Great nos. went from country last June to explore the Spokane and Nez Perce countries for gold. . . ." Further incentive for travel to the region came in the fall of 1850, when Congress passed the Oregon Donation Land Law three years before treaties liquidating tribal titles to their land, in order to "provide for the survey, and make donations to settlers of the said public lands." This legislation granted every eligible citizen who had settled prior to 1852 a half-section (320 acres) while those occupying lands before 1855 were able to obtain quarter sections. News of these liberal settlement provisions led to an onslaught of pioneers across the Oregon Trail, and in five years the territorial population rose from approximately 8,000 in 1850 to nearly 30,000 in 1855. This dramatic increase led to the creation of a separate Washington Territory in 1853 with the capital located at Olympia near Simmons's historic homesite.

In 1851 Seattle was founded by Arthur Denny, Dr. D. S. Maynard, and others who aggressively set about to create a regional supply center by the deep harbors of Elliott Bay. That same year a native of Holland, Henry Van Asselt, settled on the lower Duwamish River where he cleared a farm and squared timber and piling for the San Francisco market. In 1852 the early Seattle residents were joined by Henry Yesler, a Maryland native of German ancestry, who shrewdly acquired the best land on the shoreline (the base of present Yesler Way) in order to build the first sawmill directly on Puget Sound. Sometimes called the "Father of Seattle", Yesler went on to become the city's mayor and a King County official in later years. German immigrant Henry Roeder and Russel Peabody arrived in Seattle in 1852 with similar plans to construct a sawmill. Finding Yesler's already in operation, the two men canoed north to Bellingham Bay where they received permission from the local Lummi Indians to construct a mill near the falls on Whatcom Creek. The millsite provided the nucleus for settlement in the area which eventually grew to merge the three communities of Sehome, Fairhaven, and New Whatcom into Bellingham.

The year 1851 also marked the origin of European American settlement on Commencement Bay as a Swedish immigrant, Nicholas Delin, selected a homesite at present Tacoma, while John Nelson, a native of Norway, helped establish the White River settlement at Auburn in 1853. Neither Seattle nor Tacoma experienced any significant growth, however, until the late 1860s when coal was discovered at Issaquah and explorations were undertaken for bituminous deposits along the Cedar and Puyallup Rivers. By that time Tacoma was also emerging as a serious contender for the western terminus of the first northern transcontinental line, the Northern Pacific Railroad. In both Washington mining and railroading, European immigrants were to play a major role as these developments were concurrent with forces overseas that were contributing to a mass emigration from Europe.

Europe's "First Wave" Migrations to Washington: 1840 to the 1880s

Between 1840 and 1914 nearly 52 million Europeans left their homelands for new opportunities abroad; approximately 35 million of them journeyed to the United States. The reasons for discontent in

Europe were manifold: economic, social, political, and religious conditions unique to each country; personal circumstances unique to each individual. Up to the 1880s emigration was predominantly from Great Britain, Ireland, Germany, the Netherlands, and the Nordic countries of Sweden, Norway, Finland, Denmark and Iceland. From the 1880s to the outbreak of World War I emigration shifted to the nations of south and east Europe: Italy, Greece, the Balkan states, Poland, Russia, and Austria-Hungary.

Emigrants from Great Britain and Canada have always constituted the most populous European American community in Washington with broad dispersion throughout the state. English and Scots encountered few barriers to assimilation with native-born Americans, given their shared language, political institutions, and religious heritage. During Washington's territorial period (1853-1889), Irish tended to cluster in Clark, King, and Walla Walla Counties where many were associated with military posts and mining activity at a time when thousands of their countrymen were migrating to America in search of a more prosperous life.

By 1880 Washington's first generation Irish were the territory's second largest European group with 2,243 listed in the dicennial census (Canadians totaled 2,857). Due to a relative lack of education and their Catholic faith, the Irish had a more difficult time in early Washington communities than the Scots or English. Less accepted in the social or economic mainstream, most Irish found employment as urban laborers, freighters and packers, and on the railroads.

Nineteenth century European emigration levels generally correspond to eras of vigorous industrial and economic activity in America and great economic stress in Europe: Ireland presents such a case. This inextricable link between the forces of "push" from the Old World and "pull" toward the New was rooted in the relation of the European farmer to the land. In Ireland at mid-century, for example, a little over half of the population was directly dependent on the soil. Those who actually labored on the farms, the tenants, formed by far the largest social class in Ireland in the 1840s.

Further subdivision of tenant lands among a father's sons was no longer economically viable. Since it was customary for the eldest son to inherit, the other children were forced to go elsewhere to find economic security. Ireland at mid-century, however, had little industry so the system "predisposed it to disperse population" which led to massive and prolonged emigration. When the Irish Potato Blight first struck in 1846, the people already had developed a tradition of migration with the majority journeying to America and employment in the industrial cities of the East. The famine of 1846-1848 swelled the number of those immigrating to American shores in 1848 to 151,000 and this increased to over 219,000 in 1851—the most ever to emigrate to the United States in a single year from Ireland (Schrier, 1958).

Pioneer Washington residents Nicholas and Catherine Whealen were among those who emigrated. He had come to the United States as a young man in the 1840s and settled in Illinois, a state which boasted one of the highest concentrations of Irish-born residents. Crossing the plains to California a short time later, he had mined for three years, then returned to Pennsylvania and had married Catherine O'Neil, a native of Wexford, Ireland, in 1854. The day after their marriage the couple embarked on a journey by steamer to the northern California mines and settled in Siskiyou County where they eked out a living for eleven years.

In 1856 in response to a general Indian uprising in protest of the heavy-handed negotiation of inequitable treaties in Puget Sound, the Yakima Valley, and the Palouse and Walla Walla areas, Governor Stevens and military authorities directed establishment of a new series of military posts throughout Washington's territory to protect white interests, thus expanding Washington's European American presence. The warring tribes were finally forced to surrender by 1858 and most were relocated to Northwest reservations. Eastern Washington's lower Snake River country was suddenly transformed into a whirlwind of frontier activity as the Colonel Wright, Tenino, and other lower Columbia and Snake steamers transported hordes of eager souls from Portland to the newly opened jumping-off points of Wallula, Walla Walla, and Lewiston: 15,000 in 1861, 24,000 in 1862 and 22,000 in 1863. Miners were flocking to new gold deposits found along the Coeur d'Alene, Clearwater and Salmon Rivers in present Idaho and to the Bannock district in what is now Montana.

The dramatic increase in the region's population had led to a strong local market for livestock and agricultural produce. Many of those coming up from the California mines had witnessed the same situation before and decided more money could be gained by supplying the miners than by digging with them. About 1867 Nicholas and Catherine Whealen and their four sons joined others in heading north and settled in the Waitsburg area north of Walla Walla to begin raising cattle for the new Lewiston markets. The Whealans relocated to Whitman County in 1869 after pasturing a herd of cattle in the Palouse country. Encamped on the bunchgrass prairie of Union Flat Creek (named with neighboring Rebel Flat by Civil War veterans), Catherine announced to her husband that the place offered everything they had ever looked for and if he was going to "keep wandering" he would have to do it alone. Nicholas complied with his

wife's wishes and their entire family moved to the area in the spring of 1870 (Whelan and Kissler, 1980). Other Irish engaged in the freighting business, operated restaurants and saloons, farmed, or found other work to establish a significant presence in southeastern Washington by the 1870s. A large number of Irish families also were included in the surge to the Northwest after the Civil War. Many located in the Walla Walla Valley and in the Dublin district of Clark County where they took advantage of the liberal provisions of the 1862 Homestead Act.

Among the millions of European emigrants who entered the United States during the nineteenth century, by far the largest number came from Germany. In contrast to emigrant groups such as the Irish and Southern Europeans who often preferred to live in American cities, many Germans actively sought a rural life and were among the first European Americans to settle on Washington's virgin prairies and in its mountain valleys. As noted by a newspaper reporter near the turn of the century, "Cheap lands, light taxes, the need of laborers, and the opportunity to gain a competence in a short time by toil—these were the conditions that attracted the Germans."

One of the first Germans to take up residence in Central Washington was "Dutch John" Galler, who emigrated to the United States from Baden, Germany in 1849. As a youth, Galler had learned to hunt and trap from his father who supervised state game preserves. These skills would later prove valuable in Washington's Cascade Mountains. Against his father's wishes, Galler had married a young widow shortly before leaving but she died soon after their arrival in Philadelphia leaving him with her two small sons. Relatives took the children and Galler headed west. Following the pattern of most European immigrants to the Northwest prior to the railroads, he settled first in the Midwest. After six years in Nebraska, Galler moved to Montana Territory where he first heard about the beauty and climate of the Puget Sound country. Enroute to the coast, Galler became enamored with the broad, grass-covered Kittitas Valley and was the first settler near present Ellensburg. The restless German longed for both freedom and seclusion but in a short time others were settling nearby. In 1868 he headed north across the Colockum Trail to the Wenatchee Valley where he lived at various locations near present Cashmere and Peshastin before settling at the mouth of the Squilchuck Creek just south of present Wenatchee. He planted a small vineyard of Malaga grapes and a fruit orchard, which he irrigated, and married a local Indian, Semultalks. Their home soon developed into a hospitable rest stop for freighters and immigrants traveling along the Columbia River. Other Germans soon followed Galler to the area including Phillip

German Community's
Stridsbaner Lodge, Number 278.
Aberdeen, n.d.
Polson Museum, Hoquiam

Miller (to Wenatchee in 1872), Alexander Brender (to Cashmere in 1881), and John Emig (to present Leavenworth about 1885). Ten children were born to the Gallers and remarkable "Dutch John" lived to the age of 108 (Hull, 1929).

A large rural German presence was also established prior to the 1880s in Spokane County and in Whitman County where Michael Schultheis led a group of German Catholics to the Uniontown-Colton area in 1875. Nearly half of Washington's 2,188 native-born Germans in 1880 preferred the opportunities afforded in the territory's rapidly expanding cities where they found employment as merchants, saloon keepers, bakers, millers, and brewers. Referring to the pioneer German businessmen of Seattle, historian Spencer Polland wrote that they had "contributed more to the business growth of Seattle and more to its enlivenment with the graces of living than any other group their size."

Many of Washington's most successful businessmen were German Jews who came to the Northwest in the 1850s with the mining advance to supply clothing, tools, and other supplies to the fortune seekers. Among the earliest of these entrepreneurs were Martin, Adolf, and Sigmund Schwabacher, brothers from Germany, who first opened a general merchandise store in the boomtown of Walla Walla in 1860. With the completion of the Mullan Road across the Northern Rockies in 1862, Walla Walla became linked with Ft. Benton, Montana to facilitate traffic from the Missouri River to the Columbia River and Pacific Coast. This route had a significant impact on population growth in eastern Washington which, according to a territorial memorial, directed "a constant stream of population flowing into the region" as immigrants arrived intent upon mining, farming, stockraising and other enterprises.

The Schwabachers expanded their operations to Dayton and Colfax and put their brother-in-law, Bailey Gatzert, into business at Wallula. Gatzert, a native of Worms, Germany, soon demonstrated a remarkable talent in merchandising and moved to Seattle in 1869 to find greater opportunities more suited to his abilities. During the years of Seattle's transformation from a muddy village into the Pacific Northwest's preeminent city, Gatzert made a fortune in the wholesale business; helped form Schwabacher Brothers, of which he became president; and organized Puget Sound (Seattle-First) National Bank with Austrian immigrant Jacob Furth in 1883. Many other enterprises launched by Washington's pioneer German-Jewish businessmen thrived in Seattle, Tacoma, and in other cities. Louis, Moses, and Sigmund Bettman, brothers from Bavaria, opened a general merchandise store in Olympia in 1853; Marcus Oppenheimer and Herman Friedlander had stores near Fort Colville and at Camp Chelan, respectively,

Moving the Torahs.
Seattle, 1925
Jewish Archives, Special
Collections Division,
University of Washington
Libraries. Negative number:
UW1181

43

in the early 1870s; and in 1879 Simon Berg arrived in Spokane to open the first Jewish merchandise business in that city.

Prior to the 1880s the vast majority of Jews in Washington were Ashkenazim from Northern Europe who had come as single men. During Washington's territorial period they were rapidly acculturated into the dynamic life of emerging Northwest cities and towns. Through hard work and mutual support they attained middle class income levels in a relatively short period and adapted very well to American political and educational institutions. Their culture emphasized public responsibility and from 1870-1872 the territory was served by a Jewish governor, Edward Salomon, while other Jews were elected as city mayors and other officials. Cultural traditions remained strong through the formation of religious associations. Washington's first B'nai B'rith chapter was organized in Seattle in 1883 and the first congregation, Ohaveh Sholum, was organized in 1889. Later in that year a group of Orthodox Jews organized a burial society, Chevra Bikur Cholum, which led to the founding of the Bikur Cholum Congregation in 1891 (Droker, 1983 and Buttnick, 1988).

Norway was second only to Ireland in percentage of her population immigrating to the United States. Although the number of Norwegians who entered the United States in the nineteenth century was not great when compared to the total emigration from Europe, they did constitute a major foreign-born element in areas of the upper Midwest and Pacific Northwest. The first significant Norwegian immigration to North America began in 1825 with the voyage of the tiny sloop *Restauration* which transported fifty-three passengers and crew to New York. The main stream of Norwegian immigration to all parts of this country, however, did not begin until 1836 continuing at a highly variable rate until 1866 when the first period of mass immigration began which was to continue until 1874. A second and larger mass immigration began in 1879 and lasted until the early nineties. A third major wave began in 1899 and lasted through the following decade.

Lack of farmland was a principal factor in emigration from Norway where three-fourths of the land could not be cultivated. Half of Norway's population in the early nineteenth century lived in rural areas where society was rigidly divided into several classes. The lowest and most populous class was composed of renters, farm workers, and servants who had little opportunity in a land where their toil resulted only in perpetual poverty. Guidebooks distributed throughout Norway in the 1860s, much to the dismay of the local clergy and officials, explained the conditions of settlement in America: they depicted

Norway Day, Alaska Yukon Exposition.
University of Washington,
Seattle, 1909
Nordic Heritage Museum

a bountiful land of immense size reinforcing a popular image created through letters Norwegians already in America had sent home describing a life of prosperity in a haven of freedom.

Economic and social conditions were similar in neighboring Sweden where the economic problems of the rural landless, and particularly the laborers and servants, had become acute by the middle of the nineteenth century. A financial depression in the 1860s, high unemployment in both the countryside and industrial districts, crop failures and famine cast a shadow across Sweden from 1866 through the 1890s. During these years approximately 800,000 Swedes immigrated to the United States and many came to the Pacific Northwest. Iceland, suffering from overpopulation, social unrest, and natural disasters, also witnessed an exodus to North America between 1870 and 1914. This movement led to the formation of Icelandic communities in the Dakotas and Manitoba which soon spread to Washington at Point Roberts, in Blaine, and Seattle although relatively few Icelanders entered the state before the 1890s.

Conditions in Denmark and Finland were less severe, nevertheless, unemployment rose in Denmark with the industrialization of the 1860s and the first wave of emigration followed as servants, artisans, and landless manual workers sought better lives in America. Finnish emigration also began in the 1860s when workers were recruited for copper mining in Michigan. Many Finns had also worked on the Baltic fleets and for other maritime nations actively pursuing international trade in the nineteenth century. Several hundred Finns worked Russian Alaska ports in the 1860s and a few Finnish sailors visited Seattle during this time.

In 1868 pioneer Finn Charles Tollber began working as a ship carpenter at Port Blakely on Bainbridge Island. The following year he filed on a homestead in Skagit County but relocated to a farm near LaConner in 1872. A Finnish colony was established near Centerville in Klickitat County in the summer of 1877 after the families of Lars Mattson, John Crocker, and John Hagen, who had originally settled in Michigan, were advised by the Russian vice-consul in Portland (Finland was under Russian control at the time) to homestead in The Dalles area. Finns began homesteading at Brush Prairie near Vancouver in 1879 and over the next three decades an extensive Finnish presence developed across southeastern Washington. By the 1880s Finns were living around Ilwaco, Naselle, and the Willapa Valley where loggers from the great Karelian forests found massive stands of fir, spruce, and hemlock to cut while fishers from the Gulf of Bothnia entered the Pacific for salmon and halibut (McDonald; Apsler, 1952; Mattson, 1977; and Connelly, 1960).

Swedish funeral.
Preston area, 1917
Nordic Heritage Museum

Nordic settlement gradually spread across America in the mid-nineteenth century from New York to Wisconsin and Minnesota and beyond. A pioneer Norwegian clergyman in North Dakota reported, "Those who live in the older settlements learn that great reaches of fertile and free lands are to be had to the westward, and so they again turn toward the new and unseen." As the frontier pushed west, Norwegian and Swedish immigrants moved with it in search of new opportunities. In 1850 among those leaving from Norway's Trondheim district for the Pacific Coast, a song of future expectation was sung which ended sadly with the following verse:

> To thee, beloved land, I bid farewell.
> Soon I no longer shall view thy beauty nor hear the music of thy waterfalls.
> The snow-capped mountains will fade from sight and slowly thy coast will sink away in the mists
>   like a mother being lowered in the grave.
> No glimpse then of thy tallest peaks; only a lonely sail on the boundless deep.

This lament reflects the profound spiritual attachment that many immigrants shared with the homeland. The decision to leave was rarely made without regret. Distinctive to the European immigrant experience in Washington, however, was that "fading" snow-capped mountains and serene coasts reappeared in all their former grandeur. This impact on the immigrant mind was profound as Germans beheld Bavarian splendor in the Wenatchee Valley while Scandinavians marvelled at the familiarity of placid inlets on Puget Sound.

"The jagged summits of the Olympics now appeared clear and cold," wrote Oliver B. Iverson of his arrival on Puget Sound in the 1870s, "sticking out of the dark, green banks of firs on the foothills. I thought of Norway. This scene was different, but just as beautiful. . . ." Iverson, a native of Hardanger, Norway, had emigrated in 1867 to Iowa and had undertaken travels throughout the Dakotas and Montana before settling in Snohomish County in 1874. An expert surveyor, Iverson developed a reputation for meticulous work and assisted in locating property claims for Norwegians who had been settling since the 1860s in the lower Stillaguamish River Valley. This area near present Stanwood became the region's first Norwegian settlement and Iverson gained election as Snohomish County's delegate to the territorial assembly in 1876. He later gained the support of Governor Elisha P. Ferry to recruit Scandinavians from the Dakotas for settlement in Washington.

Although Stanwood, Silvana, and Poulsbo emerged during Washington's territorial era as predominantly Norwegian communities, the greatest numbers of Norwegians later settled north of Seattle in Ballard and in Tacoma. Other important enclaves of Norwegian and Swedish settlement appeared at Bellingham, Everett, throughout smaller communities encircling Puget Sound, and in southwestern Washington where work was available in fishing, logging, lumbering, and farming. Fewer numbers found employment in the cities as day laborers and street builders; some like the Swedish immigrant John W. Nordstrom, who drifted to Seattle in the 1880s, went into merchandising. Unlike most others he parlayed his last three dollars into a fortune through the shoe business. Unfamiliarity with the language and a lack of formal education and capital kept most Nordics from professional careers during their early years in the Northwest (Hansen, 1975; Flatin, 1975; and Dahlie, 1970).

East of the Cascades, Scandinavian settlement appeared in farming districts around Ellensburg, Walla Walla, and throughout Spokane County. By 1880 Washington's native-born Norwegian and Swedish population registered 1,228 (data on other Nordics were not included), or approximately 11.5% of the total foreign-born element. Their numbers skyrocketed during the next decade, however, when a transcontinental railroad linked Washington with the East. Substantial credit for its completion must go to Washington's first territorial governor, Isaac Stevens, and Eastern investors who initially backed the risky venture, the toil and blood of immigrant labor built the line under the direction of the legendary magnate Henry Villard, himself an immigrant from Europe.

The Northern Pacific Railroad and "Second Wave" Migrations: 1880s to World War I

Henry Villard.
Minnesota Historical Society

Henry Villard had come to the United States from Bavaria in 1853 as a young man. After several years at various occupations he studied law and then worked in the offices of several United States senators from the Midwest. A talented journalist, he reported various political campaigns which led to personal acquaintanceships with Abraham Lincoln, Horace Greeley, and others in influential circles of American and European business. He became increasingly interested in the subject of railroad securities and finance and, in 1873, was asked to advise and subsequently join a German investment partnership which had substantial interest in Western railroads. In 1874 Villard journeyed to Oregon as a representative of the committee to examine the situation and later wrote that the trip changed the course of his life: "I felt that I had reached a chosen land, certain of great prosperity and seemingly holding out better promise to my constituents than I had hoped for."

To bolster the region's developing transportation industry, he was supplied with the distinction of "Oregon Commissioner of Immigration" and by 1875 had established offices in Boston, Topeka, and Omaha which cooperated with the main Northwest Immigration Bureau in Portland in directing immigrants to the Pacific Northwest. It was the duty of railroad officials there to provide them with employment on construction crews or sell them company lands on which, in turn, agricultural produce and livestock would be raised for shipment by rail to regional market centers. Special displays were circulated of Northwest grains, fruits, and vegetables; large advertisements regularly appeared in English, German and Scandinavian newspapers throughout the United States and in Europe while thousands of circulars extolled the virtues of life in the Pacific Northwest. Villard's clever manipulation of several indebted concerns soon led him to the presidency of a number of Northwest transportation lines and acquisition of the Oregon Steam Navigation Company which operated a fleet of steamers on the Columbia and Snake Rivers.

To facilitate the orderly settlement and exploitation of his companies' holdings, Villard incorporated the Oregon Improvement Company in 1880. This move had far-reaching consequences on European immigration to Washington; the company acquired several enterprises requiring a capable labor supply including the Columbia River and Puget Sound Railroad, the Seattle Coal and Transportation Company, timber properties, and 150,000 acres in the heart of eastern Washington's fertile Palouse Hills. Villard appointed retired general Thomas R. Tannatt, who had advised him on European recruitment for several years, to handle the affairs of the Oregon Improvement Company and Tannatt directed thousands of laborers to company operations which included many Irish for railroad construction, Scandinavians in logging and lumbering, Italians to the mines, and Germans on farmlands. Villard's grandiose scheme for his railroad empire reached its ultimate fruition in 1881 when he collected an $8,000,000 "blind pool" to purchase the stalemated Northern Pacific Railroad. Work on both ends of the line resumed again and a passenger train inaugurated travel from St. Paul to Portland in the fall of 1882. A separate link from the Snake River over the Cascades via the Yakima Valley to Tacoma was completed in 1887 (Villard, 1944).

The completion of the Northern Pacific Railroad in 1882 marked a watershed event in the movement of European Americans to the region. Prior to the 1880s immigrants from Europe generally arrived without particular destinations for permanent residence. Unlike Blacks, Asians, or American Indians whose settlement was frequently restricted, European immigrants roamed widely until economic opportunities, salubrious climates, or topographic features conjuring up images of the Old Country combined to yield a decision to stay. As was the case with the Whealans from Ireland, this process could involve considerable peregrination before settling down. As some of these outposts spawned a localized ethnic identity they evolved into destination points for entire colonies of European immigrants from the 1880s who, through correspondence and newspaper reports, had learned of conditions in Washington while the railroad promoted group travel.

European immigrants to the Northwest prior to this period were from Northern and Western Europe who, as with the German John Galler, usually arrived in the region unmarried. For the non-English speaking vanguard this condition often led to marriages with women from other European backgrounds or with local Indians although this practice was common only among the early French Canadians. The advent of the railroad brought significantly more women to Washington which fostered customary family and cultural life and strengthened the work force, particularly in urban areas. Southern and Eastern Europeans also came to the Northwest in considerably larger numbers beginning in the 1880s although ethnic groups that predominated in the first wave predominated in even greater numbers during the period from 1880 to the First World War.

Railroad strategy to populate their vast land grants with dependable colonists led to a shift in their recruitment patterns directly to Europe. No longer did Oliver Iverson or other Scandinavian promoters only seek settlers from the Midwest nor did immigrants necessarily have the chance to adjust to life elsewhere in the nation before coming to Washington. Henry Villard's Northern Pacific Railroad employed over 900 agents in Europe by 1882 who distributed thousands of pamphlets in various languages extolling the Pacific Northwest as the "best wheat, farming and grazing lands in the world." To landless peasants throughout the continent the appeal of a new life in a free land spanned by railroads impelled a new generation to accept the challenge of emigration. Washington's European-born population rose steadily from 1880 to 1910 in terms of both constant numbers and as a percentage of the state's total population. Fourteen percent of Washington's 75,116 residents in 1880 were from Europe or Canada while that proportion rose to a remarkable twenty-one percent in 1910 (241,197 of the total 1,141,990 inhabitants).

The emigrant experience during the Atlantic crossing could be as miserable for the adults as it was exciting for the children. Steerage rates relegated them to the cheapest and most crowded quarters

on ship. An emigrant of 1866 wrote, "We lie among one another, Swedes, Norwegians, Danes, Germans and Englishmen like animals, some sick, some singing. It's like an auction." After enduring these conditions for about two weeks the huge vessels finally reached America, usually entering at New York, where immigration officials at Castle Gardens, or Ellis Island after 1892, inspected the newcomers for medical clearance and queried their political leanings before admission could be approved. On the average, immigrants in the late 1800s arrived to begin their new life in America with money valued at roughly seventeen dollars in their pockets.

Of Washington's 241,197 foreign-born white residents in 1910, those from Canada, Great Britain, and Ireland numbered 74,218 (31% of the total foreign-born whites) and remained widely dispersed throughout the state. Associating themselves with a culture that had served as a principal source for the one in which they were now living, the English-speaking immigrants found little difficulty in adapting to American society and little need to settle in distinctive enclaves. The greatest concentrations of these peoples were in the urban areas of King, Pierce and Spokane Counties where Catholic, Episcopal, Congregational, and other denominations maintained their religious heritage while such organizations as the Knights of Columbus, Caledonian Society, and Daughters of Scotia promoted social and cultural ties.

Immigrants from Nordic countries overshadowed all European groups by 1910 when they claimed 32% of the state's foreign-born whites (77,080 persons). Over three-quarters of Washington's Nordic peoples lived in the eight counties on Puget Sound, Grays Harbor County, and Spokane County where most retained their traditional occupations of fishing, lumbering, and farming. Nordic emigration remained greatest from Sweden and Norway during this era of the second wave to Washington, with the 1910 census reporting 32,195 Swedes and 28,363 Norwegians living in the state.

Significant numbers also kept coming from Finland during this period while other immigrants relocated to new areas within the Evergreen State. In 1884 Aksel Seaborg moved from Ilwaco to Aberdeen to build a salmon cannery and Finnish settlement soon spread to Hoquiam, Raymond, and other areas in Gray's Harbor and Pacific Counties. Eastern Washington enclaves appeared south of Almira and Govan in the Big Bend wheat country where Finns began homesteading in the 1890s while others settled about the same time in Spokane's Peaceful Valley and in the Woodspur district and Deep Creek Valley near Northport. By 1910 more Finns were living in Washington than in any other Western state and nearly one-half of the state's 8,718 first-generation Finns were living in the five counties along Washington's

Popular Finnish boarding-house.
Hoquiam, 1910
Polson Museum, Hoquiam

southwest perimeter from Gray's Harbor to Vancouver. Other concentrations were in King and Pierce Counties where some worked as coal miners at Coal Creek, Newcastle, and Carbonado or followed specialized trades in the city. Finns began settling in the Grayland area south of Grays Harbor in 1914 where they pioneered the area's cranberry industry and were prime movers in the formation of Washington's Cranberry Growers Association. (Hagin, 1988 and Howard, 1973).

Nordics also established many fraternal and benevolent organizations which provided fellowship and maintained cultural identity during this time of adjustment to American life. Groups to which Washington Nordics frequently belonged included the Sons of Norway, Vasa Order of America, Leif Ericson Society, United Finnish Kaleva Brotherhood and Sisterhood, and the Danish Aid Society. Nordics were also quick to establish Lutheran churches soon after their arrival in the Pacific Northwest and their synods, now free from state domination, flourished. The Swedish Augustana, United Norwegian, Suomi Lutheran, and Danish Lutheran Synods were all active in Washington. The most popular Nordic newspapers in the state included the Tacoma *Tidende,* Seattle's *Washington Posten,* and Spokane's *Svenska Nordvästern.*

Prior to the 1890s Dutch settlement in Washington was light and largely confined to the Puget Sound area where Henry Van Asselt had settled when Seattle was born in 1851. Other pioneer Dutch residents later clustered in Spokane where most farmed although a few engaged in the banking business. The Northwest glistened as an investment opportunity for European financiers prior to the 1893 depression and Spokane became the headquarters for several banks established with Dutch capital including the Northwestern and Pacific Mortgage Company and the Holland-Washington Hypotheek Bank. As these banks held title to more than a dozen blocks in the heart of the city, the popular saying arose during this period that "the Dutch own downtown Spokane." Investments were made in properties across the state and on Whidbey Island alone 18,000 acres were acquired for resale to new settlers. These opportunities, combined with adverse weather conditions in the Dakotas and Montana where they had settled earlier, caused a surge of Dutch immigration to Washington in the early 1890s. This movement was primarily directed to Puget Sound where lands were taken near Oak Harbor and Coupeville. The early immigrants wrote to relatives comparing the mild climate and fertile soil to Holland's polder region and others from the Midwest and Europe were induced to come.

People in Dutch Costume at the First Holland Days. Lynden, 1986
Photo by Michael Lewis
Courtesy of *The Lynden Tribune*

In 1895 Gerrit Veleke of Oak Harbor scouted Whatcom County's Nooksak Valley for settlement potential and returned a year later to lead others from Whidbey Island to the area where the Hollanders engaged in dairy and poultry farming, lumbering, and flower bulb culture. Lynden, Sumas, and Mount Vernon became centers for Dutch life in Whatcom County and settlement expanded at the turn of the century to Bellingham and Everett. Henry Wayenberg was a Midwestern transplant who immigrated to the Yakima Valley in 1896 and purchased a small farm on Moxie Creek. He became an ambitious promoter of Dutch settlement and interested dozens of his countrymen in moving to the newly irrigated lands of the valley including colonies from Iowa and South Dakota which arrived in the fall of 1900. Congregations of Dutch Reformed, Christian Reformed, and the Reformed Church of America were organized in many of Washington's Dutch communities and by 1910 the state contained 2,157 immigrants from Holland (Vander Ende, 1963; Lyman, 1919; and Powers, 1985).

The number of German-speaking immigrants in Washington grew substantially after 1880 and approximately 42,000 first-generation Germans, Austrians, and Swiss lived in the state in 1910. Slightly over half the Germans lived in King, Pierce, and Spokane Counties where they remained employed in merchandising, food-related businesses, and professional work. Most of Washington's Swiss were native to the German-speaking cantons of Schwyz, Uri, and Unterwalden. Those who were employed as craftsmen, machinists, bakers, and in other occupations in Swiss cities typically settled in Seattle and Tacoma while the rural Swiss established dairies and farms elsewhere around Puget Sound and in Pacific, Clark, and Spokane Counties. Many Swiss established their Catholic and Anabaptist churches in the Northwest; the Germans were predominantly Catholic or Lutheran joining the German Evangelical Synod of Missouri, Ohio and other States or the Joint Synod of Ohio and other States. Some Germans joined other Protestant denominations such as the German Congregational Church which established its first congregations in the West among Germans from Russia in Walla Walla, Ritzville, and Endicott in 1883. The state's first German language newspaper, *Die Washington Tribuene*, began publication in Seattle in 1883 where a Washington branch of the American Turnerbund Lodge was established two years later. Its members aspired to the classical ideal of a healthy body and sound mind. Sons of Hermann Lodges were also organized as cultural and mutual-aid societies throughout the state beginning with the Tacoma Sons Lodge in 1889. Affiliated lodges, Evergreen Sisters, were also instituted in several cities. (Giese, 1983; Wirsing, 1977; and Chebuhar, 1978).

"Second Wave" Emigration from Eastern and Southern Europe

While German immigration diffused throughout Washington, the rural element was especially predominant in the Big Bend country where most were engaged in dryland farming. Over 5,000 first-generation Germans were living in this region in 1910 and with their children constituted nearly one-third (1,721) of the entire population of Adams County. Adjacent Lincoln and Grant Counties were also heavily German. Characteristic of the second approaching wave of immigrants to America, however, many of these Germans had not come from western Europe but were known as the *Russlanddeutschen* (or Russian-Germans). Beginning with the invitation of Tsarina Catherine the Great in 1763 to settle on the wild steppes of southeastern Russia, their ancestors were among the Germans who migrated to three colonial enclaves in Eastern Europe: the lower Volga River, the northern Black Sea and Ukraine regions, and the eastern Polish province of Volhynia. Russian-Germans from all three areas began emigrating following the abrogation of settlement privileges in 1871 that had guaranteed exemption from military service and reduced taxes.

One group of Volga Germans led by Phillip Green and Peter Ochs and another guided by Frederich Rosenoff entered Washington independently in 1882 following their communication with agents of the Northern Pacific Railroad. They were directed to Walla Walla where the Oregon Improvement Company arranged for scouting expeditions of the region. The Green-Ochs party chose to settle in the Endicott-St. John-Colfax area of Whitman County, while the others selected land between Ritzville and Odessa (named for the Black Sea port) in Adams and Lincoln Counties. Others decided to remain in Walla Walla though a few of these families later moved to the Bickleton Plateau in Klickitat County. Again the newcomers were struck by a sense of familiarity with the undulating bunchgrass prairies in the Palouse, Big Bend, and Horse Heavens which they set about to transform into productive grainlands. Even the name of the distinctive soil in which many planted their crops, *chernozem,* was Russian in origin.

Black Sea Germans led by Louis Pflugrath began settling near Lind in 1887 and spread northward while the railroad induced a colony of Volhynian Mennonites to settle on its lands near present Schrag (named for their leader, Jacob Schrag) in 1899. After the turn of the century Germans from Russia also immigrated to the wheatlands of Grant and Douglas Counties, the Wenatchee Valley orchard

Jacob Weber family, Russian German immigrants.
Passport photo
Russia, 1910
Courtesy of Emily Weber

56

districts, and to the sugar beet fields in the Yakima Valley. Prominent German immigrant Frederick Weyerhaeuser acquired 900,000 acres of Northwest timberlands in 1900 from the Northern Pacific Railroad. Relocating his headquarters from St. Paul to Tacoma, the Weyerhaeuser Timber Company built an international empire which brought thousands of European immigrants to work in Washington's forests (Scheuerman, 1979; and Scheuerman and Trafzer, 1980).

Reflecting the national trend, Washington's second wave of immigration from the 1880s to the First World War brought many other Southern and Eastern Europeans to the state with the majority coming from Italy, Greece, and Yugoslavia. Some of Washington's first Italian families were able to establish themselves in farming although later immigrants from Southern Europe frequently had to abandon their traditional agrarian pursuits since employment opportunities had changed significantly. By the turn of the century, when Southern European immigration surged, most potential farmland in Washington had been claimed and unskilled laborers were compelled to move to cities where industrial growth and available service occupations meant employment. Moreover, wages in factories and mines were generally better than the income from farming or fishing and required no investment.

Among Seattle's pioneer Italians was George Colello who arrived in 1875 and established a vegetable farm near present-day First Avenue and South Jackson Street. As the city swelled in population from 3,500 in 1880 to 155,000 in twenty years, Colello was forced to move progressively south until he secured land in South Park on which he and other Italian and Japanese truck farmers raised a variety of fresh produce. They transported the tomatoes, leeks, and other vegetables almost daily during the growing season to Pike Place Market which came under the ownership of another Italian immigrant, Joe Desimone, and developed into one of the largest fresh food outlets on the West Coast.

Italian settlement in the Walla Walla area likely began in 1876 with the arrival of Pasquale Sturno. Sturno had immigrated to America a year earlier from an island near Naples and together with Joseph Tachi, who also arrived in the mid 1870s, became a pioneer truck farmer in the fertile valley. In 1888 Sturno brought his family to Walla Walla where dozens of Milanese and Calabrese also settled and contributed to the cultural diversity of eastern Washington's first city. By 1910, first-generation Italians living in the area numbered 259. The Walla Walla Italian community established its own church, St. Francis of Assisi, in 1915, as well as the Italian Workingmen's Club to promote fellowship and cultural identity.

Mr. and Mrs. J. A. Weber.
Quincy, 1982
Photo by *Wenatchee World*
staff photographer
Courtesy of Emily Weber
(Jake Weber is the child in
the passport photograph)

Left: Italian wedding.
Roslyn, circa 1913
Oral History Program,
Washington State Archives

Right: Greek Community
baptism.
Tacoma, circa 1922
Courtesy of Chris Tolias

58

Elsewhere east of the Cascades, Italians were often recruited to work railroad section gangs which led to a predominance of Southern Italians in Spokane where rail connections fanned out throughout the region. In most Washington cities where Italians settled, however, those from the north were in the majority. In places like Renton, Issaquah, and Roslyn, the Italians worked in the coal mines while those living in Seattle and Tacoma at the turn of the century found employment as merchants, laborers, and fishermen. Most of Seattle's several hundred Italian fishermen in 1900 were from Sicily and they congregated near a small but colorful houseboat community of Greek fishermen on the Duwamish River just south of the Spokane Street Bridge (Nicandri, 1978).

As with the Italians, many of Washington's first Greeks traveled the rails as unmarried laborers whose homes were kitchen, dining, and sleeping cars. Others relocated to the city where they operated tobacco, fruit, and candy stores, shoe shine parlors, and restaurants. The popular Greek coffee house provided a social center where immigrants gathered over Turkish coffee mixed with Greek Metaxa brandy for discussions of mutual interest. Of Washington's 4,177 Greeks and 13,114 Italians in 1910, the largest concentrations were in Seattle and Tacoma. Although the majority were still unmarried, more women began coming to the United States from Southern Europe after the turn of the century as the male population became stabilized in certain localities. Some women found employment in textile mills and other factories but fewer Italian and Greek women worked outside the home than other Europeans due to the strong cultural emphasis on the domestic household. Seattle's Mount Virgin Parish was among the first organized in the state by Italian Catholics while prominent ethnic associations included the Mazzini Society, Greek American Protective Association, Italian Commercial Club, and Spokane's Fratellenza Marconi-Columbo Society (Reddin, 1961).

Steeped in ancient traditions, Yugoslavia in the late nineteenth century was the fractious domain of the "South Slavs": Croatians, Serbians, Slovenes, and Montenegrins. Most of these hardy Mediterranean peoples were peasants who struggled in the foothills of the Dinaric Alps in the 1800s to make a living on small plots of rocky land, often rented at exorbitant rates, using antiquated farming methods. Others were small fishermen along the Dalmatian Coast who plied the warm waters of the Adriatic and Mediterranean for daily catches. Since the problems of nineteenth-century Europe's food shortages and population increases were not as acute in this region, large scale emigration to America did not occur until the 1890s. In 1867 Sam Jerisich and Peter Goldsmith had settled on Gig Harbor with John Farrangue, a

Croatian wedding party.
Old Town, Tacoma, 1904
Courtesy of Mary Babare
Love

61

Spaniard, to become the first two Yugoslavians known to live on Puget Sound. The two men fished from San Francisco to Vancouver Island in search of a new home before selecting the protected shores off Point Defiance which likely reminded Jerisich of his native Kotor Bay in Montenegro. They were followed by dozens of other Dalmations who started coming to Puget Sound in larger numbers in the 1880s. Tacoma's Old Port soon developed into the Dalmatian fleet's headquarters on the Sound where purse seiners with cotton nets sailed throughout the year for salmon, smelt, herring, and bottom fish in the rich fishing grounds off the San Juan Islands. In 1896 Antoine Glenovich from the island of Viz off Dalmatia landed in Bellingham and later encouraged many Yugoslavians to settle in Whatcom and Skagit Counties. In this area dozens fished for the Pacific American Fisheries plant at Bellingham, the world's largest canner of salmon by the early 1900s, and joined other purse seiners in the annual voyages to Alaska and the Bering Sea. By 1920 Yugoslavs were operating out of ports at Bellingham, Anacortes, Everett, Seattle, Tacoma, and Hoquiam (Petrich, 1984).

The earliest Slovenes in Washington were probably Mathais Malneritch and Joseph Paschich, natives of the Austrian province Carniola, who homesteaded at present Krain near Eatonville in 1881. Krain's namesake was the Austrian hometown of the local Catholic priest, Father F.J. Seminich. Like most immigrant Slavs in the area, Malneritch and Paschich were unmarried and found work during the winter with Italians, Croatians, and other Slavs in the coal mines at Black Diamond, Carbonado, Wilkinson, Ravensdale, and elsewhere in Pierce and King Counties where the Slovenes became the largest Slavic element by the turn of the century. High grade bituminous deposits had been discovered in this district in the 1880s at a time when demand by the Northern Pacific Railroad and various Puget Sound steamship companies was booming. Proximity to the coal mines also led to construction of the Tacoma Smelter in Ruston which caused many Croatians and Austrians to settle there. Explorations east of the Cascades for coal also revealed a large field near Roslyn and Cle Elum in Kittitas County where coal exporting began in 1886. These developments brought the first Croatians to Roslyn where Philip Ozura and Ignaz Francisovich arrived in 1891. Often beginning as strike-breakers, the Croats and other Slavs joined Italians working in the mines as loaders, drill operators, and in other hazardous labor. By 1920 the Croatians were Roslyn's largest nationality as nearly one-quarter of the city's 4,000 inhabitants were of this Slavic group (Green, 1974; and Buerge, 1988).

Cornishmen, Welsh, and other English speaking Americans usually served as foremen and superintendents in the Washington coal fields. This dichotomy characterized most Washington mining operations as upward mobility was often a function of assimilation in language and culture. Racism was also a factor, denying Southern Europeans access to other professional work during this period as their darker complexions distinguished them from most other Americans. Consequently, many Slavs and Italian immigrants, from an Old World culture that had stressed formal education for the privileged class only, remained unskilled laborers who tended to live in more tightly organized ethnic neighborhoods. Here their rich heritage remained evident in Catholic and Orthodox religious observances, distinctive Mediterranean cuisine, and other unique elements of their diverse cultures. By 1910 Washington was home to about 4,500 South Slavs and many joined the Slavonian-American Benevolent Society, Croatian Fraternal Union, (Slovene) St. Barbara Lodge, and Serb National Federation.

Slavs and Greeks found traditional religious fellowship in Orthodox churches located where they clustered. The state's first Orthodox parish, St. Spirodon, was organized in 1892 among Russian and Greek immigrants in Seattle by the Russian Orthodox missionary Sebastian Dabovich. They met in a small white church until a magnificent multi-domed cathedral was completed at the base of Capitol Hill in the 1930s. As Slavic immigration to the city increased the church came to serve Serbians, Bulgarians, and Ruthenians as well as Gypsies and Syrians. Seattle developed into the center for Washington's Russian community which began in the 1880s when immigrants from Alaska sought employment in area coal mines. By 1910 approximately 2,500 Russian immigrants were living in Seattle and an influx of Greeks during the next decade led to a division of the Orthodox parish in 1915. St. Demetrios Greek Orthodox Church, organized that year, completed its cathedral in 1918. Greek Orthodox congregations were also organized in Tacoma and Spokane. Other Eastern European Slavs immigrated to Washington during this period and by the turn of the century Ukrainians and Slovaks had established a colony at Wilkenson where they worked in the stone quarry and Polish communities of loggers and mill workers developed at Aberdeen and in cities on Puget Sound.

Those immigrants who had first spied Seattle as a bustling settlement of 3,500 in 1880 must have found it incredible to be living in an international crossroads of a quarter-million residents in 1910. Spurred on by the coming of the Northern Pacific in the 1880s, the Great Northern in 1893, and the Klondike Gold Rush beginning four years later, fully half the city's population in 1910 was foreign-born   *63* or of foreign parentage. Forays through its neighborhoods filled the senses with sights, sounds, and smells of European culture. Reflecting the state's profile, Nordic peoples predominated with their heaviest concentrations north of the ship canal in Fremont, Phinney Ridge, and Ballard where Norwegian and Swedish shopkeepers and Lutheran churches served community needs. Germans proliferated throughout Seattle but operated many downtown hotels and saloons while Italians lived in residential areas in Youngstown, South Park, Georgetown, and the Rainier Valley. Flotillas of small Greek and Yugoslav fishing boats assembled near their home ports on Elliott Bay and kosher butcher shops, delicatessens, and other Jewish stores lined their business district in the Yesler Way-Cherry Street neighborhood. Ladino-speaking Jews from Turkey and the Isle of Rhodes began arriving there at the turn of the century and, though a small percentage of the local Jewish population, by 1910 they had become the third largest Sephardic community in America and later formed the Sephardic Brotherhood. In 1924 *The Jewish Transcript*, an Ashenkanzic newspaper, began publication for the Northwest Jewish community.

The 1910 census recorded the highest number of foreign-born residents in Washington's history with nearly a quarter-million individuals or twenty-one percent of the population claiming that status. The outbreak of World War I in 1914 substantially reduced emigration from Europe as travel across borders and the Atlantic Ocean became increasingly restricted. Furthermore, virtually all of the state's fertile lands had been claimed by 1910 and, in the following decade, Congress enacted legislation that placed entry quotas on all foreign groups. By that time, however, unsettling changes had begun to appear upon Northwest lands and waters. European American zeal to exploit the region's bounty contributed to the depletion of coastal fish runs, the clearing of the state's old growth forests, and widespread erosion of eastern Washington's irreplaceable cropland. These conditions would present challenges to future generations seeking to renew the land's natural resources.

Twentieth Century Patterns of Migration

The distinctive cultural identity of some American-born groups also grew as their populations expanded around the turn of the century. The influx of Southerner highlanders to the western Cascade slopes began with the journey of Rufus Siler from the hills of Louden County, Tennessee to the upper Cowlitz country of Lewis County, Washington in 1884. Siler came west on the Union Pacific Railroad following a brother to Portland since their native Clinch River Valley was becoming overcrowded. "We were educated enough to know that out in the Oregon country we could get good bottom land free," he said of his motive for moving. Siler relayed favorable reports about southeastern Washington back home where the work of aggressive railroad agents was paying dividends for the newly opened lines to the Northwest. Siler was soon followed by fellow Appalachian highlanders Richard Ormsbey, Evans Blankenship, John Osborne, and dozens of others who clustered in the quiet valleys above Morton, Mineral, Randle, and Riffe. The latter two communities were named for natives from Tennessee and West Virginia, respectively. As a steady stream of the newcomers, sometimes called "Tarheels," flowed to Washington from about 1900 to 1930, the course forked into a general pattern directing Appalachians from Kentucky and the Virginias and Ozarkians from Missouri and Arkansas to Lewis and northern Cowlitz Counties, while highlanders from eastern Tennessee and North Carolina's Great Smoky Mountains migrated to Skagit and northeastern Snohomish Counties. Settlement in Lewis County soon spread to the Willapa Hills and northwestern Washington enclaves developed around Sedro Wooley, Marysville, Hamilton, Rockport, and Darrington. Many of these people also settled east of the Cascades in the Kittitas, Wenatchee, and Okanogan Valleys.

Appalachian and Ozark culture in Washington reflected the primal values of family clans which perpetuated respect and support for relatives and prized rural isolation. As had been the tradition in the South, the families were largely self-sufficient and drew their livelihood from hunting, logging, and subsistence farming. Initial experiments in planting familiar crops of corn, sweet potatoes, and tobacco were disappointing in the cool, moist climate where small grains, potatoes, and other root crops soon became staples. Secondary income came through the sale of mountain blackberries, huckleberries, cedar shakes, and other wood products. Most of the highlanders remained faithful to the Old Regular Baptist Union and New Salem Union of Kentucky while others belonged to Pentecostal fellowships. These congregations remain active in the small towns and valleys of the Cascade slopes where country Gospel singing rises each Sunday morning while mountain ballads and folktunes are still sung and fiddled on summer evenings (Clevinger, 1938,1942).

America's entrance into World War I in 1917 fostered enmity toward the Germans which was often transferred to German-American immigrants and their children. Washington's legislature prohibited the teaching of German in schools and some families came under public harassment where Germans were a minority. In efforts to prove their loyalty to their adopted country, Germans in many churches

Missouri women quilt-makers.
Lynden, 1988
Photo by Wilhelma Cowin
Courtesy of the Missouri Club, Lynden and the Washington State Folklife Council

converted from use of their mother-tongue in services and instruction to English, and newspapers in the state carried advertisements proclaiming their patriotism. In Seattle a chapter of the Stueben Society of America was formed to promote public appreciation for the contributions Germans had been making to the United States since the nation's inception. All European immigrant groups in Washington, however, generally prospered with the entire nation as American involvement in the war effort bolstered the economy. Puget Sound shipyards hummed with activity while wheat prices doubled and other commodity prices rose to strengthen the state's economy on both sides of the Cascades.

After the war ended, members of several European groups entered the Northwest including French and Belgian war brides, Armenian refugees from atrocities in Turkey, and Russians fleeing after the 1917 Bolshevik Revolution. Six thousand Russian emigres who had made their way across Siberia to Harbin, China, passed through Seattle alone in 1923. Most journeyed to other destinations but some remained to work in Seattle or in Puget Sound area logging camps and mines.

Washington's largest Bulgarian and Romanian enclaves have been in Seattle where several hundred Balkan immigrants settled soon after World War I. Although they formed no formal ethnic associations, the popular Radost Ensemble has performed Balkan folk dances and songs throughout the region featuring the distinctive music of the pan flute and stringed cymbalon. Romanians point proudly to the remarkable collections in the Maryhill Museum near Goldendale which display priceless Orthodox icons and regalia from the magnificent throne room of Romania's Queen Marie. The museum was built by railroad magnate Sam Hill and was dedicated in 1926 by the queen herself in tribute to Hill's postwar relief efforts in Eastern Europe (Chebuhar, 1978).

The state's swelling numbers of second-generation European Americans contended with both external and internal pressure to "not be different" among their peers. Children of the foreign-born often grew up bilingual but public schools and the workplace militated against the perpetuation of native language and Old World custom. Anti-Catholic feeling and "Red Scare" sentiment were directed against Italians in Northwest cities during the twenties since they were widely regarded as being heavily involved in Washington's trade union problems of that period. Although many Italians were members of the United Mine Workers organizations in the Cascade coal mines, they also comprised the majority of the labor force at many locations and their actual membership rate was no higher than that of other nationalities. Through the efforts of the union's Italian, Slavic, and other members, Washington's miners helped lead the struggle for standardized wages and safer working conditions in mines throughout America. Italians and Germans were also targets of Prohibitionists since their use of wine and beer had been a cultural trait for generations. The consumption question has been characterized as a "Puritan debate," not a Mediterranean or German one, but the distinction usually was not recognized by authorities or public crusaders (Pellegrini, 1970; and Nicandri, 1979).

The American entry into World War II brought trends in ethnic sentiment and economic opportunity similar to those evident earlier in the century. Racist attitudes were more harshly directed against immigrants from America's new adversary in the Pacific, Japan, but prejudice was also directed against Germans and Italians in Washington, although in many areas members of these groups led native-born Americans both in enlistments and the purchase of war-bonds. Wartime contracts for military aircraft transformed the Seattle-based Boeing Company into a world-leading manufacturing industry during the 1940s. Company officials were enabled to gather a skilled production force with outstanding engineers attracted from states throughout the nation as well as Canada, Western Europe, and Turkey. An unprecedented influx of families to the Tri-Cities area began in 1943 as work began at the Hanford Nuclear Reservation. Within months the tiny farming hamlet of Richland was transformed into one of Washington's largest cities as authorities struggled to keep its existence a secret during the war. Many technicians at the plant were from Europe and the general workforce was assembled by government contractors from all parts of the country. German prisoners of war were also brought to Washington where they were detained in a sprawling compound at Fort Lewis. Under Army supervision these men were organized into labor brigades which were directed to Walla Walla area truck farms, Wenatchee Valley orchards, and elsewhere in the state to help take in the annual harvest. Some, like an aspiring young artist named Albert Weirich, returned to the Northwest from Germany after their repatriation. In 1953 he and his German-born wife, Hilde, returned to Washington to make their home near Peshastin where the industrious Weirichs soon acquired an orchard of their own.

After the war the International Refugee Organization worked with several Washington religious organizations to resettle European refugees in the state. Jews from Central and Eastern Europe who had survived the trauma of the Holocaust found sanctuary among Seattle's Jews who began expanding into suburbia during the post-war period. The city's Jewish population doubled from ten to almost twenty thousand between 1945 and 1980. The I.R.O. also worked with Lutheran churches to find homes in

Washington for refugees fleeing Communist repression in the Baltic republics and with other organizations on behalf of Polish, Czech, and Hungarian refugees. In 1949 several hundred Latvians and Estonians were resettled in Seattle, Olympia, Longview, Spokane, and Naches. In Seattle they joined Lithuanians, who began settlement there around the turn of the century, in forming organizations dedicated to restoring the independence of their homelands and maintaining cultural identity (Howell, 1959; Berkholds, 1983; Howell, 1961). In 1980 approximately 10,000 people in Washington were of Czechoslovakian descent, about 5,000 indicated a dominant Baltic ancestry, and a similar number were Hungarian. Some 22,000 claimed a singular Polish ancestry in 1980 but this number soon rose slightly as intensified government repression of the Solidarity labor movement from 1981 to 1983 caused many Poles to emigrate to the West. Most who came to Washington were resettled through church organizations in Puget Sound and Spokane.

With a presence in the region stretching back to the genesis of the Northwest fur trade, Canadians moved to Washington during the first half of the twentieth century in record numbers and have remained the state's largest foreign-born group. Present estimates place their population in the Puget Sound area alone at 70,000 and while they comprise a significant group in all Washington counties, their concentrations are also heavy along the northern tier of Whatcom, Skagit, Okanogan, Stevens, Ferry, and Pend Oreille Counties. Economic opportunities south of the border have attracted most Canadian immigrants whose culture and language so closely resemble American that they have been called the "invisible minority." Differences are perceptible, however, in certain pronunciations as well as political sentiment given their historical associations with Great Britain. Robert Greer of Seattle's Canadian Imperial Bank, a native of London, Ontario, has observed that North American culture is more vertically related than horizontal and that citizens of British Columbia and Alberta probably have had more in common with Washingtonians than with their counterparts in the Eastern provinces. Recent Canadian legislation has also facilitated residence and since 1977 citizenship can be maintained by Canadians who also request this status in the United States. This right also extends to children born here to Canadian mothers with dual citizenship. Groups like Seattle's Royal Canadian Legion and the Granite Curling Club provide Canadians with opportunities to gather together on a regular basis. The club is one of several in the state zealously devoted to playing this ancient Scottish game. The Canadian Society of the Northwest was formed in 1983 by the Canadian Consulate to maintain ties with Canadians in the region and to engender

Richard Dekshenicks family, first displaced persons from Latvia.
Tacoma, 1948
Courtesy of the Dekshenicks Family

greater understanding between the people of two nations who have much in common (Case, 1983).

Though smaller in numbers than many other ethnic groups in Washington, other peoples with a distinct European heritage have entered the state in recent years to enrich the regional culture. Isolated enclaves of Basques have existed in the Seattle and Spokane areas throughout most of the twentieth century and Basque numbers increased after 1952 when a foreign sheepherder recruitment bill strongly supported by the Washington Wool Growers Association was passed by Congress. This legislation allowed 500 young Basque immigrants to enter the United States where dozens of skilled herders like Alfonzo Barber and Fernando Arbea from the rugged Valle de Salazar in Spain's Navarra province were directed to eastern Washington rangelands. Their abilities were highly regarded by the region's large sheep operators and many were induced to remain in Washington beyond their initial three-year contracts to become American citizens (Douglass, 1975; McGregor, 1982). In 1956 Hutterite leader Eli Wollman brought a small group of his kinsmen from Pincher Creek, Alberta to establish Washington's first Hutterite colony at Deep Creek near Spokane. With a religious heritage rooted in the Anabaptist traditions of pacifism and communalism, the Hutterites fled persecution in sixteenth century Germany to begin a series of successive moves to Moravia, Wallachia, the Ukraine, and in the 1870s, North America. After building a prosperous and virtually self-sufficient agricultural commune near Espanola on Deep Creek, a second colony was begun at Warden (1971) and others followed near Wilson Creek (Marlin, 1976) and Odessa (Stahl, 1980) (Gross, 1981; Brandmarker, 1979).

That Washington's European American communities retain a vibrant ethnic identity is evident in religious life, occupational patterns, folk traditions, and other cultural expressions. Visitors can catch a glimpse of these distinctive features at annual celebrations held across the state ranging from Scandinavian festivals at Naselle, Poulsbo, and Ballard to Oktoberfests in Odessa, Leavenworth, and Seattle, along with Lynden's Holland Days, Soap Lake's Greek Festival, and Italian Heritage Days at Walla Walla. These events present a kaleidoscope of activity with colorful folk costumes of performers who sing and dance to traditional music in an atmosphere rich with the aroma of ethnic delicacies. Yet these scenes only highlight the vitality and resilience of Washington's European American communities that abides throughout the year. Ethnicity still bears a strong relationship to denominational affiliation with Catholic, Lutheran, Episcopal, Presbyterian, Reformed, Anabaptist, and Jewish congregations serving spiritual needs and providing traditional fellowship among ethnic communities in Washington.   *69*

Peter, Augustina and Lilia
Vashchenko,
Soviet émigrés.
Puyallup, 1984
Photo by Natalie Fobes
Courtesy of the *Seattle Times*

In the tiny Endicotts and Silvanas across the state, families who know fast food also know wurst and kuechen, lutefisk and lefsa. The children who sometimes wince when forced to indulge will soon be joining the perennial debate on the best wood for smoking or oven temperature for baking. Similarly, ethnic musicians regularly meet to sing and play for pure enjoyment and in preparation for public performances as residents of the state and nation are frequently treated to the talents of such groups as the renowned Vela Luka Croatian Dancers of Anacortes, Seattle's "Alpenroeshi" Swiss Chorus and the Dobar Dan Tamburitza Orchestra while Spokane boasts the famed German Arion Choir. Ethnic historians and authors work to chronicle the heritage of European American peoples through numerous journals published in the region; notable examples include the *Newsletter of the Washington State Jewish Historical Society* and *Journal of the Finnish-American Society of the West;* ethnic newspapers include the Ethnic Heritage Council's *Ethnic News,* the *Western Viking* (Seattle), and *Pacifische Rundschay* (Blaine). Home societies of various national origin exist throughout the state for community elders in retirement while many local ethnic organizations have joined forces with universities and museums to create programs with a European focus for young people and the general public. These innovative approaches have led to the development of the Scandinavian Cultural Council at Pacific Lutheran University, the Germans from Russia Archive Collection at Washington State University, and Kursa, the Latvian Cultural Center for high school students near Shelton. Museums featuring distinctive ethnic themes include the Nordic Heritage Museum in Ballard, the Lynden Pioneer Museum, Odessa's Historisches Museum, and the Polson Museum in Hoquiam.

Though altered by the American experience, European American cultural traditions in Washington are as varied as Europe itself and are reflected in daily living, ethnic associations and celebrations, and in education and preservation efforts. From the Pyrennes Mountains of Spain to the endless steppes of the Ukraine, immigrants of virtually every European nationality have come to form ethnic communities in Washington. Based on the 1980 federal census, nearly one-third of the state's 4.1 million residents still claim a single European ancestry. Those from Northern and Western European backgrounds continue to predominate with the greatest numbers associated with the Canadian English and British (8.9%), Germans (7.9%), Irish (3.3%), Norwegians (2.6%), and Swedes (1.6%). Southern and Eastern Europeans appear in smaller numbers as individuals of single ancestry but their presence is considerably larger through intermarriage with other groups. Working as individuals, families, and communities, the

European Americans of Washington built a home on the varied Northwest landscapes that reminded many newcomers of the Old Country. But they had come primarily to find a better way of life. Washington promised no riches but opportunities abounded along the coastal waters, in the evergreen forests, and on the plateau prairies for hardworking souls to enjoy a good life. The promise endures for Europeans and others who continue to find a home in Washington.

WORKS CITED

Apsler, Alfred. 1952. "Finns of Southwest Washington." *Sunday Oregonian,* 28 September, 10-11.

Berkholds, Arvids. 1977. "Latvians in Washington State." Manuscript.

Brandmarker, Alan. 1979. "Hutterites Cling to Old Lifestyle." *Wenatchee World,* 1 April, 1.

Buerge, David M. 1988. "Russian Seattle." *Seattle Weekly,* 30 March, 26-34.

Buttnick, Meta. 1988. Interview with author. Seattle, 16 December.

Case, Frederick. 1983. "Our Largest Ethnic Minority Is Hard to Find." *Seattle Times,* 17 April, E1.

Chebuhar, Teresa. 1978. "Balkan Immigrants Here Are Few but Enthusiastic." *Seattle Times,* 9 December, B1.

_____. 1978a. "40,000 Strong, the Swiss Are Still Here." *Seattle Times,* 30 September, B1.

Clevinger, Woodrow R. 1938. "The Appalachian Mountaineers in the Upper Cowlitz Basin." *Pacific Northwest Quarterly,* (29: 2): 115-134.

_____. 1942. "Southern Appalachian Highlanders in Western Washington." *Pacific Northwest Quarterly,* (33: 1): 3-25.

Connelly, Dolly. 1960. "Blaine's Little Iceland." *Seattle Times,* 20 March, 16-23.

Dahlie, Jorgen. 1970. "Old World Paths in the New: Scandinavians Find Familiar Home in Washington." *Pacific Northwest Quarterly,* (61: 2) 65-71.

Douglas, Jesse S. 1950. "The Origin of Population of Oregon in 1850." *Pacific Northwest Quarterly,* (41) .

Douglass, William A. and Jon Bilbao. 1975. *Amerikanuak: Basques in the New World.* Reno: University of Nevada Press.

Droker, Howard. 1986. "A Coat of Many Colors: A History of Seattle's Jewish Community." *Portage,* 4/2: 4-9.

Flatin, Kjetil. 1975. "Nordmenn ved Kysten." *Western Viking,* Supplement, 10 October.

Gibson, James R. 1985. *Farming the Frontier: The Agricultural Opening of the Oregon Country, 1786-1846.* Seattle: University of Washington Press.

Giese, Hans-Otto. 1983. "The Germans in Seattle." *German American Tricentennial: 1683-1983.* Seattle: German Tricentennial Committee.

Green, Roger H. 1974. *South Slav Settlement in Western Washington.* San Francisco: R. and E. Associates.

Gross, Jacob. 1981. Interview. Marlin, Washington, 10 April.

Hagin, Ellen S., Erma S. Hagin, and Allen Hagin. 1988. "Finnish Settlement in Eastern Washington." Manuscript.

Hansen, Bob H. 1975. *Norse to the New Northwest: A Sesquicentennial Saga.* Seattle: Norwegian American Anniversary Commission.

Howard, Marjut. 1973. "First the Indians—Then the Finns." *Aberdeen World,* 7 November.

Howell, Erle. 1959. "Seattle Area's Czechoslovakians." *Seattle Times,* 31 May.

_____. 1960. "Seattle's Lithuanians." *Seattle Times,* 16 April.

Hull, Lindley. 1929. *A History of Central Washington.* Spokane: Shaw & Borden.

Lyman, W. D. 1919. *History of the Yakima Valley, Washington, comprising Yakima, Kittitas and Benton Counties.* Volume 2. Chicago: S. J. Clarke.

Mattson, Mrs. Otis. 1977. "Centerville Finns, Klickitat County, Washington." *Journal of the Finnish Historical Society of the West.*

McDonald, Lucile. 1958. "Washington's Finnish Settlers." *Seattle Times,* Magazine Section, 13 July.

McGregor, Alexander C. 1982. *Counting Sheep: From Open Range to Agribusiness on the Columbia Plateau.* Seattle: University of Washington Press.

Nicandri, David L. 1978. *Italians in Washington State.* Washington State American Revolution Bicentennial Commission.

_____. 1979. "Washington's Ethnic Workingmen in 1900: A Comparative View." Manuscript.

Pellegrini, Angelo. 1970. "Italians in a New Land." *Seattle Times Magazine,* 6 September, 10-11.

Petrich, Mary Ann and Barbara Roje. 1984. *The Yugoslav in Washington State.* Tacoma: Washington State Historical Society.

Powers, Dorothy. 1985. "All of Us: Spokane Dutch Brought Beauty and Money." *Spokesman-Review,* 17 January, 1, 5.

Reddin, John J. 1961. "Faces of the City: Greek Fishing Fleet Evokes Fond Memories." *Seattle Times,* 15 January, E.

Scheuerman, Richard D. 1979. "From Wagon Trails to Iron Rails: Russian German Immigration to the Pacific Northwest." *Journal of the American Historical Society of Germans from Russia,* (2: 2) Fall, 37-40.

Scheuerman, Richard D. and Clifford E. Trafzer. 1980. *The Volga Germans: Pioneers of the Northwest.* Moscow: University of Idaho Press.

Schrier, Arnold. 1958. *Ireland and the American Emigration, 1850-1900.* Minneapolis: University of Minnesota Press.

Vander Ende, Gerrit. 1963. "History of Dutch in State Told." *Everson News,* 22 August.

Villard, Henry. 1944. *The Early History of Transportation in Oregon.* Eugene: University of Oregon Press.

Whealan, Richard and Loretta Kissler. 1980. Interview. Colfax, Washington, 31 July.

Wirsing, Dale R. 1977. *Builders, Brewers and Burghers: Germans of Washington State.* Washington State American Revolution Bicentennial Commission.

Most of Washington's Black population is African American

Washington's largest population of African ancestry is composed of Americans, whose ancestors were brought to the Western Hemisphere as slaves before the end of the eighteenth century. African Americans from all parts of the United States came to Washington in two great waves, the first in the late 1800s, the next during World War II. The majority of Washington's more than 91,000 Black residents live in Seattle, Tacoma, and Spokane.

WASHINGTON'S AFRICAN AMERICAN COMMUNITIES

Esther Hall Mumford

In 1961 I came to Seattle from a small, hill-country town in northern Louisiana. I had come at the invitation of my aunt and her husband who, like thousands of other Black people, principally from the southern states, came to the Pacific Northwest during World War II. It was a quietly exhilarating experience for me.

The war had brought enormous change to Washington. Between 1940 and 1950 census data shows the state's population increased thirty-seven percent, almost four times the increase of any of the three previous decades (Schmid, 1969). Thousands were attracted by an economic boom based on wartime shipbuilding, airplane and aluminum manufacture, and the Hanford Plutonium Project.

An even more dramatic change had taken place in the state's African American population which, in 1940, had numbered about 7,000. By 1950, allowing for some postwar decline, the Black population numbered around 30,000 concentrated in Seattle with smaller groups in Tacoma, Spokane, Yakima, Pasco, and Bremerton. There was also a sprinkling of Blacks in small towns and around the countryside. During World War II a variety of industrial jobs opened up for Blacks for the first time once available White workers had been absorbed by the war effort. Nearly 3,000 Blacks were recruited from Southern states as temporary labor for construction of the United States government plutonium production plant at Hanford (Droker, 1974). Boeing Aircraft Company recruited Black Southern laborers as did some construction and lumbering concerns.

These were some of the people I met, a part of the ongoing history of Washington's African American population. When they first arrived, they were the most recent in a succession of immigrants who had been looking, not only for a better life and an improved standard of living, but also for the freedom to live without the insults and harassment that were so much a part of daily life in the southern United

States of the 1940s. Had they achieved their goals? It appeared so. They were part of a vibrant community, suffered practically no harassment, owned their own homes, had late-model cars, and many of their children attended college.

Seeing Seattle from an automobile with family members and meeting their friends and acquaintances was very different, however, from venturing out alone and finding one's way around an unfamiliar place. I soon learned that my relatives' Beacon Hill neighborhood, although easily the most racially diverse in the city, was almost as inhospitable to Black people as any place in the deep South. (I was made even more painfully aware of this when I returned to Seattle in 1974 as a married woman with two small children. We spent six months in an apartment building with families of various ethnic groups, but few Blacks, while we searched for a house to purchase. Occasionally I allowed my son, who was then seven, to go out to play. After a few bewildering experiences of all the children disappearing when he came outside, I realized their parents would keep them inside rather than allow them to play with my son.)

As I became more familiar with the community in the 1960s I began to notice that there was a gap between those people I knew and many other members of the African American population. While I had seen numerous examples of skill, talent, and resilience I also found sizable numbers of Black people who were experiencing problems that seemed, both then and now, to be intractable: welfare dependency, teenage pregnancy, drug addiction, and crime. University of Chicago sociologist William Julius Wilson, in his 1988 book, *The Truly Disadvantaged*, attributes all of these problems to the fundamental circumstance of unemployment. A *Seattle Times* article of March 20, 1988 describing people living on Washington's minimum wage recently discussed the growing gap between well-educated Americans who are working and doing well, and less well-educated ones who work, yet remain in or near poverty. The article takes note of the disappearance of large numbers of well-paying blue collar jobs and the opening of many new jobs that pay less than the living wage for a family. This has been the situation many of Washington's Black families have faced over the past forty years. The Black community of which I was a part was both the product and the victim of its history and its present. But, while the present was there before my eyes, the past was more elusive.

As I became aware of the gaps, not only in my knowledge but also in that of those around me, I discovered, as did Alex Haley, that the oral tradition was alive and well in America's Black communities, and that history was there waiting to be recorded. In time I began to collect the oral history of my community and put it together with the scraps of written history to find out who those Black men and women were who had first come, and those who had followed, and why.

The 19th Century

This line of people searching for economic freedom and human dignity stretches back almost 150 years to Thurston County pioneer George Bush. He had come north of the Columbia River in 1845 after learning on his arrival in the Oregon Country that a self-appointed provisional government had recently voted to prohibit people of African descent from settling south of the Columbia River. Although Bush did not find complete freedom from prejudice north of the river, and in spite of the fact that it would soon be populated by people whose ideas about race relations were often distorted, he was reasonably free of the strictures against Blacks found in the United States proper. Bush's move has been repeated throughout the decades down to the present. Black people in other areas have continued to come to Washington in search of a place with less prejudice and more opportunity. And over the years, the people who followed him have experienced a certain gain of freedom; but discrimination, while less severe than in other places, has always been a part of their lives.

The fact of the matter is that free Black people knew very little peace in either the states or the territories. For example, what appears at first to be a strong moral position barring slavery from Oregon is deceptive. Much of the related legislation contains large amounts of anti-Black sentiment, and slaves were held in Oregon, and occasionally in Washington, without much public disapproval from white settlers (McLagan, 1980). Prior to the passage of the Fourteenth Amendment to the Constitution in 1866, Black people were not citizens and could not vote or give testimony in the courts of Washington Territory or elsewhere. (Washington Territory, 1854) They could, however, legally purchase and own property there, unlike many other places, including the state of Oregon. But in general, they were subjected to white attitudes that closely resembled those of whites in the states.

Thus, although Bush was freer in Washington than in other places where he had lived, his experience was different from that of his white neighbors. In spite of his success as a farmer, his steadiness of character and his past loyalty and service to the United States, informal and legal barriers set him apart. The Donation Land Act of 1850, for instance, limited ownership claims to white males, their wives, and their male offspring, including those with Indian mothers. It was only as a result of a petition to Congress

George Washington Bush.
Illustration by Sam Patrick
Courtesy of Los Angeles
Times Syndicate

79

by Bush's friends in the Territorial legislature of 1854, a year after Washington Territory separated from Oregon, that a waiver was granted making him the only African American to receive a Donation Land Grant in Washington. He was still a person without citizenship, however, and the efforts of his friends in the 1854 legislature to allow him to vote were overruled. And so this man, who is said by some to have financed the westward journey of some of his white Missouri neighbors (Katz, 1987) and provided hospitality to scores of late arrivals, died without ever exercising that fundamental right.

As the century progressed, the number of African American settlers in the territory grew slowly. In the late 1850s and 1860s a small number of Blacks, both individuals and families, were scattered around the territory. George Washington, who came to Lewis County in 1852, and his wife Mary Jane, registered the plat of their town, present day Centralia, in 1875 according to Lewis County auditor's records, but for the rest of the century they were one of only two or three Black families in the community.

By the 1880s Blacks could be seen in ones and twos in most Washington towns and villages. And at the end of the decade African American communities had emerged in Seattle, Tacoma, Roslyn, and Spokane. With the coming of hundreds of Black miners to Roslyn in Kittitas County in the wake of miners' strikes of 1888 and 1889, the state's African American population rose for the first time to more than a thousand. The 1890 federal census listed 1,602 African American people in the state as compared to 180 in 1880.

There is evidence that the African American population has achieved major gains during or after times of national or local crisis. The most notable example is, of course, the signing of the Emancipation Proclamation during the Civil War. Labor strife has also been of benefit to Black employment opportunities. Men used as strikebreakers, on entering the labor force, generally remained as workers once the trouble was over. This held true all over the nation, whether it was in coal mining, steel production in the South, or meat packing in the midwest, or coal mining in Washington. The largest single industry employing Black laborers in Washington in the 1880s and 1890s was coal mining. The first Black miners to come to Kittitas County in 1888 were contract laborers brought to Ronald. Their presence so enraged striking white miners in Roslyn that the issue became, in the words of a contemporary newspaper account, "niggers or no niggers." (*Seattle Post Intelligencer*, 1888) An all-out strike ensued. More Black men were brought in to break the strike. In 1891 Black men were brought to King County to reopen mines that had been closed by labor strife and a series of problems in the mines themselves.

Coal miners.
Coal Creek, 1880s
Photo by Mitchell Smith
Renton Historical Society
and Museum

81

Messick Sanders family.
Roslyn, 1892
Courtesy of Esther Hall
Mumford

Left: Taylor brothers, home-steaders.
Yakima Valley, 1890s
Oral History Program,
Washington State Archives

Many talented and skilled African American men and women came to Washington. And, for the most part, they were unable to work in the areas for which they had training and skills. Labor unions were effective in closing employment to most skilled men. In interviews with older men in the 1970s, I sometimes asked about their role as strikebreakers. To a man, the response included specific examples of the difficulty, and oftentimes impossibility, of securing any kind of work with which he could support a family because of the opposition of labor unions and a pervasive pattern of discrimination in the general society. Needless to say, remorse was in short supply.

At Franklin, some of the dreams of newcomers of all races were achieved by Black miners. They came in May of 1891 and by October, two Black men had been elected to serve on the local school board. In Seattle, by contrast, the school district did not elect a Black board member until 1963. Gideon Bailey, one of three Black people in the state to serve as justice of the peace in the nineteenth century, was elected at Franklin in 1894 (Cayton's, 1896). (The other Black person elected that year was Kitsap County homesteader Nathaniel Sargent, who became justice of the peace at Seabeck [Kitsap County, 1985]). In 1900 William Shaffroth served as justice of the peace in Snohomish County (Snohomish County, 1900). Black people remained in the mining areas in large numbers for about ten years, and in smaller numbers, until the 1940s. In Roslyn today, only a few members of the Craven family remain, including William Craven who became Washington's first known Black mayor in 1975. Some of the Roslyn miners, as well as those from Franklin and Newcastle in King County, left, with a few dozen families moving to homesteads in the Yakima Valley and farms in the Kennydale area of King County. Most of them practiced subsistence farming. In addition, some grew hops, fruits, and vegetables, marketing the surplus of the latter as well as the hops (Taylor, 1976).

As the homesteaders died, most of their children sold the land and moved to towns and cities. Today only three of the families still live on homestead land; one in the Yakima Valley, one in Pierce County and one in Stevens County (Mumford, 1985).

African Americans also came to Washington by way of the sea. Before the turn of the century, Black men were culinary workers and members of sailing ship crews that came into Puget Sound from various places in North and South America, the Caribbean, and the British Isles. Some of them left the ships and became permanent residents of Washington. The late George Wright who was born in Tacoma in 1889 explained his father's move to Washington in a 1980 interview:

My father was born in London, and he and two of his brothers went to sea with my grandfather, so he taught them to be cooks. Eventually all three of them landed on the Pacific Coast. They were on sailing ships and would come in and out of San Francisco. William lived in San Francisco always, and Theodore was up in Tacoma with my dad.

The Role of the Church

As in all Black communities in the nineteenth and early twentieth century, churches were both social and religious centers for those living in Washington. While early Black settlers often joined existing White congregations, as more Blacks arrived the urge to create their own churches increased. As I became more aware of the Washington Black community I began to realize that churches, some dating back a century or more, served to give communities in this state their stability and continuity.

The church was the first organization that the majority in each community gathered around and supported. Traditionally the center of social life, the identity of the Black community is rooted here. Long an affirmation of its organizers, the church was independent of white domination and largely defined by its members' ideas of how religion should be expressed. Since the eighteenth century, organized religion has been the strongest institution in the Black community in America.

The earliest recorded religious affiliations of Blacks in Washington Territory were with Episcopal churches in Seattle and Olympia in the 1870s. By the late 1880s some Blacks were affiliated with white Baptist churches in cities and towns as well. George Washington, Centralia's founder, donated material, land, and labor for the erection of the First Baptist Church in that city and served on the local board of trustees of Grace Seminary operated by the Baptist Church and located in Centralia (Smith, 1942).

The African Methodist Episcopal (AME) Church was established in 1787 in Philadelphia by Richard Allen after harsh and insulting treatment by white members of the Methodist Episcopal Church that he and other Africans attended. Gradually in the eighteenth and nineteenth centuries the AME and other churches were established among Blacks throughout the United States, as well as a few foreign countries. During the late 1880s Black missionaries from California began a series of trips to the Northwest. Preaching, while at the same time surveying the numbers and locations of Black people in Washington and Oregon, they made contact with adherents or potential converts (Souvenir Program, 1962).

The movement to organize AME churches in Washington was spearheaded by the Reverend C. Augustus, a missionary from the California diocese, who organized churches in 1889 and early 1890 in Tacoma, Roslyn, Seattle, and Spokane (*Spokane Falls Review*, 1890), all of which, except the Roslyn church, still exist today. Early religious services are graphically described in the 1926 autobiography of Mrs. Emma Ray who was one of the first members of Seattle's AME church. Her description includes the emotional tone of the services as well as the supportive relationship that members had with one another (Ray, 1926).

Once sufficient numbers of African American people settled in a Washington community, they followed the Philadelphia example. Exhibiting a sense of personal moral superiority to a society seen as being steeped in greed, materialism, sinfulness, and hostility, they organized their own churches. This was so much a matter of pride and conviction that Black people who were enrolled in white churches or majority white denominations left them in order to assist the organizing effort. Although he and his whole family were Episcopalian and were members of Seattle's Trinity Church as early as 1876, Alfred Freeman is listed in 1890 as one of the incorporators of the city's First AME Church. (Trinity Parish Church, n.d.)

Partings with white churches appear to have been amicable among Baptists. In Seattle, for instance, the majority of the founders of Mt. Zion Church were members of the white First Baptist Church and were assisted at the formal institution of Mt. Zion in 1894 by officials of the former church. Calvary Baptist Church in Spokane was assisted in its institution in 1890 by a white congregation in Cheney. The moving force in organizing Baptists around the state was the Reverend J. P. Brown of Roslyn (Cayton's, 1919). The number of Washington's Black Catholics remained small until a spurt in membership beginning in the 1940s and 1950s. From the early part of the century small numbers of adherents of other denominations have lived in Washington. A few dozen people in urban areas were converted to Islam in the 1960s and 1970s (a religion which is experiencing a revitalized interest among Blacks in Washington and the rest of the United States). The first Church of God in Christ in the state was organized in Seattle in 1923.

In addition to its primary religious function, the church was the place of community meetings, socials, banquets, and musical and literary programs. From the 1890s, churches raised funds for Black colleges and gave annual scholarships to local students (Mumford, 1980). African-American history was taught and the annual community Christmas tree ceremonies were held in which the tree was decorated

Right: Calvary Baptist
Church.
Spokane, circa 1920
Charles A. Libby Collection,
Eastern Washington State
Historical Society, Spokane

Left: Gathering of Usher
Boards in Washington (AME
Church).
Seattle, circa 1955
Oral History Program,
Washington State Archives

and every child given a gift. Then, as now, newcomers to Black communities met established residents at the churches. Visiting churches was a favored activity. Members of one denomination would visit churches of other denominations for regular services and special programs. Sunday Schools of the Black Baptist and Methodist Churches in Seattle and Spokane scheduled meeting times so that children could attend both. Before the Second World War, churches planning special events would check with the other denominations to avoid a scheduling conflict and so guarantee good attendance for their own programs. In keeping with this community orientation, the orchestra organized at Mt. Zion Baptist Church in Seattle between the two world wars was called Mt. Zion Community Orchestra rather than Mt. Zion Baptist Church Orchestra. Through conferences, associations, and conventions most of the adult church members of the same denominations knew other church members around the state, and in this way were kept informed on secular matters, as well as those that were church-related. To a limited extent this is true even today.

In churches all over the state one may hear some of the most beautiful music and oratory, and witness the training of young people in such skills. Many vocal groups perform for the general public, specializing in spirituals and gospel music for concerts at festivals and fairs. The beginnings of most of these groups are found in churches.

Church members have always had high aspirations for the children of their communities and a variety of plans to realize them. In 1890 a church was built by Black Baptists at Ronald, Kittitas County. The men with families felt the necessity of a school for their children and, after raising funds among themselves and Ellensburg townspeople, a teacher was hired to teach both African American and white children at the church: Ronald's first school (Ellensburgh Capital, 1890; Operation Uplift, 1979). About 1910, several leading members of the Seattle community sought, unsuccessfully, to establish a Christian school complex in Irondale, Jefferson County (Cragwell, 1910). While this plan never came to fruition, other churches or religious groups have held similar ambitions with somewhat more success. The Smith Bible Academy in Seattle began operation of a day care center in 1959, and added a first grade class in 1962 which continued for several years. (The Feets, 1963) Seattle's Mt. Zion, which established a Saturday Ethnic School in 1975 to provide tutoring in a variety of subjects as well as Black History classes, has considered the establishment of a school for students from pre-kindergartners through high school. The Zion Christian School, established in Seattle in 1981, with classes from kindergarten through eighth grade, operates at capacity in a building formerly housing a parochial elementary school which shut down, in part, for want of students. In Pasco church members and other concerned persons founded the Afro American Academic Society in 1976 to encourage and recognize academic excellence among Black Students (Tri-Cities Ethnic Players 1984).

Black churches have traditionally been associated with protest and resistance to oppression. Civil rights meetings have been held in churches in Washington since the 1890s (Mumford, 1980). Following the lead of southern churches in the 1960s, Black churches often provided meeting space for such civil rights groups as the Congress of Racial Equality. Beginning in the late 1970s the free breakfast program of the Black Panther Party was held in the First AME church of Seattle. In the 1940s a small church in Seattle collected a donation which totaled more than the annual salary of the pastor to assist in a young man's resistance to the forced relocation of persons of Japanese ancestry (Williston, no date). Members of the clergy have been the most articulate in the campaign for equal rights and are often today the most visible in this regard.

African American Working Women

Mrs. Nettie J. Asberry.
Seattle, n.d.
Asberry Papers, Special
Collections Division,
University of Washington
Libraries

Among the people my relatives introduced me to at church were a variety of small business operators and tradespeople. Most of them had set up their dry cleaners, groceries, service stations, upholstery, barber and beauty shops in the late 1940s to serve the growing Black community. This was in keeping with the pattern established by the first Black people to come to Washington who operated small businesses or farms. Prior to 1890, however, most of their patrons were white people. The African American population was simply too small to support businesses catering specifically to their needs (Mumford, 1980).

Employment in the Washington of the 1850s and 1860s was largely a "make-work" affair. In the Puget Sound towns and in Walla Walla, Black men owned and operated barber shops, restaurants and hotels. While men were most visible as wage earners, at least one woman was known throughout the territory for the food and accommodations she provided to the public at the Pacific House Hotel and Restaurant in Olympia from the early 1860s until her death in 1881 (Mumford, in progress).

This woman, Rebecca Howard, like most African American women of the day, came to the territory as a wife. The Howard name first came to public attention with the opening of a restaurant by her husband, Alex, in 1859 (*Pioneer and Democrat*, 1859). Mrs. Howard's Spokane counterpart, Barbara Scrutchin, was well known in that town and outlying districts in eastern Washington in the 1880s. *(Spokan[e] Times,* 1880) Both of these women, listed in the censuses as illiterates, were astute business managers. At their deaths in the early 1880s, both left thousands of dollars to family members (Mumford, in progress).

Black women have always worked. This was so in Africa, where their rights have traditionally been far more limited than those demanded by women in America. After coming to America they worked as slaves, then as freed persons, then as ordinary citizens with sometimes extraordinary responsibilities. Until the 1970s African American women were more likely to work outside their homes than women from any other group in Washington. Although people said "a woman's place is in the home," African American women frequently lived without that luxury. Some, usually widows or wives of husbands who abandoned them—and there were a few—found it necessary to leave their homes and families to go and tend those of others who were more affluent. But even the woman who never left her home to work was still the first up and the last to go to bed. She was a miner's wife with a family and several extra boarders, all of whom needed her attention. Or she lived in town, taking in ironing and providing room and board to railroad porters and waiters or boat crews. With a sewing machine and an eggbeater as the main labor-saving devices up until the turn of the century, a woman's work was truly never done.

Before I came to Seattle in the 1960s, and for several years afterwards, most girls limited their ambitions to nursing, teaching, and secretarial services, and for a Black woman even those modest, traditionally women's jobs were difficult to attain. The teaching profession is a case in point. From the late nineteenth century onward several Black women were to come to Washington with both the credentials and experience necessary to teach. However, African Americans were not to obtain these positions in Seattle until after World War II. There were a few exceptions. Bremerton researcher Diane Robinson tells of Jane Archer Ruley, a graduate of Hampton Institute in Virginia, who moved to the territory following her graduation in 1875. There, with her husband Paul Ruley, she established and taught at an early Kitsap County school in their barn on the "Sleepy Hollow Ranch" in what is now Bremerton. Some time later, they established the first Sheridan School #22 (Kitsap County, 1985).

Mary Victorine Cooness moved to Centralia shortly after graduation as salutatorian of the 1890 class of Portland High School. In the following years, and after her marriage to Stacey Cooness, stepson of George Washington, she taught at Lewis County's Salzer Valley, at Cinebar, and substituted in the Centralia High School (Smith, 1942). In 1938 Helen Dundee, a graduate of Washington State College, became the first Black teacher in Spokane County (Minisee, 1938). In the Yakima Valley a few Black women taught in schools attended by homesteaders' children (Taylor, 1977). The first Seattle teachers (mostly educated elsewhere) were hired in 1947. Recent conversations and a *Seattle Times* article on these teachers reveal a very different experience from that suggested by a 1948 headline that read "Negro Teachers Like it Here" (*Seattle Times*, 1988). Their early experiences ranged from insults and harassment by principals to indifference and gradual acceptance by their co-workers. There are fewer and fewer Black teachers in the state in this centennial year; those who are in the profession are aging while the number of Black students graduating with teaching credentials is shrinking. And the number of Black students in the schools continues to increase.

For the African American woman who aspired to join the nursing profession, the experience was, if anything, more frustrating. The lone exception was Amy Bedell, daughter of Grandview homesteaders, John and Carrie Bedell, who was staff nurse at Sunnyside Hospital for many years. I have met several women who, as nursing students, were told outright by University of Washington School of Nursing faculty that they should select another major, since sharing a room with a white woman at the nursing students' residence was unthinkable. Others were left on their own to arrange the required floor practice with thoroughly resistant white hospital staffs. Maxine Haynes, a third generation Seattleite, was urged by University of Washington nursing school staff to change her major in her senior year because of the "impropriety" of rooming with a white student. She graduated with a degree in Sociology instead, but her dream was still to be a nurse. After sending scores of letters to nursing schools around the country, in which she stated in part: "I am a colored girl, and I want to be a nurse," she was accepted at New York's Lincoln School of Nursing. She graduated in 1944 (Haynes, 1987).

During World War II, Black nurses, including Ms. Haynes, were recruited from several places in the country. Since that time Black nurses have practiced in hospitals and clinics all over the state. Some have headed hospital departments and taught at other colleges as well. Ironically, in response to the demands of African American students at the University of Washington in the late 1960s for more Black faculty, Ms. Haynes was invited to teach at the School of Nursing. She held the position from 1971 until 1976. As in education, enrollments of African American students in nursing programs have declined in the past decade. Increasingly, the Black women now practicing or studying nursing are foreign-born, mainly from Africa (Mumford, in progress). A few men have entered the profession in recent years.

In spite of enormous advances made by women with education and skills since the 1960s, a disproportionate number still work in low wage deadend jobs, whether domestic work, private industry or government employment. But the human spirit is irrepressible. African American women have long joined the fight for freedom and equality in the country and the state. The nation's first comparable worth law, obtained through a landmark court ruling, was precipitated in 1973 by Josie Anthony and Betty Walker. These two women were food service workers at the University of Washington. They went out on a wildcat strike after white male members of their union, performing similar work in another location, were given $100 wage increases while the women received fifty dollar reductions in pay. The strikers were joined in their campaign by university students and staff and other interested parties. The women, who had been fired, were eventually reinstated with a raise (Hyde and Martin, 1988). The lawsuit brought by their union ultimately resulted in the historic decision mandating equal pay for equal work under similar conditions. (Federal District Judge Jack Tanner of Tacoma originally ordered back pay for employees who had been discrimnated against, although the settlement agreed upon did not provide back pay.) The African American woman in Washington today, spiritual heir of Mrs. Howard, Mrs. Scrutchin, and Ms. Haynes, often reaches beyond traditional occupations and is heading her own consulting service, law firm, garbage disposal business, medical practice (as do eight physicians), working as a railroad engineer, civil engineer, hotel manager, radio or television news reporter, college professor or serving as a city council member or, as in one instance, a superior court judge.

Working in the Twentieth Century

From the early twentieth century until the Great Depression of the 1930s African American men were increasingly shunted into service work on ships. In the early twenties, following a strike on the Admiral Lines, large numbers of Blacks were hired as waiters and bellhops. In the mid-1970s men who were interviewed for their oral histories described their surprise upon seeing Black members of ship maintenance crews on eastern-based ships, when the only work open to Washington men for decades had been in the culinary and service departments. (Yarbrough, 1975)

It was much the same for railroad workers. From 1900, work as cooks, stewards, waiters and porters on the trains provided employment to a segment of Washington's African American population. Some Washingtonians were in quiet sympathy with A. Phillip Randolph's move to organize the Pullman porters beginning in 1926. James Kirk, a Seattle resident since 1914, first came to the city as a railroad waiter. In a 1976 interview he described a day in the life of a railroad dining car waiter:

The day usually began about six o'clock in the morning and they'd work you a whole day; maybe up to ten, eleven, twelve o'clock at night, on your feet most of the time. There was no certain hours. If the train left at four o'clock every afternoon, all you had to do was serve dinner that day. Breakfast was about seven until ten, until everyone on the train was fed. You didn't have no certain time to stop; just kept working until everyone had their meals. Then you had to clean the car, sweep and mop the floors and set up for lunch. You serve lunch, then you serve dinner. After dinner you clean the car at night, make your bed down. In those days you'd put your bed—a kind of cot concern—across two chairs, and you'd sleep right on that.

The costs of silverware stolen by light-fingered passengers were borne by the waiters who had the cost of the utensils deducted from their twenty-six dollars monthly wages during the 1920s. In 1937 Mr. Kirk helped to organize the Railroad Waiters' Union, Local 516, to help address this and other grievances of the waiters. The union, now multi-racial, is still functioning.

The uniformed services have provided employment opportunities and contributed to the increase in the Black population of the state, as members of the military and their families have retired in Washington or returned to the state upon their retirement elsewhere. Myrtle Mathis Pitts, in explaining her family's move to Spokane from Tennessee in the early years of the century, during an interview in 1985 said:

I had one brother who came ahead of the family. He was in the army and was at Fort George Wright . . . it was through him that the family moved to Spokane because he thought there would be better opportunities for the younger children's education if they were in a city like Spokane (Pitts, 1985).

Like many young African American people in other parts of the country, Washingtonians have also found enlistment in the military services an avenue of hope for a better life. One of the most colorful military men, John Henry (Dick) Turpin, twice recommended for the Medal of Honor, was often mentioned to me in the course of oral history interviews during the 1970s. A master diver who was at Havana Harbor aboard the Maine when she was blown up, Turpin is best remembered for his part in the

James Kirk at Jobs, Peace, and Freedom March, Seattle, 1983
Courtesy of Esther Hall Mumford

invention of an underwater welding acetylene torch and electric arc welder (Gayton, n.d.; Gayton and Weber, 1977).

Although short-lived, World War I shipbuilding in Puget Sound opened opportunity for decent wages for African American men—and women—during the war years. Black workers were also used in meat packing plants and the construction industry during the period, but the greatest boon to Black employment in the state came with the critical need for workers in the shipbuilding, plutonium production, airplane manufacturing and aluminum industries during World War II. Residents of the state prior to the war readily volunteer that "the war made all the difference in the world." Seattle native Muriel Pollard recalls:

> Everyone worked. People who hadn't worked in years went back to work, and you could work as long as you were able to work. People with very small children worked. People who were past sixty-five worked. The young men were in the service. The women were quite often left alone, and so they were happy to work (Pollard, 1975).

Because work was plentiful, money was abundant, although goods were sometimes in short supply. There were difficulties, too. Older residents sometimes reflect on the effort to pull together during the Second World War to resolve a variety of problems: segregation and discrimination against Black troops; tensions between the established African American population and Southern newcomers with a different cultural background; and the transplanted white Southerners who sought to impose the hated mores of the South on Blacks living in Washington (Nicholas, 1976).

Since the 1890s, the government has been an important source of employment for Black people in Washington and continues to be so today. African Americans are represented in a much broader range of jobs than when I first came to Seattle, or at any time in the state's history. There are many indications, however, that this progress comes at a very high price. At every level of employment, one hears reports of brutal, stress-laden working environments. As a teenager one of my neighbors came from Arkansas to Bremerton with her family during World War II . She shared her pain with me as she told of the experience of training a young white man at the Puget Sound Naval Shipyard in the work she did. He was then made her supervisor. Although she had worked faithfully at her job for eighteen years, at no time was she offered the advanced position. Similar experiences are reported by others with depressing regularity and even more humiliating circumstances. King County workers at Harborview Hospital report that

Black professional personnel have also been pressured to train new people. Then, in some cases, they were demoted two or three levels or held at a lower level of work. All the while they continued training cadres of new people who then went on to advanced levels. (Harborview Hospital Workers, 1988)

Some of the worst treatment has been that reported by Washington State Ferry System workers. No African American has ever held a managerial position in the ferry system. Workers report the free use of racial epithets by supervisory personnel as well as discriminatory work assignments (Ferry Workers, 1988).

When I began interviewing Seattle's elderly Black population in 1975, the men I talked with, in referring to working conditions from the late 1910s through the 1920s, would often say to me "You should have seen how it was then." But by the late 1970s and early 1980s, in conversations with some of these same men, doubts that the situation was so fundamentally different had begun to arise. Based on recent conversations with contemporary working people I, too, wonder how different conditions are from what they were sixty or a hundred years ago. I have no doubt that the men need to be as tough today as were their nineteenthth and early twentieth century predecessors.

Workers in some companies have reported uncouth and provocative treatment ranging from physical assaults to nicknaming a machine the "nigger crusher." A supervisor for one company, commenting on the increase in the number of Black workers, suggested that they had "enough niggers down here to make a Tarzan movie." One man, the only African American in his department, reported that his supervisor not only kept and circulated a "nigger" cartoon book and pictures of men with Ku Klux Klan hoods, but initially announced the Black man's appearance at work by asking if anyone saw a "slow-moving black object" go by. The "object" has since been amended to slow-moving "nigger". Such conditions take their toll. Some of these men report elevated blood pressure and the need for extended psychological counselling and therapy due to the stresses and harassments on their jobs. Stress is also listed as a probable cause of the prevalence of hypertension among African Americans. Yet these men remain because well-paying jobs for Blacks are few and far between.

Oftentimes there is a tendency to dismiss incidents such as these as actions of poorly educated blue collar workers. The experience of white-collar workers has not always differed, however. In a sometimes emotional interview, Ora Avis Dennis, a 1937 civil engineer graduate of the University of Washington, recounted numerous incidents of similar treatment when he worked at the State Department

of Highways office in Olympia beginning in 1945 (Dennis, 1976). In spite of appalling treatment, Mr. Dennis remained with the department and, after relocating to Seattle, headed the design team for the elevated roadway on the Evergreen Point floating bridge, designed the welded plate girders for the Columbia River Bridge at Biggs Rapids in Eastern Washington, and designed the welded steel girders on the approaches of the Hood Canal Bridge.

Fortunately these shameful episodes are not the whole story. In other jobs a "live and let live" attitude, and even camaraderie, seems to prevail. Black workers do join their fellow workers on after-hours projects and for entertainment. Although a discrimination suit was recently brought by African American and Hispanic workers at Boeing the hostility to African Americans in the 1940s, for instance, has given way to amicable working conditions in several departments. This is true of many other places of employment. It has consistently been the case for me, even in jobs in the 1960s where I, and everyone else at the job, knew I was a token. In my judgement, African Americans are not asking for any special treatment or after-hour socializing. They are asking, however, for what a hospital worker with two graduate degrees who left his managerial job rather than be subjected to further treatment calculated to degrade him, described as the simple desire "to be treated as a human being with dignity." No other person would ask for less. Clearly in the instances cited, this was not forthcoming, and Black workers in Washington State have a long ways to go, as do their detractors.

The Civil Rights Movement

Prior to the Civil Rights Movement of the 1960s there was a saying among African Americans that white Southerners "did not care how close you got as long as you didn't get too high. White Northerners did not care how high you got as long as you didn't get too close." There is more than a little truth in that expression, though nothing is ever quite so simple. The experience in public accommodations' access, however, lends some support, for the notion. Internationally known contralto Marian Anderson was refused accommodations in Bellingham and Seattle on concert tours during the 1920s (Dennis,1976). Celebrated pianist Hazel Scott was awarded damages after she brought a suit against a Pasco restaurant in the late 1940s for denying her accommodations. Both their concerts and public appearances were great successes.

This aversion to "closeness" in Washington so angered the 1940s migrants that some of them lashed out publicly, earning the whole community the stereotype of "disturbers of the peace" (Droker,

Governor Langlie signing
Fair Employment Practices
Code into Law.
State Capitol, Olympia, 1949
Courtesy of Arline and
Letcher Yarbrough

1974). Few people noticed, or bothered to address, the fact that the peace of thousands of African Americans in the state was being disturbed on a daily basis by poor and overcrowded housing, discrimination in stores, restaurants and theaters, and, after the war, in all phases of employment. Upon my arrival in Seattle in 1961 there was not a single Black bus driver, bank teller or department store clerk. The few people in jobs that brought them into contact with the public were hired after a great deal of negotiation by such groups as the National Association for the Advancement of Colored People, the Urban League and the Christian Friends for Racial Equality and later, the Congress of Racial Equality. The State Board Against Discrimination, established in 1949, would hear numerous complaints concerning employment and access to public accommodations until well into the 1970s.

The struggle for civil rights in the 1960s and 1970s was more audible and more visible than it had been, but it was not new to Washington's Black population. African Americans have waged a continuing effort since the late 1880s to obtain constitutional guarantees of equality of access and opportunity (Mumford, 1980). Over the next seventy years Black people in Spokane, Tacoma and Seattle brought suits in the effort to obtain service in hotels, restaurants, theaters, housing facilities, and even cemeteries. For the most part those bringing suits were individuals, and they were largely successful, although the damages collected could amount to as little as one dollar. In smaller places like Wenatchee and Yakima individual acts of resistance took the form of sitting in theater seats of one's own choosing rather than those in designated areas (Roberts, 1976; and Pitts, 1985). Some people also made it known that families would be protected—with guns, if necessary. While Washington has never had laws segregating Blacks, "Whites Only" signs and those stating "No dogs or Negroes allowed" and "We reserve the right to refuse service to anyone" could be seen in places like Pasco in the late 1940s (Burgess,1949). Discrimination in urban areas was somewhat less blunt, but just as effective.

Civil rights organizations have existed in Washington since the organization of Afro-American Leagues in Seattle, Tacoma, Spokane and Franklin, beginning in 1890 (Mumford, 1980). Ad hoc committees formed to address specific concerns have been convened from time to time since then. In 1912 the first chapter of the NAACP was organized in Tacoma, largely through the efforts of Nettie J. Asberry (Mumford, in progress). It was soon followed by units in Spokane, Seattle, and Everett. The work of these organizations continues today. In the past twenty-five years they have been involved in activities ranging from open housing legislation and equal employment to school desegregation efforts. A new sense of mission regarding employment has recently infused the organization in Seattle.

The Civil Rights effort that began in the 1960s stirred the country and brought about momentous changes in Washington. Open housing ordinances in Seattle and Tacoma were passed after initial rejections. Jobs were purportedly open to all. The Federal Public Accommodations Law of 1964 corrected some of the imperfections in Washington's amendments to the provisions of the 1890 Constitution. The original clause, lobbied for by African American Civil War veterans Rudolph Scott of Spokane and John Conna of Tacoma, had been weakened by amendments in 1895 (Cayton's, 1896). The Public Accommodations Law, which has been on the statute books of Washington State for the past century, was observed more often in the breach than in fullfillment. Nevertheless, it has been of great significance to Washington's Black population in more than practical terms. It heralded hope for their new state and its peoples and it was symbolically powerful. It was promulgated at a time when Jim Crow legislation was being written all over the South to strip African Americans of the precious gains they had made in the years following the Civil War.

In 1961 Black people approached restaurants, white churches and rental housing very, very gingerly. Nor was the Federal Public Accomodations law observed instantly. Ten years after its passage some restaurants and many apartment houses refused to accommodate Black people. Recent African immigrants have reported discrimination in trying to rent apartments in the mid-1980s. Occasionally one still hears or reads of illegal practices. In April of 1988 the *Seattle Times* published an article describing the renaissance of an area owned by a Black family until 1985 that had become rundown in the years following its development as a commercial complex by Blacks during World War I. In describing a new business the writer quotes the operator as saying that "Caucasians and Asians are welcome".

There was a great deal of tension between African Americans and whites in Pasco and Richland during and after the Second World War. Living conditions of Blacks were reported to be more nearly like those in some of the poorest third world countries as well (Burgess, 1949 and Wiley, 1949). In the larger cities efforts to address the problems were made in churches, social clubs and lodges. In Seattle such groups as the Civic Unity League, whose members had been appointed by the mayor, the Christian Friends for Racial Equality, the NAACP, the Seattle Urban League, and many individuals worked diligently for the passage of a fair employment practices law (Droker, 1974). The Washington State Law Against Discrimination in Employment was passed in 1949, after two previous campaigns for such a law in 1945 and 1947. African Americans were a prominent part of that effort, particularly in the first campaign. They were discouraged from taking lead roles in subsequent campaigns because their participation antagonized large numbers of whites who were determined not to make concessions to Black people.

Arline Yarbrough was one of the participants. She shares her impression of that effort:

It was the Black community that got that law passed. We worked awfully hard on that. I can remember typing so many letters. There are so many changes—in housing, employment . . . My husband and I were very active in organizations—NAACP, Christian Friends for Racial Equality. For years we fought for FEPC. Oh, that was a struggle! You would have thought we were asking for the end of the earth. It was just terrible when you think of the opposition and the silly stories that would get around and the excuses they'd make . . . what was going to happen to them if this bill passed. Oh, my goodness! (A. Yarbough, 1975).

With determination the gains that were made during the war were maintained and people sought to advance in those and other positions. There was a time in the late forties when "ones" or "firsts" were heralded with pride and hope, but when few others were permitted to follow, they came to be thought of as tokens. By the late 1960s few people were satisfied with these milestones and the clamor for equal employment became more widespread.

In the early sixties Blacks followed the developments in civil rights in other parts of the country with rapt attention. But they were slower than their counterparts elsewhere in getting involved in the struggle, or adopting the tactics of negotiation and nonviolent resistance that were ultimately to prove successful here and elsewhere in the country.

Boycotts and picket lines were part of the strategy used to break resistance to the hiring of Black people in the 1960s. Negotiations were begun with reluctant owners and personnel managers. Gradually Black people began to be seen behind department store counters and at grocery store checkout stands. Black drivers were hired on city bus lines and they are to be seen even in cities with small Black populations. After years of resistance, African Americans began to appear in a variety of other public service jobs around the state. Today a Black person in a policeman or fireman's uniform is no longer the novelty that it once was.

In the late sixties and early seventies the nonviolent approach of the early 1960s gave way to a more militant form of resistance. It was fueled by the impatience and thwarted sense of justice of a younger generation demanding immediate access to Constitutionally granted rights and privileges enjoyed by the majority of Americans. Not all of their actions were productive or progressive. In the latter part of the sixties Seattle had one of the highest firebombing and sniping rates in the United States.

In the spring of 1969 the Seattle Black Panthers (the second chapter organized in the nation) took guns to the state capital in Olympia to demonstrate their opposition to pending legislation aimed at restricting the right to carry firearms publicly. Their action followed the shooting death of two of their members by police in Seattle coupled with the beatings, hosings, church bombings and murders of civil rights activists in the south. In recent interviews Elmer and Aaron Dixon stated their purpose was not to intimidate. Rather, the guns were for their own protection as well as a way to demonstrate to African Americans that they should stand up for their rights.

By arming themselves, these young people—some of the most idealistic in the state's history—became outlaws in the eyes of the police and much of the society. They expected to die at any time in a gun battle with the police. Yet most of them survived. They went on to establish a free clinic, prison visitation programs, a state-wide sickle-cell anemia testing program, tutoring programs, a free breakfast program for poor children which they operated for more than a decade, and to press for expanded opportunities for African Americans in the construction trades. Those at the University of Washington were joined by others from the community in a sit-in at the President's office which resulted in the achievement of their long sought-after goal: an increase in African American faculty members and the establishment of the University's Equal Opportunities Program. Hundreds of low-income students of all races have since been given the chance to obtain a college education through this program.

With the exception of persistent picketing of the home of the late South African Consul prior to his death, the demonstrations of the past are a fading memory in this centennial year. They are wistfully recalled at twentieth anniversaries celebrating foundings in the 1960s. Protest in the late 1980s is more likely to take the form of community meetings and small group negotiations.

Recent Developments

The elimination of the more overt forms of racism had a liberating effect on the thinking of African Americans . The rejection of old stereotypes that had undermined Black self-esteem with such devastating results ushered in a pride that had not been evident before. People discovered Africa and idealized it. They imitated things African, or at least their understanding of Africa. Hair was grown to enormous lengths and coaxed into the Afro hairdo that was soon taken up by fashion-conscious whites who often resorted to wigs to assure the proper coarseness and bushiness. Dashikis in tie-dyed patterns and other pseudo-African prints, and as much of the genuine article as could be obtained, became a wardrobe staple for many people across the state. House interiors began to show the influence of the newfound identity with African masks, wood carvings and fabrics adorning walls and furnishings. Swahili classes were offered. In schools, colleges and community centers, classes in African and African American history and culture were taught at the behest of Blacks. Under pressure, colleges and universities began to hire African American professors. Unfortunately, a recent survey as reported in the *Seattle Times* shows a dramatic decline in their numbers at the University of Washington. In the mid-1970s the Patillos, a couple of newly arrived Californians, established the African Village, a cultural center near Selah, which groups and individuals from all over the state visit.

Travel to Africa became the goal of Black Washingtonians of all ages. Schools with a focus on African culture were organized by parent groups. One of these, Seattle's Marcus Garvey School, now in its eighth year, is a certified K-12 school. African names were much sought after by expectant parents of the early 1970s and onward. Some adults changed their names in the effort to reclaim their African heritage. Belated recognition of the presence and contributions of African Americans in Washington State history spurred on an effort to place Black people in their proper historical context. The Congress of Racial Equality, largely through the efforts of Frances Karimu White, published a booklet on the life of George Bush in conjunction with the unsuccessful effort (spearheaded by author Ruby El Hult and legislator Bill May, and later Ms. White) to have Bush selected as one of the subjects of the two statues representing Washington in the Federal Hall of Statuary (*Seattle Post-Intelligencer* 1963).

Increasingly, heritage is of concern with groups in major population centers working to exhibit and inform their communities of local African American history. Awareness of the need to acknowledge and respect the unique culture of the Black community dates to 1890 and the creation of the Spokane Historical and Scientific Club which debated issues of the day and presented local talent in public meetings (*Spokane Falls Review*, 1890).

A succession of clubs and organizations statewide have collected autobiographies of their members and information relating to the progress of African Americans in employment and equal access. The Seattle Association of Club Women in 1984 opened their History Room, housing articles and information relating to Black history. The Black Historical Society of Kitsap County, formed in 1982, opened a center for cultural enrichment and tutoring in Bremerton in 1987. In Seattle two groups, the

Black Heritage Society of Washington State and the African American Museum Committee, in parallel efforts, are presently working towards establishment of a museum on the one hand, and a cultural center on the other. Researchers in Seattle, Spokane and Bremerton have begun to inform the public of their findings through lectures, publications and exhibits. Public art galleries have begun the recognition of major artists, as well as some who are not as well known. Churches sponsor exhibits and some have commissioned works of art, as have members of the growing middle class.

The Black Community Festival, first held as the Mardi Gras Parade in 1948, is one of the oldest community festivals in Seattle. Sundiata, a winter arts festival named after an epic from the ancient kingdom of Mali, is held annually at Seattle Center. It showcases talent and artistic achievements of people from continental Africa, as well as people of African origin in the western hemisphere, with a focus on the Northwest.

Black businesses are no longer confined to the service sector. An increase in educational levels and greater access to well-paying jobs have led to larger investments, bigger savings and increased buying power. A partial list of businesses now operated in Washington by African Americans includes: car dealerships, a helicopter service, medical and dental practices, insurance agencies, real estate offices, entertainment booking agencies, construction, building and architectural firms, nursing homes and newspapers. An array of professions are also followed including traditional as well as newer callings. The tremendous growth of the population beginning in the 1940s brought increased political power. In 1950 Representative Charles Stokes of King County became the first person of African descent to serve in the state legislature in over thirty years. In 1988, George Fleming, Washington's second African American State Senator, ran a close second for Lieutenant Governor. Art Fletcher, Pasco city council member during the 1960s, made a similarly impressive run for Lieutenant Governor in 1968. Like William Craven of Roslyn, James Chase rose from city councilman to become a mayor of Spokane. The third known Black person to hold the office of mayor was Joe Jackson of Pasco, elected in 1984. Henry Beauchamp recently served the city of Yakima. African Americans now sit on city councils in several cities. Seattle city councilman Norm Rice recently ran an unsuccessful race for Congressional representative which he lost by 10,000 votes. In 1987 Cora Pinson of Olympia became the first elected Black female to sit on a city council, although Katie Barton was appointed to fill Art Fletcher's unexpired term when he received a political appointment in the Nixon Administration. She and King County Superior Court Judge Norma Huggins are strong role models for Black women who aspire to higher office. In 1978 Attorney Jack

James Chase, Spokane Mayor, and Clarence Freeman.
Spokane, 1981
Courtesy of the *Spokesman Review*

Tanner of Tacoma was named U.S. District Court Judge for the Western District of Washington, a position he still holds. Charles Z. Smith, the first African American to serve as a judge in the State, has recently been appointed to the Supreme Court of Washington, another first. City Councilman Sam Smith of Seattle, who served five terms as a state representative, is now in his sixth term on the council and serving as council president for the fifth time.

The extraordinary presidential campaign of Jesse Jackson and the consequent formation of the Washington State Rainbow Coalition was one of the most exciting events in recent times. The Coalition, formed of idealists and ordinary people from a number of ethnic groups, has the largest African American following of any political movement in Washington. It gave fire to the imagination and fervent hopes of a large grass roots population. In the same campaign Dr. Lenora Fulani, the only Black candidate to ever have her name on the national ballot for President, developed a much smaller following in Washington.

While it is impossible to be unaware of African American participation in the arts, it is oftentimes taken for granted. Here, as elsewhere, Blacks have long been associated with music. Orchestras were formed in Washington in the late 1880s where they were in demand in the urban communities. Such notable musicians in American life as Hollywood composer Quincy Jones, Blues singer and pianist Ray Charles, the late Jimi Hendrix, "Bumps" Blackwell, Betty Hall Jones, Floyd Turnham, and New York pianist Patti Bown, spent at least part of their formative years in Washington where they gained confidence and polish playing for Black audiences. World War II brought a number of outstanding musicians to Washington. Virtuosos such as the Sand Point Navy Band, the "Jive Bombers," as well as individuals in search of work in other fields all arrived on the scene. Many of them became permanent residents. Jazz vocalist Ernestine Anderson still calls Seattle her home, and the gifted trombonist Julian Priester is also a resident, teaching at the Cornish School of the Arts. Trumpeter Floyd Standifer continues performing in jazz while teaching at a private art-focused school. The latest Washington musician to become a star of national renown is the young Robert Cray of Tacoma whose blues singing has been highly acclaimed in the national media. The dean of secular musicians in Washington is the 1940s boogie-woogie sensation "Slim" Gaillard of Tacoma. Scores of lesser-known musicians continue to live and work in Washington. The last decade has seen a growth in performers from western and southern Africa and the Caribbean, whose contributions further enrich a highly varied art form enjoyed by wide segments

of Washington's population.

In the nineteenth century occasional theater presentations were offered in African American communities as well as for broader audiences. Churches presented pageants depicting the achievements of Black people or episodes in Black history. The first theater company was formed in Seattle in 1918 by E.W. Mitchell (Cayton's, 1918). Their plays were received favorably by the Black press of the era. Frederick Darby studied acting in Portland before arriving in Seattle in 1917. He continued his studies here and was featured on radio programs in the 1920s giving dramatic readings of both Shakespearean and contemporary plays (Darby, 1976).

The most important theater experience prior to the 1960s was that of the Federal Theater Project's Negro unit in Seattle during the Depression. Cornish School graduate Syvilla Fort, who world renowned, avant-garde composer and pianist John Cage credits with the impetus for his "prepared piano," was project choreographer (Federal Theater, *Noah*, 1936 and Cage, 1977). She joined Katherine Dunham's troupe on its worldwide tours before moving to New York in 1949. There she opened her own studio and provided training for people such as dance company founder Alvin Ailey and film actor Marlon Brando (Chappell, 1976 and Cage, 1977).

The Federal Theater Project also involved African American writers. Shirley Lola Graham, who moved to Seattle with her family during World War I, was one of several Black playwrights involved in the planning of the theater's future course. She later married the great Black historian and theoretician W.E.B. DuBois, and died in China in 1976. Theodore Browne was the group's resident dramatist and assistant director. He continued writing plays after moving to New York in the 1940s (Jackson, 1975).

In 1967 the Black Arts West Theater was organized as part of Seattle's Model Cities Program. The fare ranged from controversial works of new playwrights to revivals of plays by national writers such as poet laureate Langston Hughes. During its ten-year existence it enjoyed varying levels of community support. It was an inspiring experience for its young participants, some of whom now pursue professional careers in drama or music. Others became proficient in reading for the first time and resumed educations that had been abandoned before completion of high school. Black Arts West was succeeded by the Paul Robeson Theater which presents occasional plays at the Langston Hughes Cultural Center. Ndaba Cultural Ensemble, a Tacoma performing group, was organized in 1986 in Tacoma. Its founder, Daisy McKerson-Stallworth was one of the finalists in the 1987 National KOOL Achiever Awards for inner-city leaders. Jacob Lawrence, a world-class painter, is one of the best known visual artists in Washington.

He has been a Seattle resident since 1971 when he joined the University of Washington faculty. His paintings are in a large number of private and public collections around the world. They are seen locally in buildings such as Meany Hall at the University of Washington and the King County domed stadium. Mr. Lawrence was preceded by James Washington, Jr., a 1940s arrival who began his endeavors as a painter. He is best known as a sculptor whose creations of nature express his deep religious faith. Several new artists are making their mark today, including younger generation painters Barbara Thomas, and Marita Dingus. Both of these women have been exhibited in major museums and are represented in important public and private collections. Recently arrived painter Roy Monceaux, opened a downtown Seattle gallery, Morgan-Monceaux, in July 1988 in conjunction with Terry Morgan. This is the only African American gallery north of San Francisco. Mr. Morgan is also the founder and coordinator of Sundiata, one of the state's largest Black cultural festivals. Other artists around the state continue to work in a variety of media, often while holding down other jobs.

Many of the goals sought by African Americans coming to Washington have been fulfilled. But problems, long ignored and unsolved, are now manifesting themselves in disquieting ways. Unemployment, the most serious and fundamental problem of the Black community, continues to be at least double that of the white population. In addition, high infant mortality—tied to teenage pregnancy, inadequate nutrition and little or no prenatal care, high rates of school dropout combined with discouragement, low levels of achievement, and a spiraling rate of drug addiction—are all causes for concern.

In the past when Black people got together socially, the talk was of entertainment, travel, food, and books. Today, the conversation inevitably turns to their children and how best to solve the problems they face. Across the state grassroots efforts are mobilizing the time, energy and talent of young people nurtured in the Black community in order to perpetuate the life and culture they value. Large and small churches are focusing outreach efforts in this direction, as are a variety of organizations, most of which were founded for other purposes.

For African American people Washington has been an imperfect Promised Land. But to paraphrase a 1923 Seattle migrant, Bertha Pitts Campbell, it was, and still is, "a good place to start something."

WORKS CITED

Burgess, Margaret Elaine. 1949. "A Study of Selected Socio-Cultural and Opinions Differentials Among Negroes and Whites in the Pasco Washington Community." Master's thesis, State College of Washington, Pullman.

Campbell, Bertha Pitts. 1975. Interview with author. Washington State Oral/Aural History Program. Washington State Archives, Olympia.

Cayton's Weekly. 1896.

_____. 1919. March 2.

Cage, John. 1977. Interview with author. Seattle.

Chappell, Arlie. 1976. Interview with author. Washington State Oral/Aural History Program. Washington State Archives, Olympia.

Cragwell, John F. 1910. Scrapbook, Letcher Yarbrough.

Darby, Fred. 1976. Interview with author. Washington State Oral/Aural History Program. Washington State Archives, Olympia.

Dennis, Ora Avis. 1976. Interview with author. Washington State Oral/Aural History Program. Washington State Archives, Olympia.

Droker, Howard Alan. 1974. "The Seattle Civic Unity Committee and the Civil Rights Movement, 1944-1964." Ph.D. dissertation, University of Washington.

Ellensburgh [sic] *Capital.* 1889. 28 November.

_____. 1890. 1 April.

The Facts. 1963. 30 September.

Federal Theater Project. 1936. *Noah.* Program.

Ferry Workers. 1988. "Report to the NAACP." July.

Gayton, Leonard. n.d. Scrapbook.

Gayton, Leonard, and Donald Weber. 1977. Conversations with author.

Harborview Hospital Workers. 1988. "Report to the NAACP."

Haynes, Maxine. 1987. Conversation with author.

Hyde, Fred, and Gloria Martin. 1988. Conversations with author. July.

Jackson, Sara Oliver. 1975. Interview with author. Washington State Oral/Aural History Program. Washington State Archives, Olympia.

Katz, William Loren. *The Black West.* Seattle: Open Hand, 1987.

Kirk, James. 1976. Interview with author. Washington State Oral/Aural History Program. Washington State Archives, Olympia.

Kitsap County Black History Committee. 1985. *Bremerton Celebrates Over 100 Years...A Story Untold*. Bremerton.

Lewis County Auditor. 1875. Records.

McLagen, Elizabeth. 1980. *A Peculiar Paradise*. Portland, Oregon: Georgian Press.

Minisee, Berenice. 1938. Scrapbook.

Mumford, Esther Hall. 1980. *Seattle's Black Victorians, 1852-1901*. Seattle: Ananse Press.

_____. Ed., 1985. *Seven Stars and Orion/Reflections of the Past*. Seattle: Ananse Press.

_____. In progress. "Black Women of Washington, 1850-1950." Seattle: Ananse Press.

Nicholas, Elva. 1976. Interview with author. Washington State Oral/Aural History Program. Washington State Archives, Olympia.

Operation Uplift. See: *Spawn of Coal Dust*.

Pioneer and Democrat. 1859. Olympia, September 9.

Pitts, Myrtle. 1985. Interview with author.

Pollard, Muriel. 1975. Interview with author. Washington State Oral/Aural History Program. Washington State Archives, Olympia.

Ray, Emma. 1926. *Twice Sold, Twice Ransomed*. Chicago: The Free Methodist Publishing House.

Roberts, Geneva. 1976. Interview with author. Washington State Oral/Aural History Program. Washington State Archives, Olympia.

Schmid, Calvin Fisher, Charles E. Noble, and Arlene E. Mitchell. 1968. *Non-White Races, State of Washington*. Olympia: Washington State Planning and Community Affairs Agency.

Seattle Post Intelligencer. 1888. October.

_____. 1963. 7 January.

Seattle Times. 1988. 20 March.

_____. 1988. 9 April.

Smith, Herndon., comp. 1942. *Centralia, the First Fifty Years, 1845-1900*. Centralia, WA.

Snohomish County Commissioners. 1900. Records of Proceedings.

Souvenir Program of the 50th Anniversary Service of the First AME Church Edifice. 1912/1962. 1962. Seattle: First AME Church.

Spawn of Coal Dust; A History of Roslyn, 1886-1979. Rev. 2d ed. Project of Operation Uplift Community Development Program. Roslyn.

Spokane Falls Review. 1890. 16 March.

Spokan[e] Times. 1880. 20 July.

St. John's Episcopal Church. n. d. Records. Oympia.

Taylor, Charles B. 1977. Interview with author. Washington State Oral/Aural History Program. Washington State Archives.

The Tri-Cities Ethnic Players. 1984. *Cultural Awareness: Pasco's Black Community.* Pasco.

Tri-County Tribune. 1974.

Trinity Parish Church. n.d. Records, Volume 1.

U. S. Bureau of the Census. 1943. *Sixteenth Census of the United States.* 1940. Volume 2, Part 7. Washington D. C.: Government Printing Office.

U. S. Bureau of the Census. 1953. *The Eighteenth Decennial Census of the United States.* Census of Population. 1950. Volume 1, Part 9. Washington, D. C.: Government Printing Office.

Washington Territory. 1854. *Journal of the Council of the Territory of Washington.*

Wiley, James, Jr. 1949. "Race Conflict as Exemplified in a Washington Town." Master's thesis. State College of Washington, Pullman.

Williston, Frank. n.d. Report in Felix B. Cooper Papers. Manuscripts Division, Suzallo Library, University of Washington.

Wright, George. 1980. Telephone interview with author.

Yarbrough, Arline. 1975. Interview with author. Washington State Oral/Aural History Program. Washington State Archives, Olympia.

Yarbrough, Letcher. 1975. Interview with author. Washington State Oral/Aural History Program. Washington State Archives, Olympia.

Seattle Ethiopians trying to
raise money to fight another
famine in Ethiopia.
Seattle, February 16, 1988
Photo by Craig Fuji
Courtesy of the *Seattle Times*

Morocco
76

Cape Verde
6

Ghana
35

Nigeria
604

Africa

South Africa
152

Washington's recent arrivals
from Africa

*Within the last five years a number of groups have come directly
from the African continent, their resettlement given considerable
impetus by war and political repression. The largest number of
Black immigrants are from Ethiopia, the West Indies, and
Nigeria. While some of these immigrants have experienced an
improved standard of living, others have lost the rights and status
they enjoyed as part of the dominant majority in their homelands.*

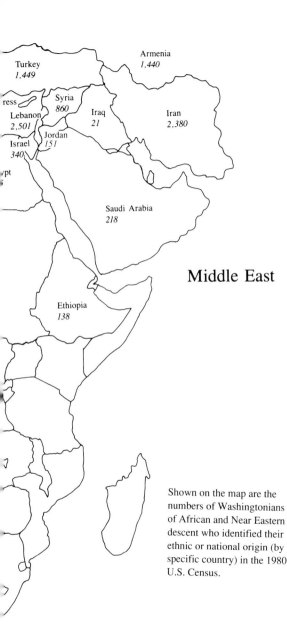

Middle East

Shown on the map are the numbers of Washingtonians of African and Near Eastern descent who identified their ethnic or national origin (by specific country) in the 1980 U.S. Census.

Turkey *1,449*

Armenia *1,440*

ress

Syria *860*

Lebanon *2,501*

Iraq *21*

Iran *2,380*

Jordan *151*

Israel *340*

pt

Saudi Arabia *218*

Ethiopia *138*

Moslem Men praying.
Seattle, August 16th, 1986
Photo by Benjamin
Benschneider
Courtesy of the *Seattle Times*

Washington's Middle Eastern communities first emerged in the 1940s

Peoples from the Middle East began to arrive in the late 19th century. They are not all of Arabic speaking heritage, nor are they all Muslim. Rather, they represent a variety of cultural and religious backgrounds created by differences in geography and history. The largest groups include Arabic speaking peoples, Armenians, Iranians and Turkish. The Armenians and Lebanese were the first to arrive, and the Iranians are the most recent. Although the original immigration started for economic and political reasons, recent immigration has included many students and professionals.

111

Washington's Asian/Pacific American community is ethnically and culturally diverse

Washington's Asian/Pacific Americans have origins in countries with varied languages, political and economic systems, religions, and customs. Yet they share a common history of struggle and resistance to oppressive legislation that sought to prevent them from finding a permanent place in Washington. Their labor was important to the economic development of the state. Hawaiians, for instance, were recruited to work in the fur trade in the early nineteenth century. Chinese, Japanese, Koreans, Asian Indians, and Filipinos were recruited to work on the railroads, in lumber-mills, in canneries, and in agriculture in the late nineteenth and early twentieth centuries. Changes in the immigration laws in 1965 and the legacy of the Vietnam War have greatly increased the numbers and changed the composition of the Asian/Pacific American community in Washington.

WASHINGTON'S ASIAN/PACIFIC AMERICAN COMMUNITIES

Gail M. Nomura

Why do people choose to uproot themselves from the land of their birth to move to an unknown and, at times, a less settled land? This is the question I ask my students at Washington State University at the beginning of each semester. Since most of them are not from Pullman, the main Washington State University campus, we explore why they chose to move from their hometowns to Pullman, and why they are in my Asian/Pacific American history class. In this way we come to understand in a personal way the continuing process of immigration and migration.

I talk about my own move to Pullman and the uprooting from Hawaii. Employment is one vital reason for a move and the life of an academic can be likened to that of a migrant worker. Like my grandparents, who were recruited from Japan to fill a labor shortage in the sugar plantations of Hawaii at the turn of the century, I was recruited to fill a labor shortage in the academic community of Washington State University. My husband, Stephen H. Sumida, a specialist in Asian American literature, and I, a specialist in Asian American history, were recruited to establish an Asian American studies program at the school. But unlike my immigrant grandparents who left their country of birth for a new adopted land where naturalization laws did not allow them to become U.S. citizens until after 1952, my husband and I are American-born U.S. citizens who chose to leave one American state to work in another. Still, I can relate to the feelings of my grandparents as they left the land of their birth for a new land. In the cold winter months in Pullman I often dream of the warmth of Hawaii and my family there. But with the birth of our daughter, Emi Fumiyo Nomura Sumida, in the college town of Pullman my husband and I, migrant academics from Hawaii, became forever tied to the land of Washington State, our daughter's birthplace, just as our immigrant grandparents had become rooted in America with the birth of their U.S. citizen children. And like my own immigrant grandparents, I, too, work for a better life for my child, a life of limitless horizons.

Matsushita family, Japanese pioneers.
Wapato, 1914
Courtesy of Kara Kondo

After discussing my own migration story, the class goes on to explore each student's migration story in the context of the immigrant experience. Education, of course, is the main reason the students have migrated to Pullman, but we go further to look at the reasons behind these choices of going to college and selecting this particular university ranging from the love of knowledge to economic improvement to a desire to escape parental supervision. The students begin to see that their experience in moving to Pullman is in its own way not so different from the universal experience of all immigrants and migrants. They have made a conscious decision to leave their families and friends to take up fresh opportunities at Washington State University. They have experienced being the stranger in a new land with its concomitant sense of rootlessness until they make a place for themselves in Pullman, temporary though it be.

It is from this common ground of understanding of the immigrant/migrant experience that we begin our discussion of the early immigration of people who came east across the Pacific Ocean to settle in what is now Washington State. The immigrants from Asia and the Pacific in the nineteenth and early twentieth centuries were predominantly young single men eager to make a better life for themselves in the new land of America. Most came to work since there was a labor shortage in the rapidly developing Pacific Northwest.

Hawaiians were the first of these immigrants to work in large numbers in Washington. Hawaii had become an important station for the Pacific sea trade soon after its contact with the West in 1778. Soon afterwards, British and American ships on their way to and from the Pacific Northwest for furs to trade in China would stop for rest and provisions in Hawaii. Hawaiians were known for their great seamanship. A system of contract labor was developed in which Hawaiians (known variously as Kanakas, Owyhees, Blue Men, or Sandwich Islanders) were employed as sailors. Thus, Hawaiians first came to Washington as sailors and accompanied the early expeditions inland. Later they were recruited to provide some of the first skilled and unskilled laborers for the fur trade. Numbering more than a thousand during the first half of the nineteenth century, there were Hawaiian communities scattered throughout the Pacific Northwest including Fort Vancouver and Fort Walla Walla. Many Hawaiians intermarried with Indians including daughters of chiefs or sub-chiefs. The town of Kalama near Vancouver, Washington was named after the Kalama River which bears the name of John Kalama, a Hawaiian who worked for the Hudson's Bay Company and married one of the daughters of the chief of the Nisqually tribe. The Kalama family once owned the land on which Fort Lewis stands. (Solberg, 1978, Duncan, 1972, Bona, 1972, Naughton, 1983).

The Chinese were the first Asians to arrive in large numbers in the nineteenth century. Since the seventeenth century immigration had been a safety valve for the overpopulated regions of southeastern China. Large numbers of emigrants went to Southeast Asia and later the Caribbean. In the mid-nineteenth century China, weakened by the impact of Western imperialism and torn by the Taiping Rebellion and clan warfare which especially devastated Guangdong saw a major out-migration occur. Formal emigration to the United States was illegal until the 1868 Burlingame treaty which guaranteed free migration of Chinese. But people around the Guangzhou (Canton) region in Guangdong province had access to the port of Hong Kong which had been controlled by the British since 1842. Tens of thousands took passage from Hong Kong to countries all over the world, including Hawaii to work on the sugar plantations and California for the Gold Rush as well as to work on the railroads and in agriculture. Those that first came in the 1860s to Washington were drawn by news of the discovery of gold in Eastern Washington, but many more Chinese were recruited in the 1870s to work on railroad construction and in the other growing industries of the area.

Japanese were similarly recruited to Washington to provide needed labor for fast growing industries. Natural disasters in the central area of the main island of Honshu along with deflationary governmental policies which adversely affected Japanese farmers led many Japanese to contract to work on Hawaiian sugar plantations from 1885. Hawaii was annexed by the United States in 1898. After the passage of the Organic Act in 1900 officially organizing the Territory of Hawaii, many Japanese plantation workers took passage to California and the Pacific Northwest, attracted by the high pay and plentiful job opportunities there. Other Japanese came directly from Japan to work initially as laborers in agriculture, on railroads, and in the timber and lumber industries. Japanese in Washington eventually sought self-employment through establishing farms, dairies, and small businesses.

About seven thousand Koreans were also recruited for the sugar plantations in Hawaii from 1903 to 1905. About a thousand of them went on to work on the Pacific west coast. The main settlements of Koreans in Washington were Seattle on the westside and Yakima on the eastside. They, too, worked mainly as laborers in Washington's industries. Korea became a protectorate of Japan in 1905 and was later annexed by Japan in 1910. Further immigration was severely restricted by Japan after 1905. More numerous numbers of Koreans would arrive after 1950. The annexation of Korea by Japan in 1910 politicized the Korean community in America for much of the period between 1910 and the liberation of

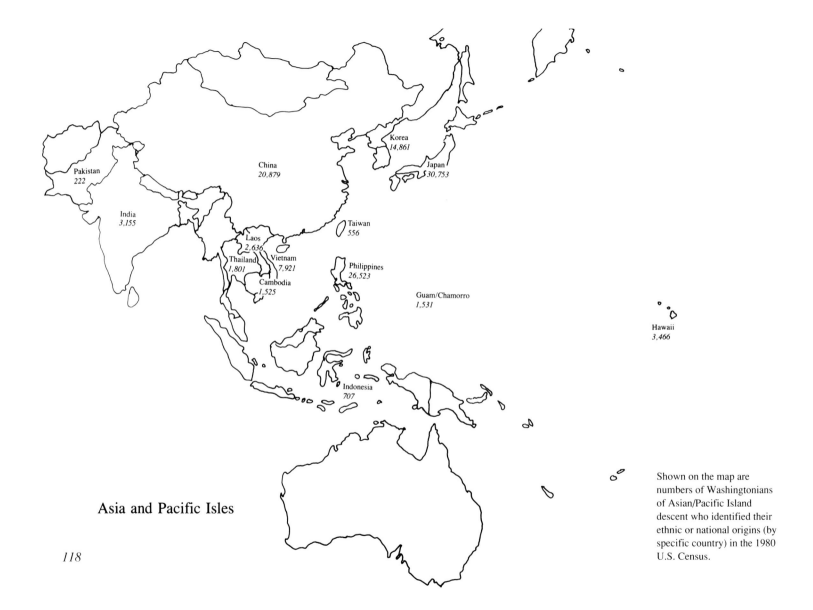

Pakistan
222

China
20,879

Korea
14,861

Japan
30,753

India
3,155

Taiwan
556

Laos
2,636

Thailand
1,801

Vietnam
7,921

Cambodia
1,525

Philippines
26,523

Guam/Chamorro
1,531

Hawaii
3,466

Indonesia
707

Asia and Pacific Isles

118

Shown on the map are
numbers of Washingtonians
of Asian/Pacific Island
descent who identified their
ethnic or national origins (by
specific country) in the 1980
U.S. Census.

Korea at the end of World War II in 1945. The Korean community in America became the main source of leadership and financial support of the nationalist movement to liberate Korea.

Most of India had been colonized by the British by the mid-nineteenth century. South Asians, as citizens of the British Empire, had the right of migration to any territory within the British empire. Poor economic conditions at the turn of the century and increased rural indebtedness had led to an influx of emigration to North America. The employment opportunities on the Pacific coast of Canada proved especially attractive. Agents for the Canadian Pacific Railway were active in recruiting Sikhs in the Punjab; Canadian Pacific steamship companies also promoted migration. Yet, once in Canada these South Asians met much hostility and eventually from 1909 the government of Canada developed a policy that effectively ended South Asian migration. For example, according to the "continuous voyage" provision of Canadian immigration law, immigrants, like most South Asians, who did not travel in a single, direct voyage from their native country could be excluded from Canada. The effect of this exclusionist policy was to deflect South Asian immigration to North America from Canada to the United States. Although most South Asians eventually settled in California, many initially worked on railroad construction and in lumber mills in Washington since Washington State was closest to Vancouver, the major concentration of South Asians in Canada. (Mazumdar, 1984; Hess, 1976).

Like imperial Britain, the United States also had colonies. In 1898 the United States annexed Hawaii and the Philippine Islands became an American possession with the defeat of Spain in the Spanish-American War though Filipino resistance to U.S. takeover continued until 1902. Filipinos were not granted U.S. citizenship but they were U.S. nationals with the right to freely migrate to any place within U.S. territories. Filipinos thus began to migrate to Hawaii and the Pacific Coast states around the turn of the century. Early Filipinos included Filipino wives of American servicemen who had fought in the Spanish-American War and students subsidized by the Philippine territorial government, pensionados. However, most Filipinos came as laborers drawn by the continuing need for labor in Washington. Educated in the Philippines under an American educational system and often taught by American teachers, Filipinos believed in the American Dream and believed themselves to be part of that dream. They took passage to Washington to seize opportunities for further education and work. Here they provided much needed labor, especially in agriculture and the canneries from the 1920s on. (Cordova, 1983).

These Asian immigrants were young, ambitious, and full of hope as they departed their lands of birth. Their hopes and dreams are well summed up in the poem, "Ode on Leaving My Home Town," by Kenji Abe, a Japanese immigrant railroad foreman in Pullman, who first began working the railroad sections in 1906:

> Over the horizon of the wide Pacific,
> Entertaining high ambitions,
> I looked for eternal happiness.
> Great love . . .
> Huge efforts . . .
> Large land . . .
> Vast sky . . .
> I survey my future path.
> On my two shoulders I bear a mission;
> In my heart hope swells.
> Goodbye, my home country.
> Farewell!
> (Ito, 1973, pp. 34-35).

Economic Role

Asian/Pacific immigrants thus left their homelands to find "Great love . . . Huge efforts . . . Large land . . . Vast sky" in Washington. It is often forgotten how important their coming was to building the regional economy. Their labor was important to such major segments of the Washington economy as the fur trade, mining, railroads, agriculture, lumbering, canneries, fishing, small businesses, and domestic services.

Hawaiians provided an indispensable source of labor for the early development of Washington. They were especially important to the fur trade. It seems that the swimming and diving skills of the Hawaiians were highly valued. They were also said to have great skill in fording rivers and handling boats. Journals of the times declared that "they had never seen watermen equal to them, even among the voyageurs of the Northwest; and indeed, they are remarkable for their skill in managing their light craft,

"Tianna" a Prince of Atooi First Hawaiian to see North America.
1790
Drawing by J. Walter in Meares, *Voyages*, p. 4a

and can swim and dive like waterfowl." (Naughton, 1983, p. 16). Their importance to the fur traders can be seen in the following testimony: "The Owyhees however are such expert swimmers that little of our effects are lost beyond recovery which accident now and then consigns to the bottom of the water in our perilous navigation: and it is next to impossible for a person to get drowned if one or more of them are near at hand . . ." (Naughton, 1983, p 18). Hawaiians were also employed in the sawmills, and worked as farmers, sheepherders, and carpenters.

Mining was one of the first major industries to arise in Washington after the decline of the fur trade, and Chinese were prominent here. In the 1860s Chinese miners were attracted by gold strikes along the Columbia River in Eastern Washington. By 1864 hundreds of Chinese miners could be found working claims purchased from whites along the Columbia River 150 miles upstream from Rock Island. Numbering as many as 1500, by 1870 Chinese miners in eastern Washington outnumbered white miners two to one. Most of the Chinese miners were contracted by San Francisco or Portland based Chinese companies. Large Chinese mining camps were established along the Columbia River from Methow to above Colville. A class of Chinese small businessmen arose to service the needs of the miners in these camps. Chinese began operating stores, laundries, and barber shops and growing vegetables and fruits for the miners. It is estimated that Chinese by working abandoned claims mined several million dollars worth of gold dust which would otherwise have been lost to Washington's economy. (Chin and Chin, 1987; Chin, 1977).

Chinese labor was also important in the coal mines of Washington. Chinese labor contractors supplied workers from the 1870s to mid-1880s to coal mines in Black Diamond, Coal Creek, Franklin, Newcastle, and Renton.

Critical to the development of Washington's economy was a railroad transportation system which could move people and products efficiently. Chinese were soon recruited to help build the major railroad lines in Washington. In 1871 the Northern Pacific Railroad, using 2,000 Chinese contract laborers from San Francisco, began laying the western part of its line from Kalama, north of Vancouver, Washington to Tacoma. More Chinese were recruited directly from China to complete the Northern Pacific. The Northern Pacific was completed when in 1883, some 17,000 Chinese laborers, comprising two-thirds of the work force, had cleared and graded the land, built bridges, and laid tracks. Laboring under harsh conditions, Chinese were instrumental in building every major railroad line in Washington   *121* including the Renton to Newcastle line which enabled Seattle to become the main coaling port on the West Coast and the tunnel through the Cascade Mountains which connected the Northern Pacific line in the Puget Sound to Spokane Falls and the states in the east. Chinese were responsible for practically all the railroad grading in Spokane, Stevens, and Whitman Counties. (Chin and Chin, 1987; Chin, 1977).

Japanese immigrants were also recruited to further build and maintain the railroad system in Washington. Railroad work on the Northern Pacific and Great Northern was one of the first jobs for many Japanese. Seattle and Portland were the main centers supplying Japanese railroad workers in the Pacific Northwest. Japanese labored to build the Stevens Pass tunnel and their presence was commemorated in the naming of a sawmill town, Nippon (later called Alpine). Japanese worked initially as section hands but later had other jobs such as engine watchmen and foremen. (Ito, 1973).

The railroads continued to be a source of employment for other Asian immigrants. Filipinos worked on the railroads, principally with the Great Northern, as cooks and porters as well as on work crews. Railroad work was one of the first jobs for South Asians entering the United States. Though some found work as section hands, most found only temporary railroad construction work. South Asians did not remain in railroad construction for long, in part because they were paid less than Italian and Greek railroad workers. In addition, since South Asians had been extensively recruited to work on railroads in Tacoma to replace striking Italian railroad workers, they were not well received by other ethnic railroad workers. (Das, 1923; Mazumdar, 1984). The railroads knit Washington together and connected Washington with the eastern half of the United States. Railroads opened new markets and facilitated the transporting of settlers to Washington. Without Asian labor to build and maintain the necessary railroad network, the commerce of Washington would not have developed as rapidly.

The Chinese were Puget Sound's first non-Indian fishermen. Using huge seine nets measuring 900 feet long and 240 feet deep Chinese fished in Elliott Bay, at Port Madison on the Kitsap Peninsula, and established a fishing colony locally called "Hong Kong" near Manzanita on the west side of Maury Island. Chinese fishermen caught, salted and dried a wide variety of fish. They also bought large quantities of fish from the Indians. The dried fish were at first shipped to San Francisco. (Chin and Chin, 1987; Chin, 1977).

Although Japanese were important in the fishing industry in California, they did not play a similar role in Washington because state law did not allow them to obtain commercial fishing licenses after 1915. The 1915 law made it unlawful for Asian immigrants, who were prohibited from becoming naturalized citizens ". . . to take for sale or profit any salmon or other food or shellfish." However, Japanese did play an important role in establishing the state's oyster industry through the introduction of the large Japanese oyster into Puget Sound.

Asian labor was important for the salmon canning industry. Canneries provided the bulk of jobs for many Asian immigrants. Chinese comprised some of the earliest cannery workers along the Columbia River and Puget Sound where most of the canneries were located. Canneries were established in Kitsap, Wahkiakum and Gray's Harbor counties. From the 1870s to the 1910s Chinese comprised the majority of cannery workers on the West Coast. Most were employed to cut off the heads, tails, and fins of the salmon, gut it, and wash out their cavities. The canneries depended on the reliable Chinese labor force that could be provided by Chinese labor contractors on a seasonal basis. (Chin and Chin, 1987; Chin, 1977).

By the mid-1890s the salmon runs in the Columbia River began to dwindle and fishing eventually shifted to the more plentiful Alaska fishing grounds. But Puget Sound remained the center of the fishing industry and Seattle was the base for the main fleet. Japanese laborers became important in the Washington and Alaska canneries when the supply of Chinese declined in the early twentieth century due to the effects of the Chinese Exclusion Act of 1882. By 1906 twenty percent of the cannery workers in Washington were Japanese. Later, in the 1920s the canneries were a source of summer jobs for the nisei or second generation Japanese Americans. From the late 1920s Filipinos became an important source of labor for the Alaska salmon canneries. These Alaskeros, Filipinos working in the Alaska salmon canneries, added to the growing population of Filipinos in Washington since Seattle was the dispatching point for the Alaska canneries. There were 4,000 Filipinos working in the canneries in 1930 with the numbers rising to 9,000 before World War II. Asian labor was of crucial importance to the salmon canning industry. (Chin and Bacho, 1985; *Alaskeros*, 1988)

The lumber industry also benefited from the labor of Asian immigrants. Asians helped meet the critical demand for labor especially in Pacific Northwest sawmills. In the early years of the lumber industry between 1857 and 1889 Chinese helped to construct early logging roads in Kitsap County and along the Hood Canal and worked in lumber mills in Port Gamble, Port Ludlow, and Seattle. The Wa Chong Co. of Seattle was the main labor contractor supplying Chinese workers for the lumber mills. Later, *123*

Japanese also worked in lumber camps and sawmills at Mukilteo, Enumclaw, Eatonville and Port Blakely. Japanese performed skilled and semiskilled labor including work as trimmers, edgermen, planing-mill feeders, lumber graders, lathe mill men, and carpenters. Other Asians also worked in the lumber industry. Filipinos worked in the lumber mills as did South Asians who were employed in Bellingham and Tacoma sawmills. Asian labor helped meet the labor shortage in the lumber industry.

Farming was a chief occupation of many Asian immigrants. Chinese in mining camps raised produce for the miners. Walla Walla became an early center for Chinese farming. Many Filipinos also farmed in Washington, especially in the Yakima Valley. Japanese were especially prominent farmers in Washington. They supplied the major cities with most of their fresh vegetables, small fruits, greenhouse products and some dairy products. Japanese cleared uncultivated land and established farms east of the Cascades in the Yakima Valley around Wapato and in Spokane, and west of the Cascades in the White River Valley, Puyallup, South Park, Georgetown, Green Lake, Vashon Island, Bainbridge Island and Bellevue. The White River Valley had by far the area of highest concentration of Japanese farmers. Many of the farmers sold their products at Seattle's Pike Place Public Market. By the start of World War I seventy percent of the stalls there were occupied by Japanese. In the prewar years Japanese supplied seventy-five percent of the region's vegetables and most of its berries and small fruits. In the 1920s Japanese dairies supplied half of Seattle's milk supply. Clearly, Asian farming was important to the development of agriculture in Washington. (Wilson and Hosokawa, 1980).

Japanese labor was also important to agriculture in Washington. Some of the earliest Japanese to come to Washington were recruited to clear land in the Yakima Valley. From the late 1920s Filipinos were an important source of migrant labor for agriculture in Washington as a seasonal work force in spring during planting and in fall during harvest; summers were spent in the Alaska salmon canneries. They were important in the apple, asparagus, and hops harvest. There was always critical need for timely, reliable, seasonal laborers at harvest.

In both urban and rural areas Asian immigrants opened small businesses that serviced both their own communities and the general public. Asians operated restaurants, laundries, general merchandise and grocery stores, tailor shops, barber shops, hotels and boarding houses. The International District was a center for many of these businesses in Seattle. Some of the largest businesses were the Wa Chong Company founded by Chin Hock, the Quong-Tuck Company founded by the legendary Chin Gee Hee who returned in 1905 to China to construct China's first railway, the K. Hirada Company, and the M. Furuya Company which had branches in Tacoma, Portland, Vancouver, B.C., and Yokohama and Kobe, Japan, in addition to banking operations.

In the cities, Asian immigrants were active in import/export trade. Trade with Asia has always been important to Washington, and Asian immigrants were important in international trade. In the late nineteenth century the Quong Tuck Company was importing Chinese products. The Wa Chong Company was exporting to China such Northwest products as lumber and flour while the M. Furuya Company had branches in two cities in Japan. With their understanding of the language and culture of the Pacific Rim nations Asian/Pacific Americans continue to play significant roles in the Pacific Rim trade so vital to Washington State.

Asian/Pacific Islander immigration has always been a vital factor in building the economy of Washington. Today, as in the past, they labor in all major industries in Washington and provide much needed labor and skills. Asian/Pacific American labor and businesses have always had great value for Washington.

Exclusion and Restrictive Legislation

Asian/Pacific Americans were instrumental in the economic growth of Washington yet they were from the start subject to exclusion and discrimination. They arrived with the great hopes and expectations expressed by the renowned Filipino American writer Carlos Bulosan in his book *America Is in the Heart*:

> We arrived in Seattle on a June day. My first sight of the approaching land was an exhilarating experience. Everything seemed native and promising to me. It was like coming home after a long voyage, although as yet I had no home in this city. Everything seemed familiar and kind—the white faces of the buildings melting in the soft afternoon sun, the gray contours of the surrounding valleys that seemed to vanish in the last periphery of light. With a sudden surge of joy, I knew that I must find a home in this new land. (p. 99).

Yet, Bulosan soon discovered that the definition of American in the pre-World War II period was exclusive, not inclusive. Asian immigrants learned to expect, though not accept, discrimination in America. As prominent Seattle businessman Dan Woo stated in a *Seattle Times* report on the 1986 centennial remembrance of the 1886 expulsion of Chinese from Seattle, "They took it for granted that discrimination was a way of life." But Asian immigrants fought for their human and civil rights through diplomatic channels, through the courts, and when those avenues failed, through creative resistance. In the process they laid the foundations for the establishment and growth of their communities.

During the territorial organization in 1849 of Oregon, which included present day Washington State, Hawaiians were denied the right to become American citizens and in 1850 they were denied the right to claim land. The racist nature of this discrimination against Hawaiians was clearly revealed by the words of the first territorial delegate, Samuel R. Thurston, who characterized the Hawaiians as "a race of men as black as your negroes of the South, and a race, too, that we do not desire to settle in Oregon." Denied citizenship and the right to claim land, many returned to Hawaii or moved to California where they were still valued for their seamanship. Many others intermarried with Indians and remained. (Solberg, 1978; Naughton, 1983).

The treatment of Chinese immigrants followed the same pattern as that of the Hawaiians and, in turn, set the pattern for later Asian immigrants. One of the first measures adopted by the newly created Washington Territorial legislature in 1853 was a law denying Chinese voting rights. Additional laws were adopted by the Territorial legislature in 1863 to bar Chinese from testifying in court cases involving whites and in 1864 to levy a poll tax on Chinese living in Washington Territory, an act whose title clearly stated its racist intent, "An Act to Protect Free White Labor Against Competition with Chinese Coolie Labor and to Discourage the Immigration of Chinese in the Territory." Chinese were constantly subjected to regulations and prohibitions which sought to exclude them from Washington. Immigration exclusion acts were the most damaging of these legal constraints.

The Chinese Exclusion Act of 1882 was the first in a series of exclusion acts passed by the U.S. Congress that stunted the growth of Asian groups in America and distorted their population composition creating, in the case of the Chinese, an aging "bachelor" society. Passed in the midst of an economic recession in which Chinese became the scapegoat for many on the West Coast, the Chinese Exclusion Act set a dangerous precedent which would have far-reaching effects for subsequent Asian immigrants. There were two major provisions of the act. The first suspended the immigration of Chinese laborers, skilled, unskilled and those engaged in mining, for ten years. The second provision denied the right of naturalization to Chinese. The Chinese Exclusion Act was extended twice with additional restrictions in 1892 and 1902 and in 1904 was extended without time limit.

Since very few Chinese women had come before 1880 and Chinese men were not able to send for wives after 1882, there was little hope for having a settled family life in America after the Chinese Exclusion Act. By the 1900 census Chinese males outnumbered Chinese females twenty-six to one. In effect, the Chinese Exclusion Act prevented family formation in the Chinese community, condemning the Chinese in America to becoming an aging bachelor society. Since no new Chinese laborers were allowed in after 1882 the population decreased dramatically with each census from 1890 to 1920.

The Chinese Exclusion Act served to legally justify further discrimination and violence against Chinese on the West Coast; they had been declared by Congress to be undesirable immigrants and had been prohibited from ever becoming American citizens. The anti-Chinese movement intensified after the passage of the Chinese Exclusion Act. With the completion of the Northern Pacific railroad in 1883 and Canadian Pacific in 1885 and the onset of an economic depression, the Chinese became an easy scapegoat for white frustrations in Washington. On September 5, 1885 three Chinese were killed in an attack on their camp at a hop farm in what is now Issaquah, a few miles east of Seattle. Later that month Chinese were driven out of coal mines in Black Diamond, south of Seattle, the Franklin mines, at Newcastle, and Renton. Chinese were driven out of the lumber mills on the San Juan Islands and at Port Townsend. In November, Tacoma residents took care of the "Chinese problem" by loading 700 Chinese into wagons which took them to trains headed for Portland, Oregon and burning the Chinese district in Tacoma which had housed the largest numbers of Chinese in the territory. No new Chinese district was ever re-established in Tacoma. Seattle held anti-Chinese rallies in September and October calling for the ouster of Chinese from Seattle. In February 1886 most of the 350 Chinese in Seattle were hauled off in wagons to the docks to be loaded onto steamers leaving Seattle. Sporadic attacks against Chinese continued until the turn of the century including attacks at Walla Walla, Pasco, and the massacre of thirty-one Chinese miners on the Snake River. (Chin and Chin, 1987; Chin, 1977).

The Chinese Exclusion Act set a precedent for the exclusion of all Asian immigrants. In 1907-1908 under pressure by the United States, and hoping to halt anti-Japanese sentiment in the United States, the Japanese Government agreed to prohibit the emigration of Japanese laborers to the United States. The Japanese Government, however, continued to allow wives, children, and parents of Japanese in the United

Anti-Chinese riot in Seattle. Seattle, February 7, 1886 Special Collections Division, University of Washington Libraries, UW527 Published in *Harper's Magazine*

States to emigrate; the Japanese community in Washington continued to grow as Japanese sent for their wives in the years after 1908, and a generation of American-born Japanese Americans resulted. Exclusionists found fault with the Japanese Government's desire to allow the formation of families in the Japanese American community. The Japanese Government believed that a healthy, stable, family oriented Japanese American community committed to permanent settlement in America would eliminate anti-Japanese sentiment in the United States. But to exclusionists the coming of Japanese wives meant an increase in the population of the hated Japanese. Even more abhorrent to exclusionists was the resulting birth of a generation with U. S. citizenship since exclusionists could never accept the possibility of a person of Japanese ancestry being American. For exclusionists, race was the key ingredient in determining who could be an American. Exclusionists were determined to once and for all end Asian immigration. (Nomura, 1988).

Further immigration restrictions were imposed against Asians by the Immigration Act of 1917 which created an Asiatic barred zone from which no immigrants from India, Siam, Indochina, parts of Siberia, Afghanistan, Arabia, and the islands of Java, Sumatra, Ceylon, Borneo, New Guinea, and Celebes could come. Then, in 1924, Congress passed a major comprehensive immigration law which prohibited the immigration of "aliens ineligible to citizenship." The only "aliens ineligible to citizenship" were Asian. After 1924 no Asian immigration was permitted. This immigration law closed the doors of the United States to all Asian immigration except Filipinos.

The racist nature of discrimination against Asian immigrants is unmistakable when one looks at the treatment of Filipinos. Since the Philippine Islands were an American possession after the Spanish-American War in 1898, Filipinos were U.S. nationals possessing the right to migrate to any part of the United States. Since they were not aliens, the 1924 immigration act that prohibited the immigration of "aliens ineligible to citizenship" did not apply to them. Therefore, when exclusionary immigration laws had cut off the supply of Asian labor from China, Japan, and India, Filipinos could step in to fill the labor needs of Washington. Filipinos became an important and visible component in Washington's migrant work labor force in agriculture and in the canneries. But, since whites did not recognize their U.S. national status, they were considered by whites to be foreigners robbing them of economic opportunities.

Filipinos were often physically assaulted by exclusionists. Some of the earliest anti-Filipino riots in the United States occurred in Washington. In November 1927 white raiders drove some Filipinos in the Toppenish area of the Yakima Valley out of their houses, beat them, dumped their produce, and dragged many to freight trains leaving the Yakima Valley. A few days later a mob issued an ultimatum to Filipinos ordering them to leave the area by six o'clock or their homes would be destroyed. This 1927 riot set the pattern for similar outbursts such as the more widely reported Wenatchee Valley incident in 1928. With the arrival of the Depression, economic rivalry increased racial tensions in the Yakima Valley leading to white vigilante activity. White unemployment made the situation more acute. In 1933 in a mass meeting in Wapato some 250 white farmers and laborers voted to "request" farmers in the Yakima Valley to stop employing Filipinos. They objected to the hiring of Filipinos on the grounds that they posed an unfair competition to white laborers and they "mingled" with white women. Notices were posted on Valley farmers' homes warning that they would burn the farms of those who persisted in employing Filipinos. There followed a rash of arson and dynamite bombings of Filipino-operated farms and of Japanese farms that employed Filipinos. In one incident, a leased tract was bombed, and buildings, crops, and equipment destroyed. (Nomura, 1986-87).

In all of the above incidents Filipinos were considered by whites to be foreigners taking away jobs from Americans, that is, whites. The basic right of a U.S. national to earn a living was not recognized. Filipinos may have possessed U.S. passports but, to whites, Filipinos were all too often just another kind of Asian to be excluded. Moreover, Filipinos posed an added threat to whites. Filipinos dated and married white women. In the Toppenish, Wenatchee Valley, and Wapato incidents Filipinos were perceived as foreigners robbing whites of economic opportunities and as "barbaric black natives" dating and marrying local white women. For local white males Filipinos posed both an economic and sexual threat to their dominance. This perceived sexual threat led in part to the attempt in 1937 by the Washington Legislature to pass an anti-miscegenation law (Senate Bill 342) prohibiting ". . . any person of the Caucasian or white race to intermarry with any person of the Ethiopian or black race, Malayan or brown race, or Mongolian or yellow race, within this state. . . ." Author Carlos Bulosan aptly states the perspective of Filipinos with regard to this travesty of American ideals:

> Western people are brought up to regard Orientals or colored peoples as inferior, but the mockery of it all is that Filipinos are taught to regard Americans as our equals. Adhering to American ideals, living American lives, these are contributory to our feeling of equality. The terrible truth in America shatters the

Filipinos' dream of fraternity. I was completely disillusioned when I came to know this American attitude. If I had not been born in a lyrical world, grown up with honest people and studied about American institutions and racial equality in the Philippines, I should never have minded so much the horrible impact of white chauvinism. (Bulosan, 1973).

Exclusionists believed the 1924 Immigration Act, which excluded all Asian immigration, should have applied to Filipinos but that Filipinos had escaped exclusion due to the technicality that they were not aliens. This technicality was remedied in 1934. Congress passed the Tydings-McDuffie Act of 1934 which made the Philippines a commonwealth and promised full independence ten years later, but limited Filipino migration to the U. S. to a quota of fifty a year. The Tydings-McDuffie Act was in effect a Filipino exclusion act. As a result there was little growth of the Filipino population from 1934 to 1946.

Community development was greatly affected by the exclusionary laws passed against Asian immigrants. The exclusion acts created aging bachelor societies in the Chinese and Filipino communities. Because immigration exclusion laws prevented them from sending for wives and children, for the most part there was an absence of a normal family life in Chinese and Filipino communities. For Chinese in particular, there was a continuous decline in population until 1920. Without such early exclusion laws Chinese might have become a populous ethnic group in Washington. Instead, until the middle of the twentieth century they remained an aging society of bachelors.

Japanese, on the other hand, experienced steady growth in population since their government was politically strong enough to prevent the passage of total exclusion until 1924. There was enough time to establish a healthy second generation in America, though the numbers of Japanese were of course severely limited by restrictive immigration policies. In contrast to the Chinese and Filipinos, the Japanese had a more normal family life and developed a growing American-born citizen generation.

The 1924 immigration law used the category "aliens ineligible to citizenship" to exclude Asians. The ineligibility to become a naturalized American is the one key feature that distinguishes the Asian immigrant experience from that of other immigrants to America. In 1790 Congress had originally set a racial condition for naturalization by restricting the right of naturalization to an alien who was a "free white person," but after the Civil War in 1870 Congress extended the right of naturalization to former slaves by making "aliens of African nativity and persons of African descent" also eligible. Naturalization laws did not specifically deny naturalization to Asian immigrants but the 1882 Chinese Exclusion Act denied Chinese naturalization rights. This Act did not specify any other Asian group.

The question remained whether Asians could be classified within the definition of free white. Some lower federal courts had issued naturalization papers to some Japanese for the 1910 census indicates that there were 420 naturalized Japanese. But the U.S. Attorney General ordered federal courts in 1906 to stop issuing naturalization papers to Japanese. Japanese took their case to the U.S. Supreme Court in the test case of Takao Ozawa, a Japanese immigrant who met all of the non-racial requirements for naturalization. In November of 1922 the U.S. Supreme Court heard Ozawa's case but ruled that Ozawa did not have the right of naturalization since he was of the Mongolian race and therefore was not judged to be either a free white person or an African by birth or descent. The Court had affirmed a racial prerequisite for naturalization which excluded all Asians.

It is interesting to note how the court handled the question of naturalization rights of South Asians who by the racial classifications of that time were considered to be Aryan. Between 1914 and 1923 some seventy South Asians had become U.S. citizens based on the criterion that they were "high caste Hindus of Aryan race" and were thus Caucasian and entitled to be considered "white persons" eligible for citizenship. Although in the 1922 Ozawa decision the court had based its ruling on the racial definition that white person meant Caucasian, in 1923 in the Bhagat Singh Thind decision, the U.S. Supreme Court further refined its exclusionary definition for naturalization now relying on the "understanding of the common man" rather than on a basis of racial classification. The Court argued that Congress never meant to include South Asians in the definition of white persons since in 1790 Congress associated the term white persons with immigrants from northern and western Europe and in 1870 Congress assumed it meant Europeans. The Court further reasoned that in denying South Asians immigration privileges in 1917 Congress was opposing their naturalization, too. The Court concluded that neither the public nor Congress ever intended that South Asians be granted naturalization rights. (Hess, 1976).

Thus, the U.S. Supreme Court affirmed the legality of the useful category of "alien ineligible to citizenship." In making Asians ineligible to citizenship, the Ozawa and Thind decisions greatly facilitated the total exclusion of all Asian immigration. As earlier stated, Congress prohibited all Asian immigration in 1924 through the prohibition of this category of "alien ineligible to citizenship." The denial of their naturalization rights led to the political weakness of the Asian immigrant communities in the prewar period. Asian immigrants were permanently disenfranchised in America. No politician sought their political support nor cared for their needs. In fact, politicians found it popular among their voters to call for further restrictions against Asians.

The permanent status of Asian immigrants as "aliens ineligible to citizenship" also served as the basis for further discriminatory laws such as the anti-alien land laws passed in various West Coast states which greatly restricted their economic opportunities. Section 33 of Article II of the constitution of Washington State prohibited the ownership of land "by aliens other than those who in good faith have declared their intention to become citizens of the United States." In 1921 and 1923 the Washington Legislature passed further anti-alien land laws that prohibited not only land ownership by aliens who had not declared their intent to become U.S. citizens, but also prohibited their leasing, renting, and share-cropping of land. Lands held by such aliens were to be escheated to the State. Forbidden by U.S. naturalization laws from becoming naturalized U.S. citizens, Asian immigrants as aliens ineligible to citizenship could not possibly own, lease, rent, or share-crop land in Washington since they could not "in good faith" declare their intention to become citizens of the United States. This law severely restricted the economic opportunities for Asian immigrants in Washington. Washington State's anti-alien land laws were not repealed until 1966.

Furthermore, despite the fact that Filipinos were U.S. nationals and not aliens, Washington anti-alien land laws were generally interpreted to apply to Filipinos. Filipinos were considered to be "non-citizens" who could not "in good faith" file their intention to become citizens since they were considered to be Asian and not eligible to citizenship. To counter Filipino contentions that the anti-alien land laws did not apply to them since they were not aliens the state legislature amended the 1921 alien land law in March 1937 to include in the definition of alien "all persons who are non-citizens of the United States and who are ineligible to citizenship by naturalization." In addition, cropping contracts with such aliens were also prohibited. Filipinos thus were prevented from setting up farms of their own and condemned to migrant labor status.

While Asian immigrants were systematically denied every avenue of legally becoming American they were faulted for being foreign. Exclusionist forces perceived Asian immigrants as being incapable of being American. In the eyes of exclusionists, somehow the highly touted melting pot of America could never be hot enough to melt Asian immigrants into the pot of America. A case in point is the editorial statement of Bellingham's *The Reveille*, after the September 1907 Bellingham anti-"Hindu" riot. On September 6, 1907, *The Reveille* stated "From every standpoint it is most undesirable that these Asians should be permitted to remain in the United States. They are repulsive in appearance and disgusting in their manners. . . .their actions and customs are so different from ours that there can never be tolerance of them. They contribute nothing to the growth and upbuilding of the city as the result of their labors."

The immigrants were not ignorant of the impossible position in which they were placed by the illogic of the exclusionists who denied them naturalization, socially discriminated against them, economically restricted them and yet demanded that they assimilate or be excluded. Japanese in the Yakima Valley wrote that

> . . . yet, the self-contradiction in the rationale of the American exclusionists is that the Japanese must be excluded since we do not assimilate. Rejecting our naturalization rights, excluding the Japanese socially and economically, and thereby closing our road to assimilation, the Americans still force us to assimilate. Such is like tying someone's feet and then ordering him to run and finally clubbing him to death because he cannot run. If this is not the absurdity of the Americans, how else can we make sense out of this contradiction? (Yakima Nihonjin-kai, 1935, p.154).

Resistance and Community Development

Yet these groups did survive and managed to build stable communities through supportive organizations. Adversity forged community organization. In the Chinese community support was provided by family associations, district associations composed of members who came from the same districts in China, and secret societies which often espoused nationalist's causes. Many of these organizations were called tongs, literally hall, parlor, or meeting place. The word was used in the names of trade guilds. The tongs were fraternal orders like the more familiar Elks Lodge, Masonic Lodge, or Moose Lodge. But in America Chinese tongs came to imply a group of criminals involved in prostitution, gambling, and opium smuggling. District associations and family associations were organized to provide for the needs of their members and promote their interests. These community organizations provided protection, shelter, employment, and loans. The Gee How Oak Tin Benevolent Association was the largest family association in Seattle. Its members consisted of families with the surnames Chin, Woo,

中華會館

CHONG WA BENEVOLENT ASSOCIATION

Chong Wa Benevolent
Association.
Seattle, n.d.
Photo by S.M. Wand
Wing Luke Asian Museum

Chan and Yuen. Most Seattle Chinese belonged to organizations whose members came from the same districts in China. Most belonged to the Sam Yap, Sze Yap, or Ning Yung District Associations of which the Ning Yung was the largest. The Hip Sing, Hop Sing, Suey Sing, and Bing Kung tongs were the four secret societies in Seattle. In 1910 the Chong Wa Benevolent Association was established as a confederation of associations to govern the affairs of Chinatown. Such a confederation was needed since there was no other local voice to protect the rights of Chinese in Washington. The associations helped to promote and support Chinese language schools, religion, and heritage, Chinese opera, and worked to stop anti-Chinese exclusion laws.

The Chinese community in Washington became more urbanized in the late nineteenth century and had its highest concentration in the Seattle area. Although the 1886 Seattle Chinese expulsion had virtually depopulated the once thriving Seattle Chinatown, a few businessmen like Chin Gee Hee and Ah King managed to stay in business and became labor contractors who brought renewed immigration of Chinese laborers. Chinese merchants dominated the Chinatown community. (Chin and Chin, 1987; Chin, 1977).

Japanese had their own community support organizations. Kenjinkai were associations whose members came from the same prefecture in Japan. The largest were the Hiroshima, Okayama, Yama-guchi, and Kumamoto kenjinkai. The kenjinkai helped both in finding employment for immigrants and providing social contacts. In the Yakima Valley the Kumamoto kenjinkai could field their own baseball team at Japanese community socials.

By far the most important community organization for Japanese were the local branches of the Japanese Association. In Washington the Japanese Association of North America consisted of represen-tatives of over thirty community groups and clubs. The chief function of the Association was to protect the interests of the Japanese community; its main efforts were directed toward fighting the numerous discriminatory and restrictive laws and regulations passed against the Japanese. The Association in Washington supported several court cases argued in the state supreme court and the U.S. Supreme Court. Association leaders in each community helped to promote better relations between the Japanese and white communities. The Associations also supported Japanese language schools. Later, the American-born

generation, the nisei, established the Japanese American Citizens League (JACL) in Seattle which helped to develop nisei leadership.

The cultural focal point for the Japanese community was the Nippon Kan in the International District of Seattle at Yesler and Seventh Avenue. Constructed in 1909, the Nippon Kan functioned as the community center for the Japanese community with the upper floors used as a hotel, other areas for offices and meeting rooms, and the main area as a theater. The Nippon Kan hosted plays, dances, puppet shows, musical performances, martial arts, and other forms of entertainment by local performers as well as performers from Japan. The hall was also used for public meetings to discuss community issues and for religious teachings.

Baseball seems to have been one of the most important recreational activities of the Japanese. Japanese immigrants organized their own teams. In Seattle these teams played in both their own ethnic league and with the City leagues. The mutual love of baseball was one element that bound the immigrant generation and the American-born generation as immigrant fathers could coach and publicly cheer their sons playing on the baseball diamond. Here on the baseball diamond at last Japanese Americans could compete equally without discriminatory restrictions. For many Japanese families Sundays were devoted to watching Japanese American baseball teams play. In fact the biggest social gathering of the year for the Japanese American community of the Pacific Northwest was its annual Japanese Northwest Fourth of July Baseball Tournament. Thousands gathered each year from all over Washington, Oregon, and Idaho.

For Filipinos, discrimination and oppression led to organization and community growth. Though condemned to largely a bachelor's existence, the Filipino community created an extended family system wherein single Filipino men were adopted as "uncles" into existing families presided over by Filipino women who functioned as surrogate mothers, sisters, and aunts to the men. As "uncles," the single men could share in the warmth of family life with children and share in the family celebrations. During the Depression and other hard times Filipinos survived because of a willingness of other Filipinos to share their lodging and food with another countryman. (Cordova, 1983).

Organization is the key word to characterizing Filipino community development. Realizing that more could be accomplished through an organization of united Filipinos, Filipinos organized a union to improve cannery working conditions and community organizations to promote the interests of Filipinos

Wapato "Nippon Juniors"
baseball team.
Wapato, n.d.
Courtesy of Gail M. Nomura

137

138

in Washington. Exploitative conditions in the cannery system led Filipino cannery workers to organize the Cannery Workers' and Farm Laborers' Union Local 18257 in 1933 in Seattle. Chartered in 1934 by the American Federation of Labor, the union brought an end to the labor contractor system. Seattle remains the general headquarters of the union now known as Local 37 of the ILWU. The pioneer Alaskeros, Filipino laborers in the Alaska salmon canneries, were characterized by Filipino American scholar Peter Bacho as proud, defiant, and tough. Their legacy of proud defiance of labor contractor and cannery owners' oppression continues to inspire the Filipino American community to take action against injustice. (*Alaskeros*, 1988).

Filipino community organizations were often successful in fighting off exclusion efforts. One of the most successful efforts was the Seattle Filipino community's efforts to establish their right to own land in Washington. In 1939 Pio DeCano, a Filipino immigrant, challenged the 1937 amendment to the anti-alien land law which had sought to include Filipinos within the definition of alien. He purchased a tract of land in Seattle to be used as the future site of a Filipino clubhouse but his purchase was immediately contested by the State Attorney General. Through the united efforts of Filipinos across Washington, DeCano was able to successfully fight his case to the State Supreme Court.

Similar efforts were made by the Filipino community in the Yakima Valley to secure leasing rights on the Yakima Indian Reservation. Though Filipinos were not allowed to directly lease reservation land before World War II, they were able to farm through labor agreements with Indian allottees. Farming was seen by Filipinos as a means of creating jobs for themselves in the poor economy of the Depression. But as Filipinos began to leave their migrant labor status and become independent reservation farmers, they came into direct competition with white farmers who sought to exclude Filipinos from leasing rights on the reservation. After the passage of the 1937 amended alien land law there was a crackdown on Filipino reservation farmers. The Filipino Community of Yakima Valley, Inc. organized a campaign to settle the issue of their legal status and rights once and for all. They circulated petitions, sought the support of labor unions and civic groups, wrote to President Franklin D. Roosevelt, the Speaker of the U. S. House of Representatives, to President Quezon of the Commonwealth of the Philippines, the Resident Commissioner of the Philippines and other officials, and worked out an agreement with the Yakima Tribal Council. Finally in 1942 due to their determined efforts, the Yakima Valley Filipinos secured leasing

Cannery union officials and members at Labor Day gathering.
Seattle, 1936.
Courtesy of the Espe Family and the *International Examiner*

139

rights on the reservation and assured themselves of a permanent home in the Yakima Valley. (Nomura, 1986-87).

In Seattle by the 1930s the bulk of the Asian American community lived in the area now called the International District. Landlords would not rent to Asian Americans outside the district and restrictive covenant practices further limited the residential mobility of Asian Americans. Most Seattle real estate agreements specified that the owners could not sell their property to non-whites. First Hill and Beacon Hill were not covered by such covenants and became the first areas in Seattle where Asian Americans were able to buy homes outside the International District. (Chin, 1977).

The cultural life of these communities was stimulated by significant writers and artists who were able to express the collective experience of these groups. In particular the writings of Sui Sin Far, Carlos Bulosan, and Monica Sone give glimpses into the lives of their ethnic communities in the years before World War II. The art world of Washington State was greatly enriched by Asian American artists. In particular photographers Dr. Kyo Koike, Frank Kunishige and other photographers of Japanese ancestry of the Seattle Camera Club received international recognition for their work in the 1920s and 1930s. Japanese American painters in the 1930s such as Kakuichi Fujii, Kenjiro Nomura and Kamekichi Tokita and members of the Chinese Art Club like Fay Chong and Andrew Chinn contributed their aesthetic sense to the art world of Washington. Asian American artists like George Tsutakawa, internationally known for his fountain sculptures, Paul Horiuchi, known for his collages made of Japanese handmade papers with Japanese calligraphy, Roger Shimomura, who is especially known for his mock ukiyoe style graphic paintings, and Val Laigo, known for his strongly religious-influenced paintings, continue this Asian American art tradition today. (Tsutakawa and Lau, 1982)

On the eve of World War II there seemed to be great hope that perhaps these communities had achieved some permanence. The U.S. born children of the early immigrants grew up as Americans in Washington State and their parents took special pride in the achievements of their children whose success marked a rectification for past and present injustices. The hopes and aspirations of the immigrants rested in the future of their American children. These hopes and aspirations are encapsulated in the words of the Yakima Valley Japanese who wrote on the occasion of the graduation of the first two Yakima Valley university graduates with honors along with the graduation of Valley nisei high school students also with honors:

Our graduates struck the children of 'superior' whites dumb with astonishment. The whites were amazed; the Japanese were ecstatic. No matter how arrogant the Americans may be, they were aware of the self-contradiction of condemning the excellence of the young citizens of America. They must praise the nisei children with applause; they must be thankful to the Japanese fathers and mothers who have produced fine American citizens. Under this logic, the excellence of the Japanese nisei became an absolute fact, and the long years of hardship of the issei were finally rewarded for the first time. (Yakima Nihonjin-kai, 1935, 252).

World War II

World War II proved to be a turning point for Asian American communities in Washington. For Japanese Americans World War II was a time of incarceration and near destruction of their ethnic community; for other Asian groups it was a time of improving their legal status.

With the outbreak of World War II on December 7, 1941 Japanese immigrants in Washington became enemy aliens. It must be remembered that Japanese had fought their case all the way to the U.S. Supreme Court trying to obtain naturalization rights. They had been denied naturalization on racial grounds and had been condemned to being permanent aliens in America. Moreover, exclusion laws had ended the immigration of Japanese laborers in 1908 and all Japanese in 1924. Therefore, most Japanese "aliens ineligible to citizenship" living in Washington in 1941 had been in the United States for more than three decades. They had chosen to set down roots in America and tied themselves permanently to America through the birth of their U.S. citizen children. Yet despite their commitment to America they were perceived by exclusionists as never becoming part of America. After the outbreak of war with Japan they were viewed with great suspicion. They and their citizen children were subject to a myriad of restrictions and with the issuing of Executive Order 9066 by President Roosevelt on February 19, 1942 they were all forcibly rounded up, removed from their homes and interned in inland concentration camps in California, Idaho, Wyoming, Utah, Colorado, Arizona, and Arkansas. This removal started with Bainbridge Island Japanese Americans on March 30, 1942. They were sent to Manzanar in California. Most Seattle Japanese Americans were sent to Minidoka, Idaho. Some were sent at first to Tule Lake in northern California. Yakima Valley Japanese Americans were sent to Heart Mountain, Wyoming. Two-thirds of those so interned were U.S. citizens.

Evacuation from Bainbridge
Island.
Bainbridge Island, 1942
Seattle Post Intelligencer
Collection,
Museum of History and
Industry, Seattle

142

Yet though the United States was at war with Germany and Italy, German Americans and Italian Americans were not rounded up and interned nor were German and Italian aliens who were also enemy aliens. Clearly the difference in treatment was based on race. The internment of Japanese Americans in World War II marked the culmination of a century of a racist policy of discrimination and exclusion of Asians in Washington. Always considered foreign because of their race even the American-born, second generation Japanese American, the nisei, were interned in inland concentration camps during the war along with the immigrant, first generation, the issei.

It has been argued that Japanese Americans were interned for their own protection, but there were few if any acts of violence against Japanese Americans in the immediate months after Pearl Harbor when war hysteria was highest. Besides, in America we lock up the criminal not the victim. Rather than imprisoning all Japanese Americans west of the Columbia River in Washington, measures should have been taken to prevent any violence against Japanese Americans and prosecute any who committed acts of violence.

Others claim that internment was a military necessity, that there was no time to determine who were loyal and who were not. In a celebrated instance Gordon Hirabayashi, a University of Washington student who contested the curfew and evacuation orders, was convicted of resisting internment on the basis of the government's claim of military necessity. His conviction was upheld by the U.S. Supreme Court. There was apparently time to determine the loyalty of German and Italian aliens who were never interned en masse even if there was not for Japanese Americans. Japanese Americans were never charged with a crime. There are no documented cases of sabotage attributed to Japanese Americans, but even if one or even a thousand had been proven to be disloyal this would not have justified the imprisonment of all Japanese Americans. Our judicial system does not convict the group for the actions of a few. The individual criminal is punished. Moreover, Japanese Americans fought with distinction in the U.S. armed forces in World War II in both the European and Pacific theater. The 100th Battalion and the 442nd Regimental Combat team were the most decorated units of their size in American military history. Furthermore, government documents uncovered in 1981 through the Freedom of Information Act revealed that the initial recommendations for mass internment of Japanese Americans were based on racial considerations and that in later cases argued before the U.S. Supreme Court the government knowingly suppressed, altered and destroyed evidence proving that there existed no military necessity for the removal of Japanese Americans from the west coast. On the basis of this uncovered evidence of government duplicity, Gordon Hirabayashi's conviction was overturned in 1987 by the U.S. Court of Appeals, Ninth Circuit. It took forty-four years for justice to be carried out.

It is exactly in times of crisis that Americans expect the U. S. Constitution to protect them. Yet in the case of Japanese Americans the Constitution folded its protective wings and in so doing jeopardized the future civil rights of all Americans. It seemed that no group would be safe in the future if there were another crisis and they became an acceptable target group. By 1987 the lower courts had finally overturned the convictions of Hirabayashi and the other test cases of Korematsu and Yasui, yet the U.S. Supreme Court has not moved to rewrite their World War II decisions. On Halloween Day, 31 October 1988, the U.S. Supreme Court refused to hear the class action suit for reparations in *Hohri v. United States*, the last case in which it could reconsider its wartime decision. However, due to the vigorous educational campaign by the Japanese American redress movement, the legislative and executive branches of the U. S. government moved to correct this injustice. In 1988 Congress passed, and the President signed legislation to apologize and pay monetary compensation to redress the relocation and internment of Japanese Americans during World War II. Yet, there still continues misunderstanding by many as evidenced by some groups who claim that no monetary compensation should be paid until Japan pays American World War II prisoners of war. These people fail to acknowledge the difference between an enemy nation imprisoning captured enemy soldiers and the U. S. government imprisoning in concentration camps its own citizens and permanent residents without charges.

The Japanese American community suffered incalculable economic loss as a direct result of wartime internment. They lost property, businesses, jobs, and savings. The economic gains of a half a century of work by the immigrant generation was wiped out. After the war the Japanese American community had to start up the economic ladder from the bottom rung again. The immigrant generation already nearing retirement age in 1945 had to begin their lives over again. Many ended their lives as they had begun as day laborers. The psychological losses were perhaps greater than the economic losses. Particularly for the second generation Japanese Americans who as citizens believed in the American democratic system, internment pulled the rug out from under them. But the Japanese American community in Washington did survive this ordeal and slowly rebuilt.

In contrast, World War II brought some improvements in the lives of other Asian groups. The

United States began to change its racist policies against other Asians in the U.S. in response to pressures by the Chinese Nationalist government to repeal the Chinese Exclusion Act and in response to Japan's wartime propaganda that pointed out the hypocrisy of America's claims to be fighting for liberty and democracy for Asians abroad while discriminating against Asians in America. After all, Chinese, Filipinos, and South Asians were allies in arms in Asia. In December of 1943 Congress repealed the Chinese Exclusion Act establishing a token quota of 105 per year for China and granting naturalization rights to Chinese already residing in the United States. Despite the great symbolic elimination of total Chinese exclusion, this new law was intricately designed to maintain the almost total exclusion of Chinese immigration. Not only was the inadequate quota of 105 for all of China ridiculous, even insulting, especially in comparison to the quota of 67,721 for whites from Great Britain, but there were other restrictions attached that further limited even this low quota of Chinese immigration. Any person of one-half or more Chinese ancestry was charged to the Chinese quota regardless of place of birth. Thus a British citizen who was by blood half Chinese was charged to the quota for China. Furthermore, Chinese wives and children of U.S. citizens were charged to the 105 quota for China even though European wives and children of U.S. citizens were considered non-quota immigrants. Still, World War II did cause the United States to end total Asian exclusion and grant naturalization rights to Chinese in America. More job opportunities opened up for Chinese outside of Chinatown, too. Chinese were recruited to work in the aircraft and shipbuilding industries.

The start of World War II dramatically changed the general public's attitudes toward Filipinos. News of the defense of the Philippines by Filipino and American troops fighting side-by-side against the Japanese enemy in the Bataan Peninsula and on Corregidor in Manila Bay changed American perceptions of Filipinos. Against the enemy Japanese, Filipinos were viewed as allies in arms.

Most young Filipino men joined the armed forces serving especially in the First and Second Filipino Infantry Regiments. As a result of their courageous and loyal service, they were granted the opportunity to become naturalized citizens. On the home front they were able to get jobs previously closed to them. Of major importance, Filipinos finally acquired the right to possess land in Washington. In February of 1941 in the Pio DeCano case the Washington State Supreme Court had ruled unconstitutional the 1937 amendment to the alien land law which extended the definition of alien to include Filipinos as non-citizens. But just before war broke out the legislature was about to act quickly to pass a bill to amend   *145*

the title of the 1937 Act since the court had merely ruled that the technicality of an incorrect titling had nullified the law not the intent and effect of the law. Given the wartime change in American attitudes toward Filipino brothers in arms, no legislation to correct the title of the 1937 Act was passed and the alien land law was thus not applicable to Filipinos. Furthermore, the Commissioner of Indian Affairs finally issued a ruling in January of 1942 allowing Filipinos to lease land on the Yakima Indian Reservation. It thus took a world war to secure the property rights of Filipinos in Washington.

Postwar Era

The postwar era has brought further changes. Changes in immigration and naturalization laws and the legacy of the Vietnam War have greatly increased the numbers and changed the composition of Asian/Pacific Americans in Washington.

In the immediate aftermath of World War II, Congress passed several more pieces of legislation that further helped end Asian exclusion. In 1946 Congress sought to remedy some of the inequities of the 1943 act to repeal Chinese exclusion by allowing Chinese wives of American citizens to enter on a non-quota basis. Congress also granted Filipinos the right of naturalization. South Asians were granted naturalization rights and natives of India were given a quota of 100 per year with husbands, wives, and children of American citizens entering on a non-quota basis. Thus Congress had legislatively reversed the 1923 Thind decision and removed India from the barred zone.

Starting in December of 1945 Congress also passed measures to accommodate the immigration of wives of American servicemen serving abroad. In particular the Act of August 19, 1950 made spouses and minor children of members of the American armed forces, regardless of the alien's race, eligible for immigration on a non-quota basis if marriage occurred prior to March 19, 1952. Then from 1948 to 1959 Congress passed several emergency and temporary laws to permit certain numbers and types of displaced persons, refugees, escapees, orphans, and relatives to be admitted to the United States and allowed an adjustment in status to that of permanent resident for students, visitors, and skilled aliens who were not able to return to their own country for fear of persecution. As a result of these measures numbers of Asian war brides and particularly numbers of Chinese refugees and displaced persons were able to have their status adjusted to permanent resident or allowed to enter the United States.

Baptism on Palm Sunday.
Seattle, circa 1949
Courtesy of Fannie Sumoang
and
The Demonstration Project
for Asian Americans

In 1952 Congress passed the Immigration and Nationality Act which eliminated race as a bar to immigration and naturalization. Known as the McCarran-Walter Act of 1952, this law ended the total exclusion of Asian immigration to the United States by giving every country a quota and made all races eligible for naturalization. However, this act still perpetuated a discriminatory barrier to Asian immigration by giving only a token quota to Asian countries. China had a quota of 105. Japan had a quota of 185 and most Asian countries had a maximum quota of 100. Moreover, aliens with at least fifty percent Asian ancestry were still charged to the country of ancestry regardless of where they were born or lived. Yet despite these severe limitations, 1952 marked an end to the era of total Asian exclusion. With the granting of non-quota immigrant status to wives and close relatives of U.S. citizens there was a slow growth in Asian population as Asian Americans sent for relatives.

Korean students comprised most of the Korean community in Seattle in the 1950s though there were also increasing numbers of Korean wives of Americans and Korean adopted children entering Washington after the Korean Conflict ended in 1953. A great increase in numbers of Koreans immigrating to Washington came after 1965.

There was a steady increase in numbers of Pacific Islanders especially from Guam and American Samoa, with the granting of full citizenship rights to Guam in 1951 and the moving of the U.S. naval base from Pago Pago in Samoa to Hawaii in 1951. Many Guamanians and Samoans sought better paying jobs in the mainland United States. Enlistment in the U.S. armed forces was the easiest route for many to obtain better economic opportunities. Particularly in Samoa, the loss of the military base and its attendant jobs along with a severe drought led many Samoans to come to Washington looking for a better education or as enlistees in the armed forces. Most Samoans in Seattle are U.S. nationals from American Samoa, which is a U.S. trust territory. Christian churches and a council of chiefs have played an important role in the Samoan community. Washington State has the nation's third largest concentration of Samoans after California and Hawaii.

The most dramatic changes in Asian American population growth and composition came with the passage of the Immigration and Naturalization Act of 1965 which gave equal quotas to all countries and favored the immigration of the professional classes. From July 1, 1968 when the law took effect, each independent country outside of the Western Hemisphere was granted a quota of up to 20,000 per year with the alien's quota chargeable to the country of his birth. The law exempted from the quota immediate relatives of American citizens including minor children, spouses, and parents. Within the limits of the quota preference was given to other relatives of American citizens and to workers with skills deemed necessary to the American economy.

As a result of the 1965 Immigration and Naturalization Act, there was a sharp increase in Asian immigration leading to a rapid increase in the Asian American population. Asian Americans are the fastest growing ethnic population in the United States. The 1980 census showed a doubling of the population from the 1970 census. The largest numbers of Asians immigrating to the United States now are Filipinos and Koreans. To these can be added growing immigration of Chinese and South Asians. This newest immigration is composed of relatives of U.S. citizens and a high percentage of the educated, professionals and businessmen since immigration laws give preference to this class. Because of the years of exclusion and low immigration quotas, there is a tremendously long waiting list of Asian immigrants wanting to enter the United States. While the immigration quotas for European nations are never filled there are more applicants for immigration to the U.S. from Asian countries than the quotas allow each year. The backlog of Asian applicants for immigration increases with each year.

The Asian/Pacific American population was also greatly affected by the Vietnam War. The Vietnam War generated a new wave of immigrants from Southeast Asia who entered the United States as refugees. This has led to great numbers of Southeast Asians settling in Washington. A massive evacuation of Vietnamese took place in the last weeks before the war ended in 1975 with the collapse of the Saigon regime. Washington State officially sponsored the first group of Vietnamese from their evacuation holding station in Guam and this group formed the core Vietnamese community in Washington, a community which includes a mixture of Vietnamese, Hoa who are ethnic Chinese from Vietnam, and Cham who are Moslems from Vietnam and Cambodia. Cambodians who had close ties to the United States as former government officials and civilian and military employees of the United States also began to settle in Washington in 1975 with the fall of Phnom Penh to the Khmer Rouge. Numbers of Laotians also began to arrive in 1975 including the Hmong, Lao and other tribal groups from this ethnically diverse country. This was followed by further waves of Southeast Asian refugees created by the new government policies in their countries. The crackdown on ethnic Chinese in Vietnam after 1975 led to an outpouring of Hoa "boat people" in 1979 and 1980. Because of their past close military association with the United States, Laotians had to flee the increasing dominance of the North

Ajit, Nalini and Anthony Kottioth, East Indian family. Spokane, 1979
Courtesy of *Spokesman-Review*

150

Vietnamese. Cambodians fled in increasing numbers by 1980 from the atrocities of the Pol Pot regime. Each Southeast Asian refugee has a compelling story of immigration and settlement in Washington.

Their uprooting and flight was filled with death and suffering. Boat people tell of floating for days on overcrowded boats with no water and surviving by drinking urine or dying by making the mistake of drinking ocean water. The bodies of the dead were thrown overboard and one Vietnamese says he can never forget the sound of the splash as bodies were thrown overboard. They speak of pirate raids and countries refusing them sanctuary. One Vietnamese said that as his boat load of refugees clung to a small island outside a port city in Malaysia hoping to be allowed entrance, he could see the lights in the city. He suddenly recalled what Saigon used to look like before the war. Cambodian refugees in particular say the film *The Killing Fields* did not depict the horrors of Cambodia badly enough. A young Cambodian recalls the feeling of malnutrition in which there is a tremendous tightness of the skin as the belly swells and the great fatigue that overtakes you. He also recalls trying to slip food to his parents but one night finding them dead in the jungle. They grieve for the deaths of loved ones and worry constantly about relatives and friends left back in their war torn countries. Aerial bombing by the U.S. laid barren much of Vietnam. As one Vietnamese student told me, "How can I enjoy life freely while my family still does not have enough food to eat?" The traumas of war are exacerbated by loss of country, family, culture, language, job, status, and respect. Many find it difficult to find employment, security, and identity in America.

Most of the problems of resettlement are intensified by language differences. Dropped suddenly into a new culture requiring communication in a new language, older immigrants find it difficult to quickly acquire the necessary language skills to successfully pass job interviews and even more difficult to maintain good working relations with co-workers after obtaining a job. One Hmong remarked that when people ask him questions he can only smile and say yes no matter what they are asking since he cannot understand them. Even those who can speak English often cannot write well. This makes it difficult to fill out the myriad of forms that flood our lives in America from job to car insurance applications. Even shopping is difficult when one cannot easily read labels and products are unfamiliar. There exists a constant strain on the refugee of daily trying to think and talk in a language not familiar to them. More adaptable young children often become intermediaries for adults as the young more quickly learn the language at school.

Lee Family, Hmong
immigrants.
Seattle, 1986
Photo by Olan Mills
Courtesy of Chia Thao and
Ann Tippit

One of the biggest emotional problems for the refugees is the loss of status in the community since many had some sort of higher status in their country be it a government or military rank, community leadership role, businessman or professional status. Now they are refugees at the bottom of the social structure and people no longer respect them even among their own ethnic society. Their children often are made to feel ashamed of their parents.

Perhaps the greatest pain for the refugees is the realization that their suffering may not be at an end in this land of freedom. Southeast Asians have inherited the legacy of anti-Asian exclusion history. Instead of peace and freedom they find themselves targets of physical violence, hate, and discrimination. Entering the United States in a time of economic recession, they are perceived by some as foreigners competing for American jobs or easy scapegoats to vent the frustrations of thwarted hopes and aspirations. They hear shouts of "Go back to where you came from" though they know that the legacy of American involvement in Vietnam makes it impossible for them to return from where they came. They bear the grief and hope for a better future for their children through hard work and education.

ASIAN/PACIFIC AMERICAN COMMUNITY

From the early 1970s, as a matter of political expedience, grew a political coalition of Asian/Pacific Americans who realize that they must be united to have their voices heard and their needs and perspectives addressed. Community activists and organizations began to call themselves Asian/Pacific Americans (APAs). Asian/Pacific American political caucuses have been organized to gain recognition of and action on issues of concern to the Asian/Pacific American community. This community worked for the establishment of the Commission on Asian American Affairs in the governor's office. In learning to work the political system, the community has worked to elect local, state, and national candidates sensitive to these issues. Qualified Asian/Pacific American candidates have been identified and backed for elected and appointed offices. In particular the Seattle area has produced bright Asian/Pacific American candidates that have widespread inter-ethnic support within the diverse Asian/Pacific American community as well as in the larger community. From the early Asian/Pacific American candidates such as Wing Luke, elected to the Seattle City Council in 1960, to Ruby Chow who served on the Seattle City Council from 1973 there was an increase in Asian American politicians from 1979 to include Dolores Sibonga on the Seattle City Council, Lloyd Hara, Seattle City Treasurer, and Gary Locke and Art Wang in the State Legislature. Asian American politicians in Washington are not viewed as merely ethnically based but as viable, effective governmental officials for the whole community.

Political empowerment is not the only reason for a growing awareness of Asian/Pacific American identity in Washington. There is also the recognition of the commonality of discriminatory treatment that binds their histories in America. Out of the civil rights movement and social activism of the 1960s and 1970s and the domestic and international turmoil resulting from the Vietnam War emerged a movement to recognize and promote Asian/Pacific American history and culture. Asian American studies was recognized as an academic field in universities across the nation as there arose an awareness of the importance of studying and valuing the diversity of America in order to truly understand the multicultural nature of America. The University of Washington Asian American Studies Program and the Washington State University Asian/Pacific American Studies Program were established in the 1970s through pressure from the Asian/Pacific American community. Finally, American history became inclusive rather than exclusive and American literature studies were enriched by including the voices of the likes of Sui Sin Far, John Okada, and Carlos Bulosan. The canon of American literature continues to be enriched by the voices of Washington Asian American writers and poets like Mitsuye Yamada, Laureen Mar, Alan Chong Lau, James Mitsui, Alex Kuo, Lonny Kaneko, and Shawn Wong. Never silent, though often ignored and suppressed, these voices need to be heard to more fully understand the complexity of Washington State's multicultural heritage in this centennial year.

The Asian/Pacific American community continues to grow with the state of Washington, and its diversity increases each day. The community is not cohesive and deep schisms divide groups. There are splits along political lines between Chinese Americans supporting Taiwan versus the Peoples Republic of China, between Filipinos supporting Marcos versus Aquino, and Koreans supporting the current regime versus reform elements. The numbers of new immigrants since 1968 have changed the composition from two-thirds native born in 1960 to two-thirds foreign-born in 1980 though the 1990 census should show an increase in native-born. Immigration legislation and the English Only movement are issues of vital concern to the Asian/Pacific American community due to this change in composition. Tensions exist between the American-born and immigrants who often have differing world views.

Yet out of these differences a new and vital Asian/Pacific American community is being forged in Washington State. Symbolic of this new unity and vitality is the rejuvenation of the International   *153*

District in Seattle. Unlike other major west coast cities Seattle does not have a separate Chinatown, Little Tokyo, Little Manila, Koreatown, or Little Saigon. Through inter-ethnic cooperation the International District has been saved from destruction and revitalized itself as the focal point of ethnic identity for Asian/Pacific Americans. Besides ethnic restaurants and stores like Uwajimaya, the International District houses the culturally important Nippon Kan, Wing Luke Museum, and the Northwest Asian American Theatre which under the artistic directorship of Bea Kiyohara presents to its Seattle audience some of the finest in Asian American plays. This community finds a voice in its ethnic newspaper, *The International Examiner*.

The future of these peoples is rooted in a deeper understanding of their past. Community historians like Bettie Sing Luke, Douglas Chin, and Dorothy and Fred Cordova write about the past histories of their communities but also work for the future of their communities. Luke helped to organize the centennial commemoration of the 1886 Chinese Expulsion from Seattle and works towards an integration of multicultural education in the school system. Chin is the leading historian on Chinese in Washington but is also a community activist who continues to work toward the improvement of support services for the International District. The Cordovas founded the Filipino American National Historic Society to preserve the history of Filipino Americans and have worked continuously for Filipino American youth. These people and many more like Denny Yasuhara and the Spokane chapter of the Japanese American Citizens League and the Asian American faculty and students at Washington State University who fought to establish Asian American studies at WSU are the lifeblood of the Asian/Pacific American community. They possess what Frank Shobo Fujii, Seattle artist, educator, and community leader, calls "kimochi," that special sensitivity and empathy for others—for community.

WORKS CITED

Alaskeros: A Documentary Exhibit on Pioneer Filipino Cannery Workers. 1988. [Exhibit Brochure] Project Director and Photographer: John Stamets. Text by Peter Bacho. Seattle: IBU/ILWU Region 37.

Bona, Milton. 1972. "Hawaiians Made Life 'More Bearable'." *Fort Vancouver Historical Society*. 12: 158-175.

Bulosan, Carlos. 1973. *America Is in the Heart: A Personal History*. Reprint of 1943 ed. Introduction by Carey McWilliams. Seattle: University of Washington Press.

Chin, Art. 1977. *Golden Tassels: A History of the Chinese in Washington, 1857-1977*. Seattle: Art Chin.

Chin, Doug, and Art Chin. 1987. "The Legacy of Washington State's Early Chinese Pioneers." *International Examiner*. 14, Number 5 (4 March): 9-15.

Chin, Doug, and Peter Bacho. 1985. "The International District: History of an Urban, Ethnic Neighborhood in Seattle. *International Examiner*, October.

Cordova, Fred. 1983. *Filipinos: Forgotten Asian Americans, 1763-1963; A Pictorial Essay/1763-Circa 1963*. Edited by Dorothy Laigo Cordova. Dubuque, Iowa: Kendall/Hunt.

Das, R. K. 1923. *Hindustani Workers on the Pacific Coast*. Berlin: W. de Gruyter.

Duncan, Janice K. 1972. *Minority Without a Champion; Kanakas on the Pacific Coast, 1788-1850*. Portland: Oregon Historical Society.

Hess, Gary R. 1976. "The Forgotten Asian Americans: The East Indian Community in the United States." In Gee, Emma, ed. *Counterpoint: Perspectives on Asian America*. Los Angeles: Asian American Studies Center, University of California, Los Angeles, pp. 413-422.

Ito, Kazuo. 1973. *Issei: A History of Japanese Immigrants in North America*. Translated by Shinichiro Nakamura and Jean S. Gerard. Seattle: Executive Committee for Publication of Issei: A History of Japanese Immigrants in North America.

Mazumdar, Sucheta. 1984. "Punjabi Agricultural Workers in California, 1905-1945." In Cheng, Lucie and Bonacich., eds. *Labor Immigration Under Capitalism: Asian Workers in the United States Before World War II*. Berkeley: University of California Press, pp. 549-578.

Naughton, E. Momilani. 1983. "Hawaiians in the Fur Trade: Cultural Influence on the Northwest Coast, 1811-1875." Master's thesis, Western Washington University, Bellingham.

Nomura, Gail M. 1986-87. "Within the Law: The Establishment of Filipino Leasing Rights on the Yakima Indian Reservation." *Amerasia Journal* 13: 99-117.

Nomura, Gail M. 1988. "Tsugiki, a Grafting: A History of a Japanese Pioneer Woman in Washington State." In Blair, Karen J., ed. *Women in Pacific Northwest History*. Seattle: University of Washington Press, pp. 207-229.

Solberg, S. E. 1978. "Asians in the Inland Empire." Paper read at Columbia River Watch, an Inland Empire Perspective conference, 25 March, Spokane.

Tsutakawa, Mayumi, and Alan Chong Lau., eds. 1982. *Turning Shadows into Light: Art and Culture of the Northwest's Early Asian/Pacific Community*. Art Direction and Design by Victor Kubo. Seattle: Young Pine Press.

Wilson, Robert A., and Bill Hosokawa. 1980. *East to America: A History of the Japanese in the United States*. New York: William Morrow.

Yakima Nihonjin-kai. 1935. *Yakima heigen nihonjin-shi (History of the Japanese in the Yakima Valley)*. Yakima: Yakima Nihonjin-kai.

Hispanos trace their roots to Mexico, Central and South America, and to the Caribbean

Spanish speaking peoples of the western hemisphere are proud of their distinctive national and cultural identities, while at the same time sharing diverse elements of a common heritage. Hispanos stand as Washington's largest ethnic minority. Approximately eighty-five percent are of Mexican ancestry, most of whom are American born. The Mexican American community has flourished in this State for several generations. Since the 1960s many new Hispano communities have been established by families emigrating from Latin America including Cuba, Puerto Rico, Argentina, Chile, Peru, and from countries in Central America.

WASHINGTON'S HISPANO AMERICAN COMMUNITIES

Carlos B. Gil

Beginning in the early 1940s, a stream of Mexican Americans left the warmer and drier climates of the south for the cooler agricultural communities of eastern Washington. They soon were to sustain the state's agricultural economy by harvesting important crops as no other significant labor force was available; World War II had drained the region of its regular farm workers and many would not return to those jobs after the war. The Spanish-speaking workers thus toiled under the hot summer sun picking apples, cherries, hops, and other products of the earth. From the early 1950s, many of these Mexican Americans began to find their way to the western part of the state where they took up residence in urban working-class districts, many of them south of Boeing Field in Seattle. Here they worked in a variety of industrial and service jobs and were soon joined by other Spanish speakers.

I arrived in the late 1950s as part of yet another stream of Mexican Americans. Numbering approximately 103,720 in this centennial year of 1989, we now form a part of the largest racial minority in Washington. When our cultural cousins (Cuban Americans, Puerto Ricans, Chilean Americans, etc.) are included, all of us *hispanos,* or Hispanics,[1] number 166,486. This is part of our story.

For us Mexican Americans, the pursuit of our happiness in this northwest corner of the United States represents the latest of three phases of a historic migration that began in central Mexico long ago. Few of us would have made it to Washington had it not been for the earlier migrations, each one important to the next. I knew little of this history then. But my own migration to Washington would help me understand the experiences of my fellow Hispanics.

The primeval beauty of Washington's forests overwhelmed me the first time I stood in their midst in the summer of 1957. Having recently left the warmth of my family far behind in a hot and arid valley smelling of spring sage, my appreciation of the luxuriant woodlands near the Canadian border was

Chicano wedding.
Yakima Valley, 1940s
Chicano Archive, The
Evergreen State College
Courtesy of Erasmo Gamboa

dimmed. At age twenty I had landed a summer job on Orcas Island. The exuberant green of its hillsides and the sparkling blue water that lapped its shores actually deepened my homesickness for I had no one with whom to share my feelings. Unlike most other Mexican Americans, who had come to the Pacific Northwest in groups in pursuit of jobs, I had come alone to to complete a bachelor's degree in Seattle, a city that was still strange to me. The three long years it would take to earn my degree weighed heavily on me. Melancholy clung to me through the most brilliant fall I had ever seen and lasted during the greyest winter I had ever experienced.

Even after I enrolled at Seattle University, I felt sapped by the lack of a real community and the cultural life that my hometown *barrio* had offered.[2] At home, in southern California, I had always been part of a well-known, though embattled, minority community, but in Seattle I could not enjoy the benefits of this larger identity. My educational goal encouraged me to endure, and with time I began to enjoy the coolness of Seattle's long winters and slowly I became acculturated to the Pacific Northwest. The old Mexican refrain that says time cures everything, *"el tiempo cura todo,"* slowly unveiled its bitter truth to me.

The punitive dimensions of my self-imposed exile, aimed at self-betterment, began to dissipate the first spring when I began reaching out. Feeling like a fish out of water because I believed that I was the only "Mexican" in Seattle, I nonetheless occasionally sought the support of other communities. Sometimes I visited the International District, where Filipino friends in certain cafes and card parlors made me feel at home, somewhat. At other times I entered the world of the grizzled old ship hands who abounded in waterfront cafes. I felt encouraged to wander into their rough gathering places because my own barrio back home embraced many such havens for single male workers and I had grown familiar with them. Searching for a barrio, like the one I had left behind, I discovered the hispanos of White Center and West Seattle, and while they did not live in a barrio they occasionally organized community dances. I attended some of these dances with great satisfaction.

In my search for the warmth of community I even managed to reach the "east-of-the-mountains" communities of Sunnyside and Wapato awash with migrant worker families, especially in summer. There I felt at home though I could never stay long enough. Having attended many *tardeadas* (afternoon dances for the entire family) as a boy, I searched for and found the Saturday night or Sunday afternoon community dances organized for the Mexican families in these communities. As a young bachelor I naturally gravitated toward young Mexican American women and thus met Beatriz Escalante, daughter of a migrant worker family in Sunnyside, Elaine Romero, daughter of a family that operated a tiny Mexican restaurant in West Seattle, and Maria Dena, whose family had already left field work behind—she worked as a dental office assistant in Seattle.

Susana, Elaine, and Maria came to represent the first Pacific Northwest Chicanas I would know—a group that seemed different to me from the female folk back home, even in the unsophisticated years of my youth. Later I learned that many of their families had originated in south Texas and followed agricultural harvests to the north. They had found their way through Idaho and Wyoming into eastern Washington, where they settled into small farming communities. These Chicanas and their families retained filtered elements of Mexican border culture that fuses the values of family and community with the toil of agriculture and cattle raising in special ways. The small town tradition was indeed alive in their past. The shy friendliness of these Chicanas helped lift my spirit but I soon lost touch with them.

My own family had followed the crops too, we hailed from small towns in the Mexican interior, but ended our roving life by "settling out" in southern California. Our migrant work took us no farther north than San Jose, and when we settled we did so in what became one of the world's most urbanized regions carved out of a benign desert—the San Fernando Valley. Linked to a war-time industrial foundation, including a multitude of non-agricultural jobs, the valley offered many facilities including a reasonably good school system that obligated little brown children like me to attend school and thus be exposed to forces of assimilation that differed widely from those in places like Sunnyside, Washington. I didn't know it in 1957, but I had grown up a big city California Chicano.

The very dynamism of the urban region where my family had settled, permitted (forced?) us to abandon migrant work and small town ways. I managed not only to finish high school but even, after many long detours and delays, to enter academe as a university professor in the Seattle of my youth. My professional work as a historian helped me understand that my arrival in Seattle and the presence of other Mexican Americans, like Maria and Susana, were bits and pieces of a larger mosaic. My academic work taught me that we were all part of a larger historical phenomenon.

Mexican American historical literature stresses a northward push from central Mexico, from the sixteenth century; the Mexican Northward Movement. It vies historically with the Westward Movement in the United States, though preceding it by about 200 years. Both movements represent major migratory

"We heard the tale of Washington–that there was lots of money, that they paid real well, and we thought about coming to Washington. We didn't have a car to travel in and this man, Eduardo Salinas, used to contract people and we came with him. We didn't have much money, we paid him $25.00 for us and $15.00 for each of the children. This was the first time we had traveled. This man said that he had housing and everything for the people, but it wasn't true. We left the 13th of March of 1946 and arrived in Toppenish the 18th. On the road the truck broke down–who knows how many times. In Utah we had to stay overnight because the road was snowed in and we couldn't travel–we all slept sitting up with the little ones in our arms because we had no money to rent a motel. We were about twenty-five people in the truck, plus the suitcases and blankets and a mattress spread out inside, and some tires–we looked like sardines. Then a heavy wind came and the tarp on the truck tore in half. They tied it as best they could–and the snow falling. We finally got out of the snow and then the driver lost his way–we almost turned over. But God is powerful and he watched over us–we got finally to Toppenish. He didn't have housing–nothing–all lies that he told us. He finally found some old shacks, all full of knotholes, in Brownstown–about twenty miles outside of Toppenish–and in tents he placed all the people. It was bitterly cold–with wood stoves and wet wood." *

1936 photograph of Sra. Irene Castañeda taken in Crystal City, Texas, ten years before she came with her husband and children to work as agricultural laborers in Washington State. The harsh experiences faced by Sra. Castañeda and her children are described in a letter she wrote to her daughter, Antonia, in the late 1960s. Sra. Castañeda retrospectively recalled the adverse conditions faced by Mexican workers in the region during the decade of the 1940s. Her epistle evokes the collective experience of thousands of Mexican families who came to the Northwest seeking employment and ultimately settled here to

*Complete text of this evocative letter written in Spanish has been published in Antonia Castañeda, Joseph Sommers, Tomás Ybarra Frausto (eds.), *Literatura Chicana; Texto y Contexto,* Englewood Cliffs, New Jersey, Prentice Hall Inc., 1972.

phenomena with the Pacific Coast as a common endpoint. In the Westward Movement, the people we refer to as Anglo Americans, or simply Anglos, trekked west from the Ohio Valley into what they viewed as empty land in search of opportunity and adventure. In the Northward Movement, Mexicans trudged north from central Mexico for largely the same reasons. Like its Anglo counterpart, the Northward Movement took place over many generations and it proceeded unevenly, leaving a myriad of communities in its wake. Neither Susana, Maria, nor I would have reached Washington without this early northern advance, led first by Spanish conquistadores in the sixteenth and seventeenth centuries after they overcame the Aztec Empire located in central Mexico. This advance occurred in three stages.

The first stage of the Mexican Northward Movement spawned a network of Spanish-speaking communities used later as stepping stones by our forefathers. To this day, the names (now largely simplified) of these communities are clear reminders of the advance by Spanish conquistadores in the sixteenth and seventeenth centuries: San Miguel de Allende was built first, followed by Parral, then Monclova, Laredo, El Paso, Tucson, San Antonio, Nacagdoches, Albuquerque, Española, Los Angeles, San Jose, San Francisco. All of these communities, and many others not named here, were founded before 1780; each one represents a rooting of a northwardly spreading Spanish-speaking people. This initial phase of the Northward Movement thus spread Mexican-Spanish culture as far north as San Francisco and as far east as Nacagdoches. Amazing daring, preceded by careful bureaucratic planning, helped stretch the dominance of hispanos into what was considered the wild backlands of the north—all of them constituting the "northern rim of Christendom," as one famous historian has phrased it (Bolton, 1936), and antedating all English-speaking settlers.

The industrial progress that began to spread in certain parts of Mexico in the late 1800s slowly but effectively increased the number of Mexicans who already lived in these northern communities. The Mexican dictator, Porfirio Díaz (1876-1910), unwittingly contributed to this increase, and to his own downfall, when he invited American investors and engineers to Mexico to install the grand symbols of nineteenth-century progress, the railroads. Only thus would Mexico be able to participate in the great transformation that had seized much of the western world. Built in a north-south direction, in order to export copper ore to New Jersey, for example, the trains also transported many people in search of a better life in the north. The fact that back-country peasants living in Jalisco, in the late 1800s, believed that mining jobs were available to them in the distant mining centers of Miami and Morenci, Arizona, strongly

Bermuda
110

Mexico
70,375

Bahamas
53

Cuba
1,020

Dominican Republic
113

Virgin Islands
70

Jamaica
427

Haiti
62

Puerto Rico
3,965

Honduras
201

Guatamala
99

Nicaragua
210

El Salvador
161

Costa Rica
199

Panama
566

Barbados
18

Trinidad and Tobago
134

Venezuela
276

Guyana
46

Colombia
448

Ecuador
95

Peru
586

Brazil
253

Bolivia
161

Chile
298

Argentina
177

Mexico and Latin America

Shown on the map are the numbers of Washingtonians of Mexican and Latin American descent who identified their ethnic or national origin (by specific country) in the 1980 U.S. Census.

suggests that many inhabitants of central Mexico likewise began to dream and fantasize about the bountiful but arid *el norte*. The advance made in the first stage was thus reenforced by the industrial animation of the *porfiriato* and the chaotic years that followed.

If the various north-south railroad lines intensified the Northward Movement, by more effectively funnelling the northward course of migrants, Mexico's Revolution of 1910 probably helped to push these migrants more than any other event. This revolution represents a significant chapter in the history of social change in the western hemisphere because it ended an old order and ushered in a new one. The hemisphere was not to see another event the likes of this one for many decades. Ironically, the Revolution was unleashed by excesses committed during Mexico's lurch into an uncertain industrial future in the late 1800s. The Mexican Revolution sought to repudiate the early phase of industrialization, and the drastic changes it brought to traditional society, but succeeded only in destroying any feudal arrangements surviving in the countryside. The bonds that held Mexico's peasantry to pre-capitalist estates were loosened by the turmoil. Many young, dark-skinned, male peasants rebelled against their lighter-skinned, hacienda masters on account of old wounds connected with the ways in which egotistic landowners forced their authority onto the peasantry. As a result, revolutionary forces pulled many peasants and small artisans away from the old *hacienda*s and small towns into their own ranks eventually releasing them into cities or pushing them north to the United States border and beyond.

Like stones heaved out of secure resting places and nudged over the edge of a deep canyon, two young Mexicans joined this revolutionary flux. They bounced headlong from their traditional place of birth into a foreign and modern world. One of them was Pascual Naranjo, my maternal uncle. The motives that propelled Pascual were similar to those ascribed to a well-known but fictional revolutionary, Demetrio Macías. In answer to his wife's question if he would continue to be away from her side, as he had been so often during the years of turmoil, Demetrio cast a stone into an abyss and answered "look at the stone; how it keeps on going. . . ." (Azuela, 1963, 147).

Like one of the thousands of stones released by the cataclysm of the revolution, at age fifteen, Pascual abandoned his home, a rude worker's hut on a grain hacienda in mountainous Mascota, Jalisco, in central west Mexico. He had nearly killed Juan José Mora, a cantankerous local ne'er-do-well, his senior by sixteen years, in a machete fight and he had quarrelled bitterly with Don Manuel, the landowner on whose hacienda Pascual's peasant ancestors had lived as serfs ("Criminal...", passim). He also left his   *165* mother, Carlota, his younger sister, Francisca Guadalupe, and his younger brother, Miguel, behind and vowed never to return. An adventurous though resentful dark-skinned peasant lad, he volunteered to fight the rebels as a way of leaving home. Having been assigned to guard federal trains headed to the border town of Nogales, he deserted once he got to the border where he crossed over into the United States in 1919 in search of safer adventure. Working hands were sorely needed and he found a job right away. Many years later, after the Revolution simmered, his family abandoned the hacienda and joined him in California where he worked in a lumber camp near Yosemite.

The other Mexican, who helps illustrate this stage in the Northward Movement, was a fifteen year-old orphan peasant named Bernabé Gil whose ill treatment, at the hands of a sour uncle, also forced him to leave his home in tiny Chavinda, Michoacán, about 1918. Not as headstrong as Pascual, instead of volunteering to fight rebels he simply joined one of the many families attached to the soldiers fighting the rebels. Posing as a young man travelling with his family he thus gained free passage north where he too crossed the border and landed a job after lying about his age. This was my father and he took a job at the same camp perched atop the Sierras of California where young Pascual labored milling lumber. There he met and eventually married Pascual's sister, Francisca Guadalupe, my mother, and I issued from this union many years later.

Whether or not Pascual and the rest of my relatives were actually counted in the U.S. census of 1930, they constituted a diminutive but fairly representative sample of the many thousands of Mexicans who had crossed the border during the revolutionary years. These refugees made up an overwhelming fraction of the 1.5 million "Mexican" residents in the United States that year, most of whom had settled in the old Texan communities founded in the eighteenth century (684,000) where now Anglo cotton farmers sorely needed them as laborers. My relatives joined the second most numerous group (368,000), settling in California where the jobs were more diverse than in Texas. An early analyst of the Mexican American people reported 450 Mexicans living in eastern Washington by 1920 (Gamio, 1971, 25; Moore, 1970, 25; Cardoso, 1980, 92).

The initial stage of the Mexican Northward Movement, begun in the sixteenth century, was thus fortified by Díaz's railroads and the 1910 Revolution; it also facilitated my family's entry into California along with the families of hundreds of thousands of other California Chicanos. From the lumber camp near Yosemite my relatives eventually found their way to the San Fernando Valley, which had become covered-over with citrus groves by the late 1920s. When the Great Depression encouraged federal and state governments to push nearly half a million "unwanted Mexicans" (Hoffman, 1974) back to Mexico, my family stayed on in the valley because my father had found a job picking oranges and lemons. Even though jobs were scarce, few would pick citrus fruits, not only because of the hard physical labor involved but because many people believed that the spraying of orchards caused tuberculosis among the workers (de Gil, intervs.; Gil, 1983, 64-72; Gil, 1982, 1, 31 & passim.). I was born in the city of San Fernando as the economic depression began to ease up.

As the economy improved in the late 1930s, the Texas "Mexicans" slowly and invariably became the core of a vast army of roving workers forced to migrate in pursuit of a livelihood. Cotton had become king in Texas and Mexican labor was annointed as the most important factor in its success even though it was shamelessly exploited and belittled. As one Texas farmer explained it to federal authorities, in defense of increased importation of Mexican labor,

> Farming is not a profitable industry in this country. In order to allow landowners now to make a profit off their farms, they want to get the cheapest labor they can find, and if they get the Mexican labor, it enables them to make a profit. That is the way it is along the border. . . . (Kibbe, 1946, 171).

In the absence of other jobs and needing to keep their bellies full, most Mexicans and Mexican-Americans were thus swept up in this economic whirlwind that cast them about the state like dry leaves in an autumn wind. Carey McWilliams, an imporant contributor to Mexican American history, writes that by 1940,

> Nearly 400,000 workers, two-thirds of whom were Mexicans, were following the 'big-swing' through the cotton growing regions of Texas. . . . During the Depression [these workers] made this great circle, travelling distances from 1800 to 2000 miles. Over this long and wearisome route, Mexican families travel "like the starlings and the blackbirds" (McWilliams, 1968, 172).

The "big-swing" in Texas contributed to the second stage of the Northward Movement that carried *mexicanos* beyond the warm and dry regions of the Southwest so familiar to them. In other words, a structure of low wages, designed to maximize agricultural profits yet keep the labor force strong enough to work and produce more children to attend to future harvests, impelled the Mexican Americans and their Mexican immigrant cousins to widen the migrant-worker stream. As cotton moved west into Arizona, and later California, so did the Mexican Americans. When other agro-commercial crops made their appearance in the American West, Mexican American laborers appeared there too. When sugar could be pressed economically out of sugar beets the *"corte del betabel,"* the harvesting of sugar beets, became a way of life for many Mexican Americans. The great sugar beet companies first contracted Japanese, "Volga-Germans," Poles, and other non-Mexican immigrants to do the work that required long hours of stooping, but Mexican and Mexican-American labor eventually became the mainstay. This drew them to the Rocky Mountain states in 1920, for example, when 1,215 Mexican-born residents were reported working, presumably as *betabeleros*, in three counties that served as "the heart of the expanding sugar beet industry" (Gamboa, 1984, 22; 1981, 124).

Sugar beet companies like the Utah and Idaho Sugar Company ("U & I Sugar") and the Amalgamated Sugar Company were becoming known for their recruitment of Spanish-speaking Texans (Gamboa, 1984, 23). The beet-producing states of Colorado, Nebraska, Idaho, Michigan, Utah, and Montana thus became targets for Spanish-speaking workers, and in this way solidified the second stage of the Mexican Northward Movement. Western railroad companies also employed great quantities of "Mexican" workers and served to disperse *mexicanos* throughout the West. Spanish speakers thus settled in Kansas, Ohio and other mid-Western states.

This migratory experience is captured in many Mexican-American folk songs first heard in the 1930s. Echoing the melancholy I felt when I found myself away from the bright and sunny southwest for the first time, these songs reveal a similar feeling because they confess a yearning for a favored geography and community even as they enumerate the many far away and strange sounding places to which Mexicans were shipped, or felt obligated to go on their own, in order to make ends meet. Although the translated excerpts of the song below may sound awkward, they may help the reader begin to appreciate the homesickness that these men felt as they clickity-clacked on a train at night, across long stretches of unfamiliar terrain en route to strange cities whose names were hard to pronounce. The song is called "The Beet Workers":

Año de mil novecientos	In the year 1923
Veinte y tres en el actual	Of the present era
Fueron los betabeleros	The beet-field workers went
A ese "michigá"	To that Michigan, to their
a llorar. . . .	grief. . . .

Cuando ya estabamos allá	When we get there
Empiezan a regañarnos	They begin to scold us
Y luego les respondemos:	And then we say to them:
"Nosotros nos regresamos	"We are going back
Porque allá en San Antonio	Because in San Antonio
Nosotros solo gozamos. . . ."	We just enjoyed ourselves. . . .'

(Gamio, 1971, 86-87)

From places like Idaho and Wyoming, Mexican Americans began to find their way into eastern Washington, in the third stage of the Northward Movement. Although only slightly documented so far, evidence indicates that the first Chicano families in Washington arrived via the Rocky Mountain region. We know much of this thanks to the most important chronicler of the Mexican-American people of Washington, Erasmo Gamboa, who affirms that mexicanos like Juan Ramon Salinas and Geraldo Cárdenas, were among the earliest Spanish-speaking arrivals in the state and that they were joined by hundreds of Mexican guest workers known as *braceros*.

Yakima Valley farms were literally saved from ruin, during the war, by the arrival of Mexican braceros (most of them peasants or small-townsmen who had seldom if ever worked in large-scale commercial agriculture or lived in big cities) who substantially added to the, as yet, undefined number of mexicanos already residing in eastern Washington. The "Bracero Program" was a bilateral war-time agreement between the United States and Mexico that proved to be as important to American farmers as it has been undervalued by investigators. The program played a critically productive role in the United States's ability to win the war because it was designed to fill the labor vacuum created in American agriculture by manpower requirements generated by World War II. Hundreds of thousands of men and women who might have worked in the fields were swept into uniform, or into war-related industrial work. Farmers began to worry.

Serious labor shortages were experienced as early as 1941. Local farmers pursued the proper government channels in 1942 and the long-awaited braceros began to arrive in Washington in 1943. A reported total of 1,220 of these soft-spoken men in awkward countryish clothes entered the fields and orchards of Washington to gather fruit and ground vegetables before they spoiled in the sweltering summer sun. The number increased to 4,351 in 1944 and 4,393 in 1945, the highest number recorded locally. The Mexican-American presence in the state was firmly established thanks to the braceros. *169*

Gamboa writes that "by 1949, the die was cast. . . . Mexican Americans had taken over from the braceros in eastern Washington." As the number of braceros diminished, after the war, farmers actively pursued "domestic Mexicans" instead and "by July [1950], Idaho had such a [large] surplus of help that it was referring sugar beet workers on to Washington and even Michigan." (Gamboa, 1984, 322)

The life of Roberto Gallegos, who presides over the only Washington Chicano family enjoying a full-length published history, illustrates this connection very well. Originating in New Mexico, instead of south Texas where a large fraction of Washington Chicanos come from, he and his family moved to the Amalia Valley of southern Colorado. In contrast to most Mexican Americans, the Gallegos family owned some land at one point, but they were unable to make a living from it. Consequently, they moved to Vineland, near Pueblo, where they worked in the sugar beet fields. The Gallegos family thus perfectly fits the pattern in which Mexican Americans were pulled away from a borderland residence and cast farther away from the border by sugar beet agriculture in the second stage of the Northward Movement. The Gallegos family also helped harvest potatoes in the beautiful San Luis Valley in southern Colorado. It was here that Roberto became a close member of the Vasco family. Its members had lived and worked in this valley for many years, when, in the mid-1950s, they moved to Washington as migrant workers; they joined relatives already working in Prosser and young Roberto tagged along. He and the Vascos thus illustrate the third stage when they joined the thousands of Mexican Americans who were already contributing to the flourishing commercial agriculture (potato and sugar beets) of eastern Washington with their labor (Johansen and Maestas, 1981, 6-7; 1983, 93-109). Yakima, Sunnyside, Toppenish, Granger, Royal City, and other communities in eastern Washington thus became veritable Mexican American enclaves offering me thereby a fleeting sense of belonging when I discovered them in the late 1950s. Added reflection on this phenomenon, however, reveals an ironic twist.

Dedicated to specialized agricultural production, these rural northwestern communities came to match the thousands of communities in the southwest that so many Mexican Americans had purposely left behind. In these communities, economic and political power was totally concentrated in an Anglo farmer-businessman oligarchy that shut out Mexican Americans from most non-agricultural jobs. Many of these Mexican Americans thus appeared to gain little advantage from their migration. This irony clearly invites a question: how much upward mobility did the Mexican-American people enjoy after their entry into eastern Washington as an agricultural force? Did they break into the middle class? How many migrant workers became farmers, businessmen, teachers, lawyers, managers, etc? Middle "classness" thus becomes an important yardstick that needs to be applied. Preliminary evidence suggests that the Mexican-American middle class has experienced slow growth in eastern Washington. This situation contributed further to the third stage of the Northward Movement.

Even though Roberto Gallegos was a mere teenager when he first arrived in Washington in 1955, he also handily illustrates a spill-over pattern of migration that grew in significance in the 1960s. After working on eastern Washington farms, he moved to Seattle and ultimately made it his home. Joining a type of labor union, which had allegedly denied him access in California, he became a boilermaker at Todd Shipyard and ultimately became a shop steward (still later he became a well-known activist and fought to establish El Centro de la Raza, western Washington's best-known Latino advocacy organization). He worked at Boeing shortly, then returned to Colorado, lived briefly in Los Angeles, then finally returned to Seattle. Roberto thus reflects the experiences of the thousands of mexicanos who arrived in Washington via the agricultural migrant stream indicated above, but his experience also mirrors the many who spilled over into western Washington in pursuit of better opportunities disconnected from agriculture.

The main reasons for this final migratory shift, connected to the third stage, were the perceived opportunity to gain double purchasing power and leave behind a rude and unpromising poverty ridden way of life. The 1960s witnessed dramatic changes in the life styles of America, thanks in part to the vision offered the nation by Lyndon B. Johnson's "Great Society." Even humble farm workers wanted to share in this vision and Roberto and the others in eastern Washington believed that this could only be obtained in cities like Seattle or Tacoma. Like the thousands of other Chicanos in the United States, who moved from small agricultural communities to urban centers in the 1960s, Roberto vividly illustrates this important demographic shift. Many other Mexican-Americans, however, reached western Washington directly; they did not spill over from the eastern communities.

Apart from this three-staged advance, many Chicanos arrived in western Washington communities, for the first time, by virtue of their military service. Military duty during World War II, and after, became one of the most important avenues of change for Mexican Americans because it induced geographical and socio-economic mobility in a way not possible before. It brought a vision beyond the barrio. In the thousand-and-one "little Mexicos" strewn across the American West, young men looking for ways to assert themselves and prove their male-ness, volunteered or accepted being drafted into the

Army. The travel and the discipline military service requires, plus working in large rationally ordered teams, changed their perspective forever in ways we cannot yet fully comprehend. Fort Lewis and Fort Lawton, army facilities near Tacoma and Seattle, respectively, served as conduits for many Mexican American servicemen as they travelled between their homes and overseas assignments. These bases also served as windows through which they peered out at life in the Evergreen State. Two individuals aptly stand-in for this group.

The first is Manuel Barrón, born in Alice, Texas, to a Mexican American sharecropper who cut hair in town on Sundays to make ends meet. Reluctant to attend an all-Mexican school, "because I was barefoot and already becoming interested in girls," Manuel developed an intense wanderlust early, which led him to tour the country as a teenager atop railroad cars. In this way he discovered Seattle in 1939 and learned he preferred the coolness of the Pacific Northwest to the warm humidity of the Texas Gulf. He liked its people more so. "People here were very nice in those days," he stated, "you could do anything to better yourself." Lying about his age, he joined the Army in 1942 and spent some time at Fort Lawton. When he first arrived, in the company of some fellow Chicano soldiers, he did what many Chicanos used to do when arriving in a strange community. They, "searched through the Seattle telephone directory to find other Chicanos in the area. Their searches were unsuccessful—the apparent Spanish surnames turned out to be Filipinos" (Barrón, R., 1977, 16).

The time spent in Fort Lawton persuaded Manuel to settle in Seattle after his 1945 military discharge; he thus became one of the earliest Chicano residents in western Washington. Taking advantage of the genuine openness of Washingtonians, Manuel worked in an aluminum window factory in Ballard while he studied deisel mechanics and, at night, caught up on his junior and high school studies. Like his father, he cut hair part-time for many years while working elsewhere full-time. Finally, he opened up his own barbershop that he proudly oversaw in 1989. Feeling great responsibility for his family, as the eldest child, he persuaded his mother and father and all eleven of his siblings to join him in Seattle. Gregarious and community minded, he later helped organize some of the first Mexican American organizations in Seattle including El Club Latino and El Club Social (Barrón, M., 1988). Well known in the Chicano community, the Barrón clan included at least 25 households in 1988.

The other representative is Rosalío Valenzuela. Son of copper miners in Douglas, Arizona, he broke away from his hometown by entering the military service and saw active duty in the Marshall

Islands, 1950-1951. At the conclusion of his overseas duty, he was reassigned to and finally discharged at Fort Lawton. Instead of returning to his hometown on the U.S.-Mexican border he decided to remain in Washington because he had already concluded that Seattle Anglos treated him better than those in southern Arizona. "That was the main reason; I knew that I didn't want to go back there. There was a lot of prejudice in Douglas and people treated me differently here in Seattle." Concluding that there was "more room for personal growth" in Washington, he stayed on. He worked on strawberry and poultry farms in Marysville during the day and at an Everett shingle mill at night, and saved money to go to school to begin making up for the lack of a high school diploma. He attended Everett Community College and, later, Seattle Pacific University while he labored in Seattle as a machinist and a longshoreman (Valenzuela, 1988). After much personal effort, "Leo" felt proud in 1988 because he contributed to his adopted state by teaching biology and Spanish to several thousand high school students and advising an equal number over the years. He also attracted his brother Alfonso to the Pacific Northwest, who likewise took advantage of the social climate to become a well-known radio broadcaster and producer in the state. (Alfonso Valenzuela served the Spanish-language radio listening audience of western Washington with his bilingual program, "Panorama Cultural", broadcast weekly on KUOW-FM from 1981 to 1985.) Having married soon after his army discharge, "Leo" fathered a small but active Washington Valenzuela clan.

Many other Mexican Americans made their home in western Washington because of their professional training. They did not originally arrive as part of the agricultural migrant stream, originating in Texas, nor were they connected with the military when they decided to settle here. Many in this group seem to have been college-educated Chicanos, probably coming from the states that raised the least barriers to their education in the 1950s and 1960s, such as California, New Mexico and Arizona. These were the first professional Chicanos who began arriving in the Pacific Northwest when government jobs became available in Washington and elsewhere, thanks to so-called "affirmative action" legislation championed by Democratic administrations in Washington D.C.[3]

Alan Apodaca, an Arizonian, seems to have blazed the trail. Don Morgan, the President of Big Bend Community College, invited him to direct much needed migrant worker assistance programs that were fundable, for the first time, by "affirmative action" agencies like the U.S. Office of Economic

Opportunity. Morgan had already initiated proposals to this end and all that was needed was "a Chicano with a college degree." None being available to Morgan, Apodaca, who had already earned his degree at Arizona State University, accepted the assignment and travelled to Washington, planning to return to his native state once a substitute was found for him. Beginning in 1966, he directed the Migrant Education Program in Moses Lake and, later, the Washington Migrant Affairs Daycare Program both of which were fused into the Northwest Rural Opportunities Program (NRO) some years later. In 1970 he was enticed into the Department of Health, Education and Welfare because "there were no Mexican Americans" in the regional offices (Region X) of the federal government, based in Seattle, and positions were available. He served as HEW Program Officer and steadily rose in ranks until he served as the agency's Regional Commissioner from 1976 to 1986. Apodaca attracted other urban educated Chicanos into the federal government, in the early 1970s, and these established their families in Seattle, Everett, Tacoma or Olympia just as Apodaca finally had to do (Apodaca, 1988).[4]

Ernie Aguilar is another trail blazer in the area of public service. A retired soldier looking for new challenges, he too worked in the early migrant worker programs in eastern Washington. In the late 1960s, he was hired by the Washington State Office of Consumer Protection and thus served as one of the first Chicanos in state government. (Aguilar, 1976-1988).

The idea that minority men and women would be afforded an opportunity to contribute more fully to American society via "affirmative action" legislation ultimately affected the nation's colleges and universities too. Consequently, the University of Washington widened its doors in the 1970s to admit a previously unmatched number of minority students, faculty and staff. Although other Washington colleges and universities did likewise, the number of minorities in these institutions has been a fraction of the University of Washington's and their out-of-state pull has been important but limited, comparatively speaking. In 1989, the Seattle-based University of Washington continued to receive a modest stream of Hispanics from the Southwest just as it added to the spill-over of young Chicanos from the eastern part of the state by attracting them to its classrooms.[5]

Central and South American Hispanic Communities

Hispanics of non-Mexican origin have been part of the Washington scene for a long time as well. Washington port cities, in particular, have traditionally embraced the foreigner and the presence of *latinos* in the Evergreen State underscores this openness. Census takers, for example, reported the presence of 395 non-Mexican Latin Americans living in the state in 1940, 68% of whom lived in "urban" areas of the state.[6] This situation changed considerably by 1960 when census takers reported 1,371 non-Mexican Latinos in the state (but 4,778 when Mexicans were added). Beyond the cosmopolitan pull of its port cities, what brought them to Washington?

Two general phases help explain the arrival of the "new Hispanics" in western Washington (where most remain concentrated). The watershed year is 1960. Prior to this, most Latinos coming to Washington were probably spurred by the internal motivations that propel most migrants.[7] Like most of the mexicanos residing "east-of-the-mountains," some pursued better incomes, others sought adventure, still others may have discovered the benign social climate that persuaded Rosalío Valenzuela and Manuel Barrón to stay in the Pacific Northwest; some may simply have been leaving a heartache behind or actively pursuing a sweetheart. The reasons why a migrant migrates are complex, indeed.

Biographical fragments about Aida Pelaez Edenholm help us understand the pre-1960 phase of Latino immigration to Washington. In 1960 she joined the dozen-or-so Bolivian-born Washington residents, who were accounted for in that year's census, when she quit her job as a Pan American Airlines hostess and married a Seattlite who had visited her homeland. Once married, she helped the rest of her family immigrate, especially her father, Ramón Pelaez, who had worked in Bolivia as an award-winning fiction writer and radio broadcaster. For political reasons, he took the opportunity offered in 1963 by Aida and, with the help of his wife, Hortensia, he opened up a hole-in-the-wall restaurant that prospered over the years. This is the Pike Place Market's own Copacabana, one of the oldest Latino restaurants in Seattle.[8] Loyal clients remember that Ramón's "personality attracted people" in part because "he was a born story teller" ("Copacabana...," August 1984; Edenholm, 1988).

About the same time that Aida was making her home in the Pacific Northwest, a twenty-six-year-old Peruvian woman by the name of Angela Torres enrolled at the University of Washington. Prior to emigrating, she had worked as an executive secretary and taught Spanish at the biggest American cultural institute in Lima to resident Americans. "Many of the Americans I met in Lima had studied at the University of Washington," she explained, so when she decided to improve herself by studying in the United States for two years, she elected to enroll there. Her adjustment to life in the United States was "very hard because I had been an only daughter and I didn't know how to cook or take care of myself at first. Life was very hard at the start and I still get homesick for Peru." She married a Seattle man in 1969 and besides raising her daughter, she has worked hard and thus become one of the most influential Hispanics in Pacific-Northwest radio and television. Even so, she feels homesick once in a while "because there are certain memories that always come back." (Torres Henrick, 1988; "KUOW's...," August 1984)

The second phase of Latino immigration began in 1960 but it showed up most clearly toward the end of the decade. The delirious entry of Cuban revolutionaries into Havana on New Year's Day 1960 stands as a fitting symbol of the troubling decade just starting. The people of this region began to be buffeted by the winds of change. These blew so strongly that by the mid-1960s a political whirlwind uprooted many Cubans in a way seldom before seen. The Cuban Revolution immediately produced a stream of upper- and middle-class Cubans who aimed at Florida and New York. (Camarillo, 1986; Foster, 1982) Some reached as far as Washington (seventy-three Cubans were counted in the 1960 census and a five times greater number, 369, in 1970).

The United States Government's most important attempt to control the unsettled situation, made worse by the Cuban revolutionaries, was provided in a special Latin American policy known as The Alliance for Progress. It seemed to do the opposite of what was intended. Instead of helping Latin American governments raise living standards and accept a greater degree of political pluralism, which it promised, many of these governments chose instead to repress the people in ways never seen before. Military coups appeared to sweep the region.[9]

Thousands of refugees were thus created in the 1960s and 1970s and hundreds of Latin American families arrived in the northwestern-most corner of the United States. Between 1960 and 1970, the number of non-Mexican Latinos in Washington grew 1.8 times (from 1,371 in 1960 to 2,468 in 1970); by 1980 (6,073) they increased to 4.4 times the number in 1960 (U.S. Bureau of Census, 1943; 1963; 1983).

Peruvian community celebrating *Homenaje al "Señor de Los Milagros"* (Lord of the Miracles). Santa Maria Church, Seattle, 1979
Courtesy of Angela Torres Henrick

The case of Berta González helps illustrate how someone was hurled into our community by events beyond anyone's control. Her husband, Rafael, worked in the administration of the controversial and ill-fated Chilean President, Salvador Allende, who tried to introduce revolutionary changes in Chile, all within the country's constitutional framework. Conservative forces, supported by the United States Government and International Telephone and Telegraph Corporation, blocked his efforts (Sigmund, 1977, 112-118). A few days after September 11, 1973, when Allende met his death in a military coup d'etat, Rafael was arrested in his home. Along with other Allende supporters, he was imprisoned and severely beaten. When he was finally released, Berta, Rafael and two of their daughters took asylum and fled their native land as political refugees. United Nations refugee officials directed them to Seattle in 1977. Although Rafael died in 1986 (Berta blames his death on the terrible beatings he received while in the custody of the Chilean military), she continued to face life courageously in 1988, learning English at home while studying at the University of Washington (González, 1988).

Whereas Berta and her family fled their beloved Chile because their lives were endangered by a reactionary military regime, Antonio Bermúdez and his family arrived in Seattle because he believed his livelihood was jeopardized by revolutionary Sandinistas.[10] As a lawyer, Antonio had supported the need to overthrow the staunchly pro-American dictator, Anastasio Somoza, in 1979. His support for the new Sandinista government began to evaporate with each passing day, however. In 1988 he insisted that because he worked with them the first few months after Somoza's overthrow, he soon "discovered the tendency into which they were falling." When neighborhood "revolutionary committees" near his home began scrutinizing his daily goings and comings, and when his personal belongings started to disappear and his reports of theft to the authorities fell on deaf ears, he decided the time had come. He could not continue to live in his native country despite his family's long line of professional service. "I didn't think it was right for them to scrutinize me and my family nor was it right for me to lose my belongings without appeal." Believing things would get worse, he began smuggling his family across the border into Honduras and then he finally slipped out of his native homeland in 1979. They immigrated to the United States in 1980 arriving in Tacoma where relatives awaited them.

Life in the United States has not been easy for Antonio but neither has he looked for simple solutions. Even though English has been difficult for him to learn, as it is for most Spanish-speakers, he chose not to go to Miami (where many Nicaraguans live) because it would have been harder to learn it there. Unable to command sufficient fluency in English, and having to support his seven children, he had not yet prepared to take the Washington Bar examination in 1988; he had been obligated to work first in various and sundry jobs in order to make ends meet. Even so, he had already earned a master's degree in Law and Marine Affairs, at the University of Washington, one of his daughters was expected to enroll into college as a freshman and his eldest son was reportedly doing well in the United States Navy. Working as a librarian's aide in Seattle, Antonio's hopes remained high, the year before Washington's centennial, but so did the barriers.

Besides struggling to keep their children properly clothed and fed, Antonio and Maria, his wife, also worried that the children would lose their Nicaraguan identity. She observed, "they're at an age where Spanish is a source of embarrassment; it just isn't easy." He explained further,

> It's become a problem especially when we have to give them the words of advice that all parents are obliged to give their children; they have trouble understanding us, so I have decided to give them Spanish lessons myself. We must stay in communication!

Antonio and Maria speak for many other Hispanics who have made their home in Washington State. (Bermudez, de Bermudez, 1987-1988)

Life in America is hard for adult immigrants because they realize, more than their children, that circumstances beyond their control swept them from their native land. This often produces a feeling of powerlessness and an inability to discharge parental responsibility. It is not easy to contemplate their children, who assimilate into "the American way" more easily than they do, and thus more easily claim a fuller share of the American Dream. Like the millions of other "tired and poor" adults, who arrived on the eastern shores of the United States or stepped onto its southern edges after crossing the Rio Grande, they cannot easily transform themselves overnight. They know that some degree of transformation is vital to succeed in the United States but they also realize that change is a two-edged sword; it is both good and bad. How much should they change? How much can they change?

Finding ways to slow the differences that grow quickly between the older immigrants and their younger American-born kin is probably the experience that occurs most often between the "first Hispanics" (the Mexican Americans) and the "new Hispanics" (Cubans, Chileans, Central Americans, Puerto Ricans etc.). In this sense it becomes a binding commonality. The socio-cultural fears of certain "majority" Americans who ardently support legislation that would declare English as the official language of the United States (in an effort to somehow preserve Anglo-American culture that they believe is assaulted by the immigrants in the 1980s) is both illusory and excessive. The forces of assimilation remain overpowering to any newcomer.

If Hispanics share strong commonalities it is also in the appreciation for and the need to somehow preserve Hispanic cultural ways because these represent important ingredients in the definition of self. Impossible to catalog here, the cultural ways that are so vulnerable to change include a basic sense

Maria and her daughter Lisa, Guatemalan refugees, gazing up at Seattle skyscrapers. Seattle, 1984
Photo by Kurt Smith
Courtesy of the *Seattle Post Intelligencer*

of family and community held most clearly among the immigrants and members of the first American-born generation. Ironically, this "sense" began to disappear among "Anglos" in the late 1800s and its loss has since been mourned.[11] It includes the expression of social deference and *respeto* that encourages special behavior, for example, by young people towards older folk or between adults in a mutual recognition of community status. Within the larger realm of respeto, social rules require children to yield a seat to an adult without being told to do so, encourage hand-shaking behavior even between children and adults when first meeting, require a man to take his hat off when entering a home, insist on the use of formal address modes at certain times and so on.[12] The egalitarianism inherent in American society tends to defeat this particular form of respeto. Most immigrant Hispanic parents have felt frustrated by the decline of respeto, at one point or another. They also realize how important a value egalitarianism has been in the making of modern American society (Deane, 1981).

The Latino sense of community, encouraged by outdoor urban activity, has not been easily sustained in Washington. Urban planners of late medieval Mediterranean cities always made sure to include a central plaza, surrounded by the city's most important institutions and commercial stores, that would act as the heart of the community; Hispanic cities were no exception. As a consequence, some of the most important activities in an individual's life always took place on a central plaza including, for example: the gathering of parents, godparents and the god-child-to-be before stepping into the church across the street, to take part collectively in the child's baptism; a boy's first date with the girl of his dreams in a Sunday afternoon stroll around the plaza; the gathering of mourners for a friend's funeral at church, etc. Combined with long periods of warm and dry weather, both in Latin America and the American Southwest, the plaza heritage also contributed to outdoor urban activity, which included open-air farmers' markets *(tiánguis)*, street vendors, brightly festooned bazaars *(jamaicas)*, religious processions, patriotic parades and so on. These activities, which encourage a close-knit feeling, have survived in small Southwestern communities, to some extent, but have not done well in large northern cities like Seattle.

Change preys on other cultural ways too. Nourished by family and community, old-fashioned Hispanic values hold personal loyalty as paramount. Life in the modern Anglo world, however, requires the building of important ties not based on loyalty. This inevitably gives way to a disquieting anxiety, especially for newcomers, when personal loyalty must yield to impersonal and anonymous relationships.

In the United States, success at the job is tied to performance that is often measured impersonally. Male mutual support groups (sometimes known as *"palomillas"*), for practically all ages, form a distinct aspect of old-fashioned Hispanic communities that provide a man a daily or weekly opportunity to "let his hair down" and thus purge inner tensions; these rarely survive in northern American cities. In Hispanic communities everywhere in the United States, the religious sense that our immigrant forefathers brought with them has practically died. Secularism has gained such great inroads that young hispanos, already acculturated into modern ways, find it hard to imagine the religious atmosphere that prevailed in their parents' homes and barrios even as late as the 1940s. Just as Spanish cedes to English, this religious sense dies quickly, even in the homes of immigrants, and the decline of family and community, so lamented by the "majority" community, becomes apparent once the immigrant generation passes on. Self definition, individually and collectively, is made difficult as a result. What endures, then?

It follows from the preceding remarks that most of the cultural ways identified above, and others not included here for lack of space, quietly endure nevertheless. They do so on an individual or family level and according to the degree of assimilation operating in each case within a specified period of time. Thus, an immigrant family from Chile may retain certain cultural ways especially if its members are still connected to a peasant or worker background and the children are very young. As these grow up, however, the "American way" inevitably predominates and generational conflict may emerge. A working-class Chicano family from San Antonio, living in Spokane, may retain fewer "folkways" or small town ways and accept higher levels of assimilation. A middle-class Chicano family originally from Los Angeles who moves into Tacoma or Seattle may accept the highest levels of assimilation and manifest fewer Latino values.

In more personal terms, I inherited many of the ways that both my parents learned as children in provincial Mexico in the early 1900s. These were modified: by my parents' experience as immigrants in fast-paced southern California, my family's condition of poverty, and by the responses to our needs that we, as a "Mexican" family, received from the Anglo community, as we evolved. To these inherited ways I added my own experience, first as a working class youth raised near the United States-Mexican border and, later, as a middle class professional minority person living in Washington, a region distant from the sources of Hispanic culture. My own experience becomes an essential ingredient in the world view I leave my own children who are vastly different from what I was at their age. Will their children call themselves Chicanos or hispanos? Will Antonio and Maria's grandchildren call themselves *nicaragüenses* or hispanos? Whatever the answers might be to these questions, the fact is that while we may serve as cultural vehicles, we also change as we go through life and we pass these changes to our children too.

How have the hispanos answered the challenges raised by ethnocentrism and racism whenever these have shown their ugly heads? The answers bode well for history's sake. The weakening effects produced by exploitative jobs found especially in commercial agriculture did not paralyze the hispano communities of the Southwest in the 1930s nor in Washington in the 1970s. The answer to this question also suggests that certain chapters in the history of the Mexican American people in the Southwest have made life much easier both for the new hispanos who have come into our midst since 1960 and for younger Chicanos trying to find out who they are and where they belong in American society.

Even in the early days when Mexican Americans earned their livelihood as stoop labor, an inner strength helped them defend their self-esteem. They took their place in America by fighting for it. When my own grandmother, working on the assembly line of a tomato cannery in the early 1930s, was insulted by a gruff speaking Anglo supervisor in front of her fellow women workers, she suddenly raised the hooked knife used to pit tomatoes before placing them in tin cans, and surgically slit the front of his levi jacket in an unforgettable act of defiance. My siblings and I surged with pride upon hearing this and we later memorized the confrontation along with a description of the supervisor's astonishment. Most Mexican American families probably have a similar event etched into their family history teaching the need for self-respect. On a larger scale, a more important example can be found in the southern Texas communities that sent many families to the hop and potato fields of eastern Washington. School officials regularly segregated Mexican children from their Anglo classmates despite the Caucasian category to which Mexicans had been assigned. These officials insisted that language distinctions justified the separation. An enormous effort waged by concerned Mexican American parents and large amounts of money spent on legal fees eventually served to remove the calloused restrictions that wounded mexicano self esteem and the barriers to their education. Two Mexican American organizations, active in Washington in the 1980s, rushed to the aid of these parents. In so doing they came to symbolize Mexican American indomitability in these early years: the GI Forum and LULAC (League of United Latin

Campesino.
Painting by Daniel DeSiga,
circa 1975
Chicano Archive, The
Evergreen State College
Courtesy of Joe García

183

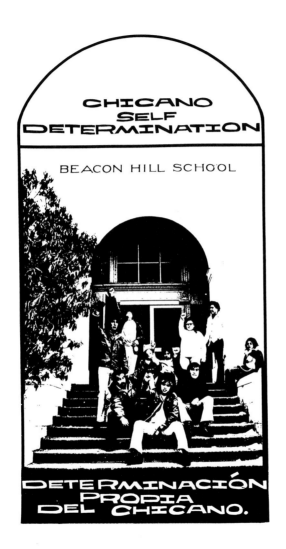

CHICANO SELF DETERMINATION

BEACON HILL SCHOOL

DETERMINACIÓN PROPIA DEL CHICANO.

184

Chicano self determination
(Determinación propia del
Chicano).
Beacon Hill School (became
El Centro de La Raza),
Seattle, 1972
Silkscreen poster by
anonymous artist
Chicano Archive, The
Evergreen State College
Courtesy of Roberto Maestas

American Citizens). Individuals of the calibre of Gus García, George Sánchez and Alonso Perales employed their hard-earned education and forged the way through several court cases that led to the Driscoll School decision of 1957. This court decision "permanently enjoined and restrained" schools from segregating "children of Latin American extraction" on the basis of language distinction. (Alsup, 1977, 27-50).

The quiet militancy of the 1930s and 1940s in the Southwest was not lost on later Mexican American generations. It may have led to the strident rebelliousness that stirred many communities in Washington beginning in the late 1960s. This rebelliousness washed up from Texas and California where young urban Chicanos joined politically minded farm workers and together they organized demonstrations, boycotts, walk-outs and trash-ins to dramatize the humiliating disparity and disadvantage that the Mexican American people had long endured. In agrarian Delano, César Chávez led the way with his attempts to finally bring union benefits to farmworkers of all racial backgrounds. In Denver, Rodolfo "Corky" González preached a semi-charismatic Crusade for Justice among ghetto youth and many youngsters in Seattle and Yakima responded to his call. Reies López Tijerina's appeal for the restitution of communal lands in New Mexico, taken away by the United States Government in violaltion of the 1848 Treaty of Guadalupe-Hidalgo, excited young Mexican Americans who were beginning to enroll in the colleges and universities in Washington. Empassioned by the emergence of their own political awareness and the rebellious rhetoric of the new leaders, many young Washington Chicanos took to the streets. They organized many acts of civil disobedience in Washington, especially in Seattle. Led by a fiery student from New Mexico named Roberto Maestas, these Chicanos and their supporters occupied the old Beacon Hill Elementary School in 1972 and refused to abandon it until the city fathers agreed to convert it into a social and educational center for the Mexican American community, the first of its kind in the region. This became El Centro de la Raza; in this light, it symbolizes Latino self-respect.

Have hispanos preserved their cultural ways, collectively speaking? Is it somehow possible to counteract the forces of assimilation that slowly seep into the cleavages of an immigrant family and its succeeding generations? The answer to this question cannot be defined crisply because cultural issues often deny specificity. The experience of the hispano community in the preservation of its cultural heritage is mixed. While individuals and families may find it difficult to resist assimilation, as discussed earlier, the community as a whole has nonetheless retained certain cultural qualities. Much of this resilience may be attributed to the many Latinos who persist in crossing the United States-Mexican border. From provincial Mexico or El Salvador, for example, they import their cultural need for music, drink, religion and a blind reliance on gregariousness and mirth that wonderously defies awesome conditions of depravation. Thus, they replenish the soul of the larger hispano community residing in the United States because they encourage, among other things, the survival of a flexible attitude toward life with its attendant ups and downs. These selected cultural rituals, often involving food and music, unfold in the privacy of the family that celebrates, for example, a baptism, a first Holy Communion, a *quinceañera* (coming-of-age rituals celebrated for fifteen-year-old girls), a wedding, a birthday *("dia del santo")*, Christmas, New Years, etc. In winter nights, the primeval gloominess that descends on western Washington or the numbing snows that sweep eastern Washington do not diminish the desire to feast on home-made *tamales* and dance to a galloping *norteño* polka, or, in some cases, Chilean *empañadas* while listening to a sprightly *cueca*.

In a more public way, certain aspects of hispano culture have been ratified and maintained by latter-day organizations in Washington, such as the already mentioned El Centro de la Raza and El Concilio for the Spanish Speaking. These leading hispano organizations, founded by Mexican Americans, have fought boldly not only on behalf of political parity but cultural continuity as well. In 1989, El Concilio continued to organize celebrations now regarded as yearly affairs that were completely unknown when I first arrived as a young man in Seattle in 1957. While these celebrations first celebrated Mexican Independence on September sixteenth, they now comprise what is known as Hispanic Cultural Appreciation Week and they continue to take place in mid-September. On those days, Seattle Center sees an amazing gathering of hispano families festively enjoying the gay musical counterpoint of *mariachi* music interspersed, in more recent years, with the vivacious rhythms of Cuban, Puerto Rican or Panamian "salsa" bands or the plaintive sounds of Peruvian flutes.

Many individuals stand out for their efforts in maintaining and developing hispano culture in the state. Because culture is multifaceted, the way in which they have upheld its continuity is multifaceted likewise.

In the realm of art, in the classical sense of the word, Alfredo Arreguín stands as its best known exponent. Born in my father's home state of Michoacán, this earthy immigrant artist has engendered a stunning collection of canvasses splashed with tropical colors and decorated with jungle figures overlaid with patterns drawn from Mesoamerican textiles. "My style comes from my childhood fascination with the artesans of my hometown," he explained one day in 1988. He received "The Palm of the People Award" in France in 1979 and the Governor's Arts Award in Olympia in 1987. (Arreguin, 1989) Ruben Sierra, a native San Antonian, has helped preserve and develop hispano theatre since 1972, when he first joined the University of Washington. Searching for a "vehicle of expression" when the Chicano Movement was beginning to crest, he abandoned the study of biology and plunged into theatre. Thousands of Washington State theatre-goers have applauded the fifty or so theatre productions he has directed for the Teatro del Piojo, the Teatro Quetzalcoatl and the Seattle Group Theatre. "Manolo" and "I Am Celso" are his best known works; he was invited to take "I Am Celso" to the Festival Latino in New York City in 1985. (Sierra, 1989)

Culture thrives outside of university halls and art galleries as well. Many outstanding singers and musicians who contributed to the dissemination and maintenance of Latino culture in Washington illustrate this pattern; they had inelegant but no less satisfying beginnings. In this genre, artists usually make their debut in assorted places that include not only church halls and school auditoriums but bars and nightclubs as well. The members of the Guzmán Family were no exception. José Guadalupe Guzmán, founder of this group, embraced music as a teenager in his native Edinburgh, Texas. After he married Maria, a childhood sweetheart, and most of their nine children were born, they followed the migrant trail to Sunnyside, Washington. There, in 1950, José began offering impromptu norteño-style concerts with five of his children when they were not toiling in the sun. Their music was cheered from the start. Though some of the children eventually went their way, in 1989 part of "Los Guzmanes" was still performing to admiring listeners favoring Chicano music. (Guzmán, M., 1989)

"New" Hispanics seeking "soul music" of their own found it in the flute and drum sounds of "Almandina," an Andean folk music group founded in Seattle about 1981. Chamaly Guzmán (no relationship to the Mexican American group above), a Bolivian who came to Seattle in the early 1970s as an exchange student, organized the six-man band and, despite some personnel changes, held it together in 1989. "Nowadays, our audiences are mostly Anglo but we performed for a lot of home-sick South Americans when we first started," he explained. "Playing is a very special hobby for us and it keeps part of our culture alive," he added. (Guzmán, C., 1989)

Guzmán Family band.
Sunnyside, 1975
Courtesy of José and Maria
Guzmán

"Let us consider, finally, whether there is anything that may separate the "first" Hispanics from the "new"? Beyond the rates of assimilation operating within each family, the immigrant experience itself may play a large role. Immigrants bring with them a sharp memory of why they migrated. Even though they may hold fond memories of old and familiar cultural ways, the memory of low wages, lack of jobs and political harrassment may act as compelling and sobering factors. The hope for a better life in the United States, than in their native country, is therefore usually sharper in the immigrant than it is in his/her descendants. This tends to produce a gap between the militancy on behalf of change in the United States, exhibited by second- and third-generation Chicanos, for example, and the cautious attitude held by most Latino immigrants. Distinctions based on class consciousness may also arise between Mexican Americans and the "new" Hispanics because the latter tend to come from the middle- to upper-classes of Latin America where social distinction plays a powerful role in society. Members of the upper class look down upon and shun those of the lower class. Most Mexican Americans, by contrast, come from small-town, peasant or working- class backgrounds in Mexico, as I do. This background often contributes to blue-collar status in the United States with its attendant poverty and meagre resources for personal improvement. When a Latino immigrant meets a Chicano worker, the former may thus step away from the latter, unfortunately.

On the whole, however, these distinctions appear to play a secondary role in the United States. Being cast into a minority role automatically dictates a struggle to achieve some degree of the parity promised by the American ideal of equal opportunity. After all, it is this ideal that constitutes the fundamental difference between the United States and other countries and it explains why many of our ancestors came here in the first place. The struggle of the few against the many binds hispanos together in the end. Most of us, however, do not lose sight of the American ideal that led us as immigrants to the United States or as internal migrants to Washington.

ENDNOTES

1. Flexibility is the rule of thumb when ethnic labels abound and this rule applies to the Hispanic peoples. In this essay the term Hispanic is synonymous with hispano(a) and latino(a) and it refers to any person living in the United States of Latin American ancestry. Chicano(a), of more recent vintage, is more specific because it refers to a U.S. resident of Mexican ancestry and it is synonymous with mexicano(a). Thus, a Cuban American or a Puerto Rican

may be referred to as an hispano or a latino but not a Chicano. See a useful and comprehensive (though now outdated) evaluation in Richard L. Nostrand, (1973) "'Mexican American' and 'Chicano': Emerging Terms for a People Coming of Age."

The population figures in the text are estimates for 1988. Ms. Ann Brooks of the Washington State Office of Financial Management provided the all-Hispanic ("Spanish Origin") figure. The number of Mexican Americans is extrapolated from the "Spanish Origin" figure using the percentage of people claiming "Spanish Origin" and Mexican ancestry in the 1980 census, 62.3% (75,598 Mexicans and Mexican-origin population divided by 121,286 persons of Spanish origin). See this census in the United States Bureau of the Census. Characteristics of the Population. *General Social and Economic Characteristics* (Washington, D.C.: G.P.O., 1983), Table 59, 49-28.

2. A barrio is a geographically defined district where hispanos reside. Most southwestern communities have barrios (most Spanish words used in this essay will be italicized the first time only)

3. "Affirmative action" legislation stems from the Civil Rights Act of 1964 and the Equal Employment Act of 1972. The first called for the creation of the Equal Employment Opportunities Commission entrusted with ending job discrimination based on race and the second recognized educational opportunites as significant as those related to employment. See *The Encyclopaedia Americana*, (1984)

4. Details surrounding Apodaca's activities in eastern Washington support the author's long held view that OEO and other "affirmative action" programs did indeed help minority Americans, despite the Reagan administration's claims to the contrary. This aid is measurable in the services provided (i.e., childcare, scholarships, food, etc.). Unstudied as yet, it also helped create a grassroots political leadership that was absent prior to the creation of OEO outreach agencies. This leadership has played an important role in minority communities in the 1980s.

Hispanics who were attracted to the state by the private sector are just as important as the others but little is known of this phenomenon so far.

5. The highest number of "Hispanic faculty" at the University of Washington was reached in 1978-1979 when 31 of these faculty members were reported out of a total teaching and research faculty of 2,534 or 1.2% The group dwindled to 23 in 1988 out of a total of 3,160 or 0.7%. Figures were supplied June 7, 1988 by the University of Washington offices of Academic Personnel and University Relations as well as memoranda of February 14, 1988.

6. The categories for Hispanic foreign-born were still quite primitive in 1940. Only three of these were offered: "Mexicans," "Cubans and Other West Indies" and "Central and South Americans." See U.S. Bureau of the Census, (1943), Volume II, Part 7, 320.

7. Explaining migration in terms of internal and external motivations is understandably risky because the two can often become confused. Roberto Gallegos, for example, may have moved to eastern Washington for better wages (an internal motivation) but the low wage scales prevalent near the Mexican border can also become an external motivation.

8. It is possible that the earliest latino restaurant in Seattle was opened in 1952. In 1977 Roger Barrón wrote that "a gentleman by the name of Chester Espinosa opened a restaurant called "El Sombrero" that served Mexican food at the New Caledonia Hotel in 1952. The restaurant is still in operation." The 1988 Seattle telephone directory, however, did not show a listing for an "El Sombrero" Restaurant nor a New Caledonia Hotel.

9. See Lieuwin (1964) for a discussion of the military coups that swept Latin America in the early 1960s, Levinson and Onis (1970) for the Alliance for Progress. Argentina went amuck when a maddening civil war tore its social fabric apart in the late 1960s. Although the insurgency was finally quelled in the mid-1970s by the infamous "Dirty War," tens of thousands of people "disappeared" as a result (Timmerman 1981, 12-13). For a discussion of the elites in the Perón and post-Perón period, see Imaz (1970); for the political turmoil following Perón see Hodges (1976). In Mexico several hundred people were gunned down in one October afternoon in 1968 after many months of political turbulence and many hundreds were imprisoned (Poniatowska 1978, 20-23). The Peruvian military overthrew the civilian government in 1968 and tried to introduce revolutionary changes (North 1981). Smouldering in the 1960s, Central America finally erupted into full-scale conflict in the 1970s with El Salvador and Nicaragua leading the way towards change (North 1985). The sense of "constitutionalism" that had filled Chileans with pride for many decades faded in 1973 when Salvador Allende, Chilean President, was assassinated; his Marxist administration was replaced by a military junta and the country was purged of many critics (many of whom also "disappeared"), and many others fled as refugees (Loveman 1988, Sigmund 1977).

10. In order to protect relatives still living in Nicaragua, the author agreed to apply a pseudonym to this informant and his wife at his request. Multiple interviews were conducted May 29, 1987 and June 12-13, 1988, Seattle, Washington.

11. "The bureacratic orientation . . . obliterated the inner man" is the way social historian Robert H. Wiebe puts it in his *The Search for Order, 1877-1920* (1976), 148.

12. Such as in *usted* (instead of the informal *tú* or the use of *don* and *doña* when a young person addresses an older one ("will you [formal voice] lend me your pen, *doña Julia?*" instead of "will you [informal voice] lend me your pen Julia?" [suggesting equality in age and experience]), etc.

WORKS CITED

Aguilar, Ernie. 1976-1988. Multiple interviews by author, Seattle, Washington.

Alsup, Carl. 1977. "Education Is Our Freedom: The American G.I. Forum and the Mexican American School Segregation, 1948-1957." *Aztlan*, 8-10.

Apodaca, Alan. 1988. Interview, Seattle, Washington. 3 August.

Arreguín, Alfredo. 1989. Interview by author, Seattle, Washington. 6 March.

Azuela, Mariano. 1963. *The Underdogs*. New York: Signet Books.

Barrón, Manuel. 1988. Interview by author, Seattle, Washington, 4 August. Handwritten notes.

Barrón, Roger. 1977. "A Social and Political History of Chicanos in Seattle." Typewritten manuscript. May. 16 pp.

Bermúdez (pseud.), Antonio. 1987-1988. Interviews by author, Seattle, Washington, 29 May, 1987, 12-13 June, 1988. Handwritten notes.

de Bermúdez (pseud.), Maria. 1988. Interview by author, Seattle, Washington, 12 June. Handwritten notes.

Bolton, Herbert Eugene. 1936. *Rim of Christendom: A Biography of Eusebio Francisco Kino, Pacific Coast Pioneer*. New York: MacMillan.

Camarillo, Alberto. 1986. *Latinos in the United States: A Historical Bibliography*. Santa Barbara: ABC-Clio.

Cardoso, Lawrence E. 1980. *Mexican Emigration to the United States, 1897-1931*. Tucson: University of Arizona Press.

"Copacabana Celebrates 20 Years." 1984. *La Voz*, 18 August.

"Criminal—Lesiones. Juan José Mora y Pascual Naranjo, Septiembre 4, 1918." Court of First Instance, Mascota, Jalisco.

Deane, Barbara R. 1981. "El Respeto: An Historical and Contemporary Value in the Interpersonal Communication of Chicanos." Paper presented at the Ninth Annual Meeting of the National Chicano Studies Association, Riverside, California, 4 April.

Edenholm, Aida Pelaez. 1988. Interview by author, Seattle, Washington, 5 August. Handwritten notes and letters.

Encyclopedia Americana. 1984. Volumes. 1, 10. International Edition. Danbury, Connecticut: Grolier.

Foster, David W. 1982. *Source Book of Hispanic Culture in the Southwest*. Chicago: American Library Association.

Gamboa, Erasmo. 1981. "Mexican Migration Into Washington State: A History, 1940-1950." *Pacific Northwest Quarterly* (72: 3): 220-230.

_____. 1984. "Under the Thumb of Agriculture: Bracero and Mexican American Workers in the Pacific Northwest, 1940-1950." Ph.D. dissertation, University of Washington.

Gamio, Manuel. 1971. *Mexican Immigration to the United States: A Study of Human Migration and Adjustment.* New York: Dover Publications.

Gil, Carlos B. 1982. *The Many Faces of the Mexican American: An Essay Concerning Chicano Character.* Occasional Papers, Number 1. Seattle: Centro de Estudios Chicanos, University of Washington.

_____. 1983. *Life in Provincial Mexico: National and Regional History Seen from Mascota, Jalisco, 1867-1972.* Los Angeles: Latin American Center, University of California, Los Angeles.

de Gil, Francisca Guadalupe Brambila vda. 1974-1985. Author's mother. Multiple interviews by author, San Fernando, California. Recorded tape, handwritten notes and letters.

González, Berta. 1988. Interviews by author, Seattle, Washington, 1-13 June. Handwritten notes.

Guzmán, Chamaly. 1989. Interview by author, Seattle, Washington. 1 May.

Guzmán, Maria. 1989. Interview by author by telephone, Seattle, Washington. 20 April.

Hodges, Donald C. 1976. *Argentina 1943-1976.* Albuquerque: University of New Mexico Press.

Hoffman, Abraham. 1974. *Unwanted Mexican Americans in the Great Depression: Repatriation Pressures, 1929-1939.* Tucson: University of Arizona Press.

de Imaz, José Luis. 1970. *Los Que Mandan (Those That Rule).* Albany: State University of New York Press.

Johansen, Bruce E., and Roberto F. Maestas. 1981. *The Creation of Washington's Latino Community: 1935-1980.* Seattle: El Centro de la Raza.

_____. 1983. *El Pueblo: The Gallegos Family's American Journey, 1503-1980.* New York: Monthly Review Press.

Kibbe, Pauline R. 1946. *Latin Americans in Texas.* Albuquerque: University of New Mexico Press.

"KUOW's Revista Latina." 1984. *La Voz,* 20 August.

Levinson, Jerome, and Juan de Onis. 1970. *The Alliance That Lost Its Way: A Critical Report.* Chicago: Quadrangle Books.

Lieuwin, Edwin. 1964. *Generals Versus Presidents: Neo Militarism in Latin America.* New York: Praeger.

Loveman, Brian. 1988. *Chile: The Legacy of Hispanic Capitalism.* New York: Oxford University Press.

McWilliams, Carey. 1968. *North From Mexico: The Spanish Speaking People of the United States.* New York: Greenwood Press.

Moore, Joan W. 1970. *Mexican Americans.* New York: Prentice Hall.

Nostrand, Richard L. 1973. "'Mexican American' and 'Chicano': Emerging Terms for a People Coming of Age". *Pacific Historical Review* (42:3). Reprinted in Norris Hundley, Jr., ed. *The Chicano.* Santa Barbara: Clio Books, 1975, 143-160.

Newfarmer, Richard., ed. 1984. *From Gunboats to Diplomacy: New U.S. Policies for Latin America.* Baltimore: Johns Hopkins Press.

North, Liisa. 1981. *The Peruvian Revolution and the Officers in Power, 1967-1976*. Montreal: Center for Developing Area Studies, McGill University.

————. 1985. *Roots of Revolt in El Salvador*. 2nd ed. Toronto: Between the Lines.

Poniatowska, Elena. 1978. "Voice of Tlalteloloc." *NACLA Report on the Americas* (12: 5): 20-23.

Sierra, Ruben. 1989. Interview by author, Seattle, Washington. 15 March.

Sigmund, Paul E. 1977. *The Overthrow of Allende and the Policies of Chile, 1964-1976*. Pittsburgh: University of Pittsburgh Press.

Timmerman, Jacobo. 1981. *Prisoner Without a Name, Cell Without a Number*. New York: Vintage Books.

Torres Henrick, Angela. 1988. Multiple interviews by author, Seattle, Washington, 9-12 June. Handwritten notes.

U. S. Bureau of the Census. 1943. *Sixteenth Census of the United States*. 1940. Volume 2, Part 7. Washington, D. C.: Government Printing Office.

U. S. Bureau of the Census. 1963. *The Eighteenth Decennial Census of the United States. Census of Population*. 1960. Volume 1, Part 9. Washington, D. C.: Government Printing Office.

U. S. Bureau of the Census. 1983. *1980 Census of the Population. General Social and Economic Characteristics*. Volume 1, Part 49. Washington, D. C.: Government Printing Office.

Valenzuela, Rosalío. 1988. Multiple interviews by author, Seattle, Washington, 15-20 May. Handwritten notes.

Wiebe, Robert H. 1976. *The Search for Order, 1877-1920*. New York: Hill and Wang.

EPILOGUE

S.E. Solberg

The preceding essays present us with a kaleidoscopic vision of Washington's ethnic heritage: shifting shapes and colors, surprising variety of tone and focus, intriguing hints of the diversity, and abundance of peoples and cultures that have enriched, are enriching, and continue to enrich our state. There has been little homogenization: the milk tastes different from place to place reflecting the character of local pasturage, just as it did when I was growing up a third-generation Norwegian in south-central Montana, and as it must if we are to be linked to the land and place of our living. A celebration then of diversity, of community, and the persistence and vitality of those community characteristics we have come to call "ethnicity". This is a demonstration of the multicultural richness of the peoples of this state and, indeed, of this nation. These remarks by no means represent "closing entries"; the ledgers remain open. To take a case in point.

On September 4, 1988 Washington's Cham Community celebrated *Katè* in commemoration of a former national glory. The auditorium in the Riverton Heights Elementary School of the Highline District just south of Seattle was the setting. I was honored to be a guest at this first tentative step toward public celebration of community-wide events in this small Southeast Asian refugee community that had first come to Washington only in the early 1980s.

Heirs of the culture and traditions of the once powerful maritime state of Champa that ruled over much of present day Vietnam and Cambodia, the Cham have been reduced to the status of ethnic minority in today's Indochina and subjected to ruthless oppression in recent years. For them, the United States, and the State of Washington, are more than way-stations on the refugee/exiles' circuitous road home; their new home represents opportunity, education for their children, equality, and respect for their elders. Being here, paradoxically, allows the Cham a greater opportunity to be more fully themselves, to preserve the memory and pride of a past glory than they once had in their "homeland."

Home village scene,
Cham Seattle Community.
Vietnam, late 1980s
Courtesy of Cham Student
Association, University of
Washington

In this one small community we find reflected some of the most enduring and endearing themes from our collective past: refuge from political, ethnic, and religious oppression, the promise of individual political, legal, and economic equality of opportunity. For the Cham, elders and youth alike, there is hope that freedom here will allow them to learn more about their past "there", to understand more about their history (which did not exist in the course of study of the nations where they lived), and to define their present as Cham within the greater community of this state and nation.

I went with one of their young men, a student at the University of Washington, in search of what written record of Champa and its people we could find in the school's libraries. The findings were returned to the community to be translated and added to the stock of memory and oral tradition that had crossed the Pacific with the elders. "Stateless Champa People's Celebration" read the banner over the stage during the program, "So long as Champa culture lives, Champa lives." Hardly the sentiments of those waiting breathlessly for the plunge into the homogenizing rush of what we choose to call the mainstream.

This commitment to protect and preserve an idealized past in celebration and daily life in no way contradicts a passionate embrace of American ideals, real or apparent. (There is, after all, nothing that says a Libyan Moslem or Irish Catholic or Therevada Buddhist from Cambodia are any the less capable of being good or better Americans than a British Episcopalian, Norwegian Lutheran, or Scottish Presbyterian.) Once again the power of the American Dream is at work, releasing the powers of the newcomer to further enrich this society of ours.

In this small Cham community there is a beginning, a tentative working out of many themes that inform the longer stories that are the core of this book: preservation, conscious or unconscious, of a cultural heritage, a sense of community as defined both from within and enforced from without. For the Cham community, as are all groups of newcomers, is also being shaped into something new by this land and its peoples. And one day the Cham will tell their own story to add to those already told here.

There can be no question that there is a great and enduring power in the revelation of self through ethnic or national group and revelation of the group through the self. The essays that make up this book suggest that the values of these self-identified ethnic or national subcommunities, in some cases no longer tangible physical reality, but lingering historical and emotional reality, define who and what they are for many of the peoples of Washington. A remarkable number of even northern Europeans, contrary to the common wisdom, continue to identify themselves with the nation or ethnic group of their ancestors. To the second, even third and fourth generations, the trip back to Norway, Korea, Mexico, or Africa remains a trip "home." I, myself, though I have spent most of my adult life working with and around peoples from Asia and Asian Americans here in Washington, still expect one day to make that trip "home" to Norway.

As Native Americans draw continuity and strength from the land, others draw it from their "histories", the common threads of custom and habit that have come down in this new land from forebears, that continue to come with the newcomers who join us daily. No matter how far from our origins, these simple things are among the fundamentals that define us: the way the coffee is poured, how the table is set, the church we attend or don't attend, the shared jokes, and most important, the shared silences. We relax, drop our guard, comfortably "at home," the ambiance familiar no matter the setting, waterfront condominium or family farm. And once we are home, we tell stories, stories of uprooting and transplanting, of fruit withered and bitter on the vine as well as the plentiful harvest, stories that usually don't wind up in the standard histories.

Peoples of Washington is a record, preliminary as it might be, of the lives, community and individual, too often ignored or unrecorded, that have, often against the heaviest odds, enriched our blood and strengthened our state. Washington's citizens, together with the citizens of this nation, are becoming more tolerant of the "strangers" in their midst, more secure in who and what they are, often through a belated return to ethnic identifications, and thus more able to comprehend, and even celebrate, difference. For Washington is today composed of an incredibly rich and diverse cultural gene pool. The way is open to a rich multi-crop harvest; the day of the single crop quick cash-out is passing.

Clarence Mandas in an
Efzone costume,
Greek Independence Day.
Seattle, circa 1910
Courtesy of Constance
Mandas

WASHINGTON'S ETHNIC HISTORIES AND CULTURES: A BIBLIOGRAPHY

Pat Matheny-White
with the assistance of Rachel Anderson

This bibliography identifies sources for information on the histories and cultures of Washington's many and diverse ethnic communities. It is an effort to document all ethnic communities, as defined in the last U.S. Census. For the first time in 1980, a general question on ancestry (ethnicity) was included in a United States Census. Census categories for national origin provide a detailed picture of the diverse population of Washington, and were used as a basis for developing bibliographic groupings.

Materials included in this bibliography are readily accessible in libraries throughout the state; it is organized in the same sequence as the essays in the book, beginning with multi-ethnic sources and continuing with sources of information on Native American, European American, African American, Asian/Pacific American, and Hispano American groups. Subsections cover specific communities within these broader categories. The bibliography will provide the user with an initial sense of the diversity of cultures within our state, and sources from which to learn more about the histories and cultures of specific ethnic groups. It is intended for the general public, students and teachers at the secondary and college level, and researchers.

This bibliography is the result of extensive bibliographic and field research for both the exhibit and book that bear the title *Peoples of Washington*. Research was carried out in cooperation with the book's authors and with the many consultants listed in the acknowledgements section. These scholars and community leaders were key to the success of the project, multiplying and authenticating sources of information. In addition to interviews with all of the consultants, library and field research was conducted throughout Washington. This research was combined with additional archival investigation that focused on the acquisition of photographs for the *Peoples of Washington* exhibits and for this book.

It was necessary to develop special methodologies in order to organize this vast array of information. The first task was to identify all of the groups, beginning with the broad categories: Native American, European American, African American, Asian/Pacific American and Hispano American. Before library research could begin in earnest, it was necessary to identify all the ethnic groups in order to search catalogs and indexes. Under Ethnology—U. S. in the *Library of Congress Subject Headings* eighty-six headings were suggested; another forty-four headings for the Native American tribal groups were listed under Indians of North America. More headings were added to the search based on the U. S. Census figures for population in the state by ancestry, and on the tribal groups listed in Ruby and Brown's *A Guide to the Indian Tribes of the Pacific Northwest*. A total of 199 headings were searched, with 116 headings leading to useful entries.

After extensive research and development of a computer database, entries were selected. The resulting bibliography is comprehensive in scope, attempting to cover as many ethnic groups as possible. It is comprised primarily of books, periodical and newspaper articles. Privately published or non-standard published works are included only when no other information was available or when the material was of significant value to the history and culture of an ethnic group. The newspaper sources included are feature articles providing historical and cultural information—their preponderance indicates they are a major source of community history. While Washington State is the focus for all materials, relevant material from books and articles on the Pacific Northwest or the West is also included. As often as possible, materials were selected that provide the voice of the particular ethnic group.

A number of significant research projects have been undertaken in the area of multi-cultural studies, producing materials that are included in the bibliography. The histories that exist have been written by free lance historians at the local level, by community historians or by university-based scholars such as Dr. Erasmo Gamboa of the University of Washington and Dr. Gail M. Nomura of Washington State University. The Washington State American Revolution Bicentennial Commission Ethnic History Series published by the Washington State Historical Society was an important publication project. This series on the Germans, Chinese, Gypsies, Scots, Native Americans, Italians, Yugoslavs and English has

laid the ground work for further research. The bibliography presents information on a number of important publications that have been carried out in conjunction with the 1989 Washington State Centennial. Books like *Roots and Branches: The Religious Heritage of Washington State* by Buerge and Rochester provide a history of the state making reference to the experiences of Native American and immigrant communities. A number of publications, video productions, and exhibits have been produced dealing with various Washington State ethnic communities and cultures under the sponsorship of the Ethnic Heritage Committee.

While we see a growing body of materials appearing in print, dealing with Washington's ethnic communities, there is nevertheless much that needs to be done. The general histories of Washington do not adequately document the history of ethnic peoples. In the light of the 1980 Census data, there are very few publications covering specific ethnic groups in Washington State that are accessible through general library and union catalogs, such as the *Western Library Network Resource Directory*. Much of the information on the histories and cultures of specific ethnic groups in Washington State has been privately published. Therefore, most of the accessible information is available in special collections which store and index periodicals, newspapers, privately published materials, and unpublished reports and manuscripts. These important sources of information are listed at the end of this introduction.

As has been said, this bibliography is a first effort to identifiy sources of information on the histories and cultures of all of the ethnic groups in the state of Washington, as defined by the 1980 U.S. Census. It should be noted that this census data is not complete, and that a significant number of new immigrants continue to come to Washington from all parts of the world, some of them from countries that have not yet been identified in the census. Thus, looking to the future, we see an ongoing need for documenting our state's increasingly diverse population as new information is developed from various sources.

Interlibrary Loan Codes

One of the major critera for this bibliography was general accessibility through interlibrary loan networks in the state. What can a public librarian in Colfax, Washington, access for their patrons or where can they refer people? To aid in providing access to the sources, the interlibrary loan codes for selected libraries in the state are noted in each entry. The interlibrary loan codes included in each entry are:

Wa	The Washington State Library
WaChenE	Eastern Washington University Library
WaEC	Central Washington University
WaOE	The Evergreen State College Library
WaPS	Washington State University Library
WaS	Seattle Public Library
WaSKC	King County Library System
WaSp	Spokane Public Library
WaSpSF	Spokane Falls Community College Library
WaU	University of Washington Library

Special Collections

Washington Room, Washington State Library, Olympia
Washington State Archives, Olympia
Washington State Historical Society, Tacoma
Northwest Collection, Tacoma Public Library
Northwest Collection, Seattle Public Library
Northwest Collection, University of Washington
Manuscripts Division, University of Washington
Northwest Collection, Spokane Public Library
Eastern Washington State Historical Society, Spokane
Archives, Eastern Washington State University
Archives and Special Collections, Washington State University Library
Oregon State Historical Society, Portland

Multi-Ethnic Sources

Various reference books contain pieces of information making some reference to ethnic groups; none, however, fully cover the ethnic history of the state in a comprehensive manner.

The *Bibliography of Washington State Folklore and Folklife* (Walls, 1987) is the first multi-ethnic bibliographic source specifically on Washington State. However, it covers folklore and folklife in a very broad sense, including ethnic sources but not focusing on ethnicity alone. *We the People: An Atlas of America's Ethnic Diversity* (Allen, 1988) is a major new resource on ethnic groups which covers all of the United States, providing detailed demographic information at the state and county level. For a broad national overview of all ethnic groups, including bibliographic sources this is an excellent reference. The standard encyclopedic source, also national in scope is the *Harvard Encyclopedia of American Ethnic Groups* (1980). An older handbook and extensive bibliographic source are Miller's *A Handbook of American Minorities* and *A Comprehensive Bibliography For the Study of American Minorities*. Other useful demographic sources are the U. S. Census publications, especially the *Ancestry of the Population by State*, and Calvin Schmid's *Non-White Races, State of Washington*. Schmid has published other demographic guides including some on non-white races in Seattle and in the public schools.

Geographic and historical material on Native Americans and immigration is contained in two atlases: *Atlas of the Pacific Northwest* (1985) and Scott and DeLorme's *Historical Atlas of Washington* (1988).

Two publications focus on Seattle's ethnic groups: *Contact* (1981) is a directory of organizations with some historical overviews. This is a major work that serves as a cultural resource guide which needs expansion to provide statewide coverage. *A Cultural Guide: Our Changing Ethnic Community* (1986) is more recent, providing brief information in a beautifully presented brochure on the new immigrants who have come to Seattle/King County.

The Washington Centennial has provided opportunities for new research and publication. *The Guide to Ethnic Washington* is a compilation of graphic and printed information on ethnic groups in Washington based on research for the *Peoples of Washington* exhibition project. The guide includes information on exhibits, films, video tapes and other media productions. Andrews's *Washington Women As Path Breakers*, Buerge and Rochester's *Roots and Branches*, Lund's *Folk Art of the Evergreen State*, *Washingtonians: A Biographical Portrait of the State*, Scott and DeLorme's *Historical Atlas of*

Washington and Ficken and LeWarne's *Washington, A Centennial History* all include references to various ethnic histories. The King County Centennial Program has published *King County and the Pacific: A Cultural Resource Guide.*

Histories published prior to the Centennial that cover ethnic materials are Clark's *Washington, a Bicentennial History* (1976), Edwards and Schwantes's *Experiences in a Promised Land* (1986), Sale's *Seattle, Past to Present*, and Shideler's *Coal Towns In the Cascades* (1986). Blair's *Women in Pacific Northwest History* covers women of various ethnic groups. Stratton and Frykman's recent book, *The Changing Pacific Northwest* also includes ethnic materials.

Northwest Mosaic: Minority Conflicts in Pacific Northwest History is important because it is the only Pacific Northwest history focusing on a wide range of ethnic groups. The Polson Museum's *Chehalis County Nationality Survey* is a model for local and regional ethnic histories. White's article covers the diversity of workers during the building of the railroads.

An important means for documenting ethnic community and personal histories is through oral histories. Of prime importance is the collection of oral histories and photographs in the Washington State Oral/Aural History Program at the Washington State Archives. Thirty-one oral histories are documented in *River Pigs and Cayuses.*

Another important venue for documenting ethnic histories is that of community newpapers and general newspapers. Two multi-ethnic newpapers/newsletters are the *Northwest Ethnic News* and the Washington State Folklife Council's newsletter *WashBoard*. Feature articles and series of articles or columns in our major regional newspapers are vital sources of information. Dorothy Powers's series in the Spokane *Spokesman-Review*, Rev. Erle Holwell's in the *Seattle Times* and features in the *Seattle Weekly* are examples. It is important when using these sources to assess the articles for biases, prejudices and accurate coverage .

Artistic production gives expression to important aspects of a community's culture and history. Multi-ethnic sources include *Gathering Ground: New Writing and Art by Northwest Women of Color* and Lund's *Folk Art of the Evergreen State*. Photographic documentation such as Matsura's historical compilation in Roe's *Frank Matsura* and Stamets's contemporary images in his *Portrait of a Market* capture the visual history of ethnic communities.

Reference Works

1. Allen, James Paul and Eugene James Turner. *We the People: An Atlas of America's Ethnic Diversity.* New York: Macmillan, 1988. 315 p. ill.*WaS, WaOE*

2. *Atlas of the Pacific Northwest.* Edited by A. Jon Kimerling and Philip L. Jackson. 7th Edition. Corvallis: Oregon State University Press, 1985. 136 p. ill., maps, charts. Bibliography. *Wa, WaS, WaSP*

3. *Contact: Ethnic Heritage Directory: A Resource Directory and Teacher Resource Manual for the Seattle/King County Area.* Developed and prepared by the Seattle Public Library [in cooperation with] the Ethnic Heritage Council of the Pacific Northwest. Seattle: Seattle Public Library, 1981. Looseleaf, ill., maps. *WaS, WaSKC*

4. *A Cultural Guide: Our Changing Ethnic Community.* [Pamphlet/Guide Book]. Seattle: Publication funded by Gull Industries; sponsorship of Leadership Tomorrow by the Greater Seattle Chamber of Commerce and United Way of Seattle/King County, 1986. 1 leaf. *WaOE (VF)*
   This guide is a description of people who have come to Seattle/King County in the last decade. The diverse peoples included are: Cambodian, Samoan, Vietnamese, Thai, Korean, Ethiopian and Laotian.

5. *A Guide to Ethnic Washington.* Edited by Sid White. Olympia: The Evergreen State College, 1988. 20 p. tabloid. *WaOE (VF)*
   This guide contains information on Washington's ethnic communities, including maps, demography, chronologies, historical overviews, personal family histories and other sources of information.

6. *Harvard Encyclopedia of American Ethnic Groups.* Stephan Thernstrom, Editor; Ann Orlov, Managing Editor. Cambridge, Massachusetts: Belknap Press, 1980. 1076 p. maps. Includes bibliographies. *Wa, WaOE, WaS, WaSp*

7. Metrocenter YMCA and King County Historic Preservation Program. *King County and the Pacific: A Cultural Resource Guide.* Project Director: Valerie Cole. Writers/Editors: Rosemary Adang and Valerie Cole. Seattle: King County Centennial Program, 1988. 37 p. ill., photos. *WaS, WaSKC*

8. Miller, Wayne Charles. *A Comprehensive Bibliography For the Study of American Minorities.* New York: New York University Press, 1976. 2 vol. 1380 p. *WaOE, WaS*

9. _____. *A Handbook of American Minorities.* New York: New York University Press, 1976. 225 p. *WaOE, WaS*

10. Schmid, Calvin Fisher, Charles E. Noble and Arlene E. Mitchell. *Non-White Races, State of Washington.* Olympia: Washington State Planning and Community Affairs Agency, 1968. 132 p. ill. Bibliographical footnotes. *WaOE, WaS, WaSp, WaU*

11. Scott, James William and Roland Lawrence De Lorme. *Historical Atlas of Washington.* Cartography by Ted R. Brandt and Patrick S. Grant. Norman: University of Oklahoma Press, 1988. 77 leaves, xxix p. ill., maps. Bibliography: pp. xi-xxii. *Wa, WaOE, WaS, WaSp, WaU*

12. U. S. Census of Population (1980). Ancestry of the Population by State. *1980 Census of Population. Ancestry of the Population by State: 1980. Supplementary Report.* Washington, D.C.: U.S. Dept. of Commerce, Bureau of the Census ; For Sale by the Superintendent. of Documents, U.S.G.P.O., 1983. 83 p. forms. *Wa, WaOE, WaSP, WaU*

13. Walls, Robert E. *Bibliography of Washington State Folklore and Folklife; Selected and Partially Annotated.* Seattle: Published for the Washington State Folklife Council by the University of Washington Press, 1987. 301 p. ill., map. "A Selected Discography of Washington and Northwest Sound Recordings, compiled by Jens Lund": p. 296-301. *Wa, WaOE, WaS, WaU*

14. Washington State Oral/Aural History Program. *Oral History.* [Microform]. [1977]. ca. 300 microfiche. ill. *Wa, WaS, State Archives*

15. Washington State Oral/Aural History Program. *Oral History Index.* Compiled by Ann Rune. Olympia: Division of Archives and Records Management, 1977. 329 p. *Wa, WaS, State Archives*

Other Sources

1. Blair, Karen. *Women in Pacific Northwest History: an Anthology.* Seattle.: University of Washington Press, 1988. 259 p. ill., photos. Bibliography: p. 246-248. *Wa, WaOE*

2. Buerge, David M. and Junius Rochester. *Roots and Branches; The Religious Heritage of Washington State.* Designed by Adrian Kalar. Seattle: Church Council of Greater Seattle, 1988. 277p. Bibliography: p. 251-259. *Wa, WaOE, WaS*

3. Clark, Norman H. *Washington, a Bicentennial History.* New York: Norton, 1976. 204 p. ill. *Wa, WaOE, WaSP*

4. Edwards, G. Thomas and Carlos A. Schwantes, Editors. *Experiences in a Promised Land: Essays in Pacific Northwest History.* Seattle: University of Washington Press, 1986. 397 p. *Wa, WaOE, WaS, WaSp*

5. Ficken, Robert E. and Charles P. LeWarne. *Washington, A Centennial History*. Seattle: University of Washington Press, 1988. 216 p. ill., photos. Bibliography: p. 187-203. *Wa, WaOE, WaS, WaSp*

6. *Gathering Ground: New Writing and Art by Northwest Women of Color*. Edited by Jo Cochran, J. T. Stewart and Mayumi Tsutakawa. Seattle: The Seal Press, 1984. 187 p. ill. *Wa, WaOE, WaS*

7. Lund, Jens. *Folk Art of the Evergreen State*. Olympia: Washington State Folklife Council, 1989. 112 p.

8. *Northwest Ethnic News*. Ethnic Heritage Council of the Pacific Northwest. January, 1984- Volume 1-. *WaS, WaU*

9. *The Northwest Mosaic: Minority Conflicts in Pacific Northwest History*. 1st Edition. Edited by James A. Halseth and Bruce A. Glasrud. Boulder, Colorado: Pruett Publishing Company, 1977. 301 p. Bibliography: p. 282-287. *Wa, WaOE, WaS, WaSP*

10. Polson Museum (Hoquiam, Washington). *Chehalis County Nationality Survey: 1848-1915*. Project Director: Joe Randich. Associate Director: Dorothea Parker. [Hoquiam, Washington] The Polson Museum, 1984. 1 volume looseleaf, ill., photos. *Wa*
    This project is supported in part by the Washington Commission for the Humanities.
    A chronicle of early immigration to Grays Harbor County (then called Chehalis County).

11. Powers, Dorothy. "All of Us: Ethnic Groups Make Spokane a Rainbow City." *Spokesman-Review*. Community News (30 May 1985): 1, 2.

12. *River Pigs and Cayuses: Oral Histories from the Pacific Northwest*. Edited and Photography by Ron Strickland. San Francisco: Lexikos, 1984. 186 p. ill., photos, ports. *Wa, WaOE, WaS, WaSp, WaU*

13. Roe, JoAnn. *Frank Matsura, Frontier Photographer*. 1st Edition. Introduction by Murray Morgan. Seattle: Madrona Publishers, 1981. 144 p. ill., photos., map. *Wa, WaOE, WaS, WaSP*

14. Sale, Roger. *Seattle, Past to Present*. Seattle: University of Washington Press, 1976. 273 p. ill. *Wa, WaOE, WaS, WaSp*

15. Shideler, John C. *Coal Towns in the Cascades: A Centennial History of Roslyn and Cle Elum, Washington*. Spokane: Melior Publications, 1986. 151 p. Bibliography: p. 147-148. *Wa, WaS*

16. Stratton, David H. and George Frykman, Editors. *The Changing Pacific Northwest: Interpreting its Past*. Pullman: Washington State University Press, 1988. 187 p., ill., notes, bibliography. *Wa, WaPS, WaU*

17. Stamets, John. *Portrait of a Market: Photographs of Seattle's Pike Place Market.* With text by Steve Dunnington. Seattle: The Real Comet Press, 1987. 95 p. chiefly ill., photos. *WaS*

18. *The WashBoard; The Newsletter of The Washington State Folklife Council.* 1985- Volume 1-. *Wa*

19. *Washingtonians: A Biographical Portrait of the State.* Edited by David Brewster and David M. Buerge. Introduction by Roger Sale. Seattle: Sasquatch Books, 1988. 520 p. Bibliography: p. 507-512. *Wa, WaOE, WaS, WaSP*

20. White, W. Thomas. "Race, Ethnicity, and Gender In the Railroad Work Force: the Case of the Far Northwest, 1883-1918." *Western Historical Quarterly* Vol. 16, Number 3 (1985): 265-283.

Native American, General

This is only a small selection from the numerous books and articles that have been published on the many tribal groups in the state. Generally accessible sources and major publishers are included. Grumet's bibliography and Ruby and Brown's books are major reference sources to consult for further research. Carpenter's *They Walked Before* is the Washington State American Revolution Bicentennial Commission Ethnic History Series book. The other books and articles are general sources with books on specific tribal groups being included in the following two sections, Plateau and Coastal. Hale's novel is partially based on her experience in Washington. Niatum's recently published book of poetry is another example of a literary work. *New Directions Northwest* documents the contemporary artists in the Northwest. For further information on historical and contemporary tribal issues, use the Regional Newspaper Index at the University of Washington Library which indexes a number of Indian newspapers (*Indian Center News, Indian Voice, Northwest Indian News, Northwest Indian Times* and others that are not included here).

1. Brown, William Compton. *The Indian Side of the Story.* Spokane: C. W. Hill, 1961. 469 p. *Wa, WaOE, WaS, WaSp*

2. Burns, Robert Ignatius (S. J.). *The Jesuits and the Indian Wars of the Northwest.* New Haven: Yale University Press, 1966. 512 p. *Wa, WaOE, WaS*

3. Carpenter, Cecelia Svinth. *They Walked Before: The Indians of Washington State.* Tacoma: Washington State American Revolution Bicentennial Commission and the Washington State Historical Society, 1977. ill. *Wa, WaS, WaSp, WaU*

Lorena Seelatsee (Yowunpum).
Yakima Tribal Elder, 1987
Portrait by Mary F. Nelson

4. Clark, Ella E. *Indian Legends of the Pacific Northwest.* Illustrations by Robert Bruce Inverarity. Berkeley: University of California Press, c1953. 225 p. *Wa, WaOE, WaS*

5. Cohen, Fay G. *Treaties on Trial: the Continuing Controversy Over Northwest Indian Fishing Rights.* Seattle: University of Washington Press, c1986. ill. *Wa, WaS, WaSp*

6. DeLoria, Vine Jr. *Indians of the Pacific Northwest: From the Coming of the White Man to the Present Day.* New York: Doubleday, 1977. 207 p. ill. *Wa, WaS, WaSp*

7. Dietrich, Bill. "Washington's Indians: A Special Report." *Seattle Times* (24 December 1985)
   Reprinted from articles originally appearing in The *Seattle Times* from December 15 - December 20, 1985.

8. "Eskimo Teenagers Learn That Life in Big City Isn't Like Movies." *Seattle Times* (16 April 1980): C2.

9. Grumet, Robert Steven. *Native Americans of the Northwest Coast: A Critical Bibliography.* Bloomington: Indiana University Press, 1979. 108 p. *Wa, WaOE, WaS*

10. Hale, Janet Campbell. *The Jailing of Cecilia Capture.* New York: Random House, 1985. 201 p. *Wa, WaOE, WaS, WaSp*

11. *The History and Culture of the Indians of Washington State: A Curriculum Guide.* Developed by the TTT Project and the Center for Indian Education, University of Washington; Principal Writers, Duane Niatum and Linda Rickman; Editors Leighanne Harris and Willard Bill. Revised Edition. Olympia: State Superintendent Of Public Instruction, 1975. 245 p. *Wa, WaOE, WaS*

12. Kirk, Ruth. *Exploring Washington Archaeology.* With Richard D. Daugherty. Seattle: University of Washington Press, 1978. 112 p. *Wa, WaOE, WaS, WaSp*

13. *New Directions Northwest; Contemporary Native American Art.* [Exhibition catalog] Producer/Editor: Sid White. Olympia: The Evergreen State College, 1987. 52 p. ill., col. *WaOE, WaS*
   Includes the folowing essays: Current Realities: A Cultural Overview of American Indian Life by Beatrice Medicine; Carrier of Culture: Contemporary Native American Art in the Pacific Northwest by Gail Tremblay; Runners Between the Tribes by Joan Randall and George Longfish.

14. Niatum, Duane. *Songs For the Harvester of Dreams: Poems.* Seattle: University of Washington Press, 1981. 64 p. *Wa, WaOE*

15. Nicandri, David L. *Northwest Chiefs: Gustav Sohon's Views of the 1855 Stevens Treaty Councils.* [Exhibition Catalog]. Tacoma: Washington State Historical Society, 1986. 96 p. ill. *Wa, WaOE, WaS, WaSp*

16. Randolph, June. "Witness of Indian Religion; Present Day Concepts of the Guardian Spirit." *Pacific Northwest Quarterly* (October 1957): 139-145. ill.
    Portraits of Madeline Covington, George Nanomkin, and Clara Moore.

17. Ruby, Robert H. and John A. Brown. *A Guide to the Indian Tribes of the Pacific Northwest.* Foreword by Roland W. Force. Pronunciations of Pacific Northwest tribal names by M. Dale Kinkade. Norman: University of Oklahoma Press, 1986. 289 p. ill. (Civilization of the American Indian series) *Wa, WaOE, WaS, WaSp*

18. Ruby, Robert H. and John A. Brown. *Indians of the Pacific Northwest: A History.* Norman: University of Oklahoma Press, 1981. 294 p. ill. *Wa, WaOE, WaS, WaSp*

19. Trafzer, Clifford E., Editor. *Indians, Superintendents, and Councils: Northwestern Indian Policy, 1850-1855.* Lanham, Maryland: University Press of America, 1986. 173 p. *Wa, WaOE, WaS*

20. Underhill, Ruth. *Indians of the Pacific Northwest.* Washington, D.C.: United States Department of Interior, Bureau of Indian Affairs. Branch of Education, 1944. 232 p. ill. *Wa, WaOE, WaS*

Native American-Coastal

We tried to include materials on all of the tribal groups west of the Cascades. The materials are selective, but the range is wide. When generally available, tribal productions are included: *The Eyes of Chief Seattle*, Gordon Hill's bibliography on the Shoalwater Bay Indians, Carolyn Marr's *The Chehalis People*, *Portrait in Time*, the Quinault Tribal Council's *Portrait of Our Land*.

1. Amoss, Pamela. *Coast Salish Spirit Dancing: The Survival of an Ancestral Religion.* With drawings by Ron Allen Hilbert. Seattle: University of Washington Press, 1978. 193 p. *WaU*

2. Boas, Franz. *Chinook Texts.* Washington Government Printing Office, 18—? 278 p. (U.S. Bureau of American Ethnology. Bulletin Number 20) *WaU, WaOE, WaS*

3. Bruseth, Nels. *Indian Stories and Legends of the Stillaguamish, Sauks, and Allied Tribes.* Fairfield, Washington: Ye Galleon Press, 1977. 35 p. ill. *WaS, other editions Wa*

4. *Coast Salish and Western Washington Indians.* New York: Garland, 1974. 5 vol., maps. (American Indian Ethnohistory: Indians of the Northwest) *Wa, WaS, WaSp, WaU*

5. Colson, Elizabeth. *The Makah Indians: A Study of an Indian Tribe in Modern American Society.* Westport, Connecticut: Greenwood Press, 1974. 308 p. Bibliography: p. 299-303. *Wa, WaOE, WaS, WaSp*

6. Deloria, Vine Jr. "The Tribe That Was Made To Be Fishermen." *Smithsonian*. Volume 55 (September 1973): 86-91.
   On the Lummi.

7. Eells, Myron. *The Indians of Puget Sound: The Notebooks of Myron Eells*. Edited by George Pierre Castile. Seattle: University of Washington Press, 1985. 470 p. ill. *Wa, WaOE, WaS, WaSp*

8. Elmendorf, William W. *The Structure of Twana Society*. Pullman: Washington State University Press and Garland, 1974, 1960. 576 p. (Monograph Supplement Number 2) *Wa, WaS, WaSp*

9. *The Eyes of Chief Seattle*. [Exhibition Catalog] The Suquamish Museum, 1985. 56 p. ill., photos., map. *Wa, WaOE, WaS, WaSp.*

10. Farrand, Livingston. *Traditions of the Quinault Indians*. Assisted by W. S. Kahnweiler. New York: AMS Press, 1975. *WaOE, WaPS*

11. Haeberlin, Herman and Erna Gunther. *The Indians of Puget Sound*. Seattle: University of Washington Press, 1930. 83 p. ill., maps. *Wa, WaOE, WaS, WaSp, WaU*

12. Hilbert, Vi. *Haboo: Native American Stories from Puget Sound*. Seattle: University of Washington Press, 1985. 204 p. Bibliography: p.183-204. *Wa, WaEC, WaOE, WaS,WaSp*

13. Hills, Gordon H. *A List of Sources on the Shoalwater Bay Indians Tribal Heritage*. 2nd Edition. [Tokeland, Washington: Heritage Committe, Shoalwater Bay Indian Tribe, 1984]. Bibliography. 22, 22, 5 leaves. *Wa, WaOE, WaU*

14. Hobuckett, Harry. "Quillayute Indian Tradition." *Washington Historical Quarterly*. Volume 25, Number 1 (January 1934).

15. "A Makah Epic Journey: Oral History and Documentary Sources." *Pacific Northwest Quarterly*. Volume 68, Number 4 (October 1977): 153-163. ill.

16. Marr, Carolyn, Donna Hicks and Kay Francis.. *The Chehalis People*. Prepared for the Chehalis Tribe. Oakville, Washington: Confederated Tribes of The Chehalis Reservation, 1980. 40 p. ill., maps. *Wa*

17. Miller, Beatrice D. "Neah Bay: The Makah in Transition." *Pacific Northwest Quarterly*. Volume 43, Number 4 (October 1952):262-272.

18. Morse, Samuel G. *Portrait in Time: Photographs of the Makah by Samuel G. Morse, 1896-1903.* Text by Carolyn Marr with essays by Lloyd Colfax and Robert D. Monroe. [Neah Bay, Washington]: Makah Cultural and Research Center in Cooperation with the Washington State Historical Society, 1987. 67 p. ill., photos. *Wa, WaS*

19. "The Nooksack, The Chilliwack, and The Middle Fraser." *Pacific Northwest Quarterly.* Volume 41, Number 4 (October 1950): 330-341.

20. Olson, Ronald Le Roy. *The Quinault Indians: Adze, Canoe, and House Types of the Northwest Coast.* Seattle: University of Washington Press, 1967. 2 Volumes in 1. ill. *Wa, WaS*

21. *Portrait of Our Land: A Quinault Tribal Forestry Perspective.* Taholah, Washington: Quinault Tribal Council, 1978. 68 p. *Wa*

22. *Quileute: An Introduction to the Indians of La Push.* Prepared for the Quileute Tribe by Jay Powell and Vickie Jensen. Seattle: University of Washington Press, 1976. 80 p. ill., photos. *Wa, WaOE, WaS*

23. Ray, Verne Frederick. "The Historical Position of the Lower Chinook in the Native Culture of the Pacific Northwest." *Pacific Northwest Quarterly.* Volume 28, Number 4 (October 1937).

24. Reagan, Albert B. "Tradition of the Hoh and Quillayaute Indians." *Washington Historical Quarterly.* Volume 20, Number 3 (July 1929):178-189.

25. Ruby, Robert H. and John A. Brown. *The Chinook Indians: Traders of the Lower Columbia River.* Norman: University of Oklahoma Press, 1976. 349 p. ill. Bibliography. (The Civilization of the American Indians, Volume 138) *Wa, WaOE, WaS, WaSp, WaU*

26. Ruby, Robert H. and John A. Brown. *Myron Eells and the Puget Sound Indians.* Seattle: Superior Publishing Company, 1976. 122 p. *Wa, WaOE, WaS, WaSp*

27. "Samish Continue Long Battle for Identity: U.S. Withholding Tribal Status." *Seattle Times* (1 June 1987): C2. ill.

28. Satterfield, Archie. "The Squaxin Tribe: 'This is Our Home'." *Seattle Times.* Pictorial (7 June 1970)

29. Smith, Marian. *The Puyallup-Nisqually.* New York: Columbia University, 1940. 336 p. (Columbia University Contributions to Anthropology; vol. 32) *Wa, WaOE, WaS*

30. State of Washington. Indian Affairs Task Force. *Are You Listening Neighbor?...The People Speak. Will You Listen?* Olympia: 1978. 100 p. *Wa, WaS, WaU*

31. Stern, Bernhard J. *The Lummi Indians of Northwest Washington*. New York: AMS Press, 1969. Reprint of 1934 Edition. 127 p. (Columbia University Contributions to Anthropology; Number 17) *Wa, WaOE, WaS, WaU*

32. Suttles, Wayne P. *The Economic Life of the Coast Salish of Haro and Rosario Straits*. New York: Garland, 1974. 512 p. ill. (Coast Salish and Western Indians; Volume 1) *Wa, WaS, WaSp*

33. Swan, James Gilchrist. *The Northwest Coast; or, Three Years' Residence in Washington Territory*. Fairfield, Washington: Ye Galleon Press, 1966. First published in 1857. 435 p. ill. *Wa, WaS*

34. Tacoma. Community College. Library. Reference Department. *Chinook Indians, a Bibliography*. Compiled by Lorraine Hildebrand. 1974. 8 leaves. ill. *Wa, WaU*

35. Taylor, Herbert C. Jr. "Aboriginal Populations of the Lower Northwest Coast." *Pacific Northwest Quarterly*. Volume 54, Number 4 (October 1963): 158-165. ill., map.

36. *Uncommon Controversy: Fishing Rights of the Muckleshoot, Puyallup, and Nisqually Indians*. A report prepared for the American Friends Service Committee. Seattle: University of Washington, 1970. 232 p. ill. *Wa, WaOE, WaS, WaSp*

37. Upchurch, O. C. "The Swinomish People and Their State." *Pacific Northwest Quarterly*. Volume 27, Number 4 (October 1936).

38. Waterman, Thomas Talbot. *Notes on the Ethnology of the Indians of Puget Sound*. New York: Museum of the American Indian, Heye Foundation, 1973. 96 p. ill., plates. *Wa, WaOE, WaS, WaSp*

Native American-Plateau

This selection covers the many tribal groups in the eastern part of the state, many of them confederated into the Colville and Yakima nations. Ruby and Brown have published books on Chief Moses, the Cayuse, and the Spokane Indians. Trafzer and Scheuerman have published on the Palouse Indians. The Yakima Nation has published a bibliography and another book on their peoples. The Colville and the Yakima have tribal newspapers that are indexed in the Regional Newpaper Index at the University of Washington Library.

1. Beal, Merrill D. *"I Will Fight No More Forever" : Chief Joseph and the Nez Perce War*. Seattle: University of Washington Press, 1963. 366 p. *Wa, WaOE, WaS, WaSp*

2. Bischoff, William Norbert. "The Yakima Indian War, 1855-1856: A Problem in Research." *Pacific Northwest Quarterly.* Volume 41, Number 2 (April 1950): 162-169.

3. Burns, Robert Ignatius. "Pere Joset's Account of the Indian War of 1858." *Pacific Northwest Quarterly.* Volume 38, Number 4 (October 1947): 285-314.

4. Daugherty, Richard D. *The Yakima Peoples.* Phoenix, Arizona: Indian Tribal Series, 1973. 104 p. *WaChenE, WaPS*

5. Esvelt, John P. "Chief Moses of the Spokanes." *The Pacific Northwesterner.* Volume 9, Number 1 (Winter 1965): 1-11.

6. Fahey, John. *The Kalispel Indians.* 1st Edition, Norman: Oklahoma University Press, 1986. 234 p. ill. Bibliography: p. 217-218. (Civilizations of the American Indian series; volume 180) *Wa, WaOE, WaS, WaSp, WaU*

7. French, David. "Wasco-Wishram." In: *Perspectives in American Indian Culture Change.* Edited by Edward H. Spicer. Chicago: University of Chicago Press, 1961. 549 p. Wa, WaOE

8. Gidley, Mick. *Kopet: A Documentary Narrative of Chief Joseph's Last Years.* Seattle: University of Washington Press, 1981. 109 p. ill. photos. Bibliography: p. 99-104. *Wa, WaOE, WaS, WaSp*

9. _____. *With One Sky Above Us: Life On an Indian Reservation At the Turn of the Century.* New York: Putnam's. 1979. 159 p. *Wa, WaSp*
    About the Colville Reservation.

10. Haines, Francis. *The Nez Perces: Tribesmen of the Columbia Plateau.* Norman: University of Oklahoma Press, 1955. 365 p. ill. *Wa, WaOE, WaS, WaSp*

11. *Interior Salish and Eastern Washington Indians.* New York: Garland, 1974. 4 volumes ill., maps. *Wa, WaS, WaSp*

12. Johnson, David P. "Last of the Wanapums." *Spokesman Review.* Magazine Section (4 February 1973): 6-10. ill.

13. Josephy , Alvin M. Jr. *The Nez Perce Indians and the Opening of the Northwest.* New Haven: Yale University Press, 1965. 705 p. ill. *Wa, WaS*

14. Kip, Lawrence. *Indian Council at Walla Walla.* Seattle: Shorey Book Store, 1971. 28 p. *Wa, WaOE, WaS*

15. Mourning Dove. *Tales of the Okanogans.* Edited by Donald M. Hines. Fairfield, Wa.: Ye Galleon Press, 1976. ill. 182 p. *Wa, WaOE*

16. Pace, Robert E. *The Land of the Yakimas.* Toppenish, Wa: Yakima Indian Media Services, 1977. 54 p. *Wa, WaSp*

17. _____. *Yakima Indian Nation Bibliography.* Toppenish, Washington: Media Services, Yakima Indian Nation, 1978. 176 p. *Wa, WaS*

18. Powers, Dorothy. "All of Us: City's American Indians Contribute in Many Ways." *Spokesman-Review.* Community News (28 February 1985): 1, 3.

19. Ruby, Robert H. and John A. Brown. *The Cayuse Indians.* Norman: University of Oklahoma Press, 1972. *Wa, WaOE, WaS, WaSp*

20. _____. *Half-Sun on the Columbia: A Biography of Chief Moses.* Norman: University of Oklahoma Press, 1965. 377 p. ill. *Wa, WaOE, WaS, WaSp*

21. _____. *The Spokane Indians: Children of the Sun.* Norman: University of Oklahoma Press, 1970. 346 p. *Wa, WaS, WaSp*

22. Scheuerman, Richard D. "The First People of the Palouse Country." *Bunchgrass Historian.* Volume 8, Number 3 (Fall 1980): 3-18. *WaPS*

23. Scheuerman, Richard D., Editor. *The Wenatchi Indians: Guardians of the Valley.* Fairfield, Washington: Ye Galleon Press, 1983. 200 p. *Wa, WaS, WaSp*

24. Schuster, Helen Hersh. *The Yakimas: A Critical Bibliography.* Bloomington: Indiana University Press, 1982. 158 p. *Wa, WaOE, WaS, WaSp*

25. Stern, Theodore, Martin Schmitt and Alphonse F. Halfmoon. "A Cayuse-Nez Perce Sketchbook." *Oregon Historical Quarterly.* Volume 81, Number 4 (Winter 1980): 340-376.

26. Trafzer, Clifford E. "The Palouse Indians: Interpreting the Past of a Plateau Tribe." In: *Spokane and the Inland Empire.* Edited by David H. Stratton. Pullman: Washington State University Press, in progress.

27. Trafzer, Clifford E. and Richard D. Scheuerman. *Renegade Tribe: The Palouse Indians and the Invasion of the Inland Pacific Northwest.* Pullman: Washington State University Press, 1986. 224 p. ill., maps. Bibliography: p. 178-197. *Wa, WaPS, WaS, WaSp*

28. Trafzer, Clifford E. and Margery A. Beach. "Smohalla, the Washani, and Religion as a Factor in Northwestern Indian History." *American Indian Quarterly*. Volume 9, Number 3 (1985): 309-324.

29. Walker, Deward E. Jr. *Conflict and Schism in Nez Perce Acculturation: A Study of Religion and Politics.* Pullman: Washington State University Press, 1968. 171 p. ill. *Wa, WaOE, WaPS, WaS, WaSp*

European American

The European American sources are of many types providing historical and cultural perspectives. The multi-ethnic sources include the reference works, such as bibliographies. Materials on early exploration are not included here as there are excellent bibliographies on this historical period in other books, most recently in Ficken and LeWarne's *Washington, A Centennial History.*

The European American section is divided into the following sections: British, North American, Nordic, Central Southern, Eastern Balkan, Gypsy and Jewish.

European American, British Isles

Materials on English, Irish, Scottish and Welsh are included in this section. The books and journal articles are very selective, including the two Washington State American Revolution Bicentennial Commission Ethnic History Series (Green and LeRoy), and key authors such as Galbraith and Winther.

Latvian folk dancers,
Camp Kursa Cultural Center.
Shelton, 1987.
Photo by Ed Circenis
Courtesy of Anatolijs and
Indra Michalovskis

1. Bond, Rowland. "Spokane Irish Retain Strong Identity." *Spokesman-Review* (6 March 1971): 5.

2. Galbraith, John S. "The British and Americans at Fort Nisqually, 1846-1859." *Pacific Northwest Quarterly*. Volume 41 (1950): 109-120.

3. _____. "The Early History of the Puget Sound Agricultural Company." *Oregon Historical Quaterly*. Volume 55 (1954): 234-259.

4. _____. *The Hudson's Bay Company as an Imperial Factor, 1821-1869.* Berkeley: University of California Press, 1957. 500 p. *Wa, WaOE, WaS*

5. Green, Frank L. *Captains, Curates and Cockneys: The English in the Pacific Northwest.* Foreword by Bruce Le Roy. Tacoma: Washington State Historical Society, 1981. 105 p. (Washington State American Revolution Bicentennial Commission Ethnic History Series) *Wa, WaS, WaSp*

6. Haigh, John. "Seattle's Welsh: A Least Conspicuous 'Minority'." *Seattle Times*. Magazine Section (8 June 1975): 10.

7. Howell, Erle. "Irish Contribute Much to Seattle Development: Thousands of Old Erin's Sons and Grandsons Have Figured in Progress of This Area." *Seattle Times*. Magazine Section (22 March 1959): 2.

8. _____. "Seattle Area's Scots." *Seattle Times*. Magazine Section (8 March 1959): 3. ill., port.
   About Rev. Dr. Turnbull, James A. Duncan, Jack Ironside, Mrs. Pat McDonald.

9. Howell, Erle. "Seattle's Bit of Cornwall." *Seattle Times* (5 July 1965): 8.

10. Keane, John F. "The Greening of the Emerald City: An Historical Overview of Seattle's Irish Clubs." *Seattle Folklore Society Journal*. Volume 1, Number 2 (1984): 32-35. New Series.

11. Le Roy, Bruce. *Lairds, Bards, and Mariners: The Scot in Northwest America*. Foreword by Robert Hitchman. Published for The Washington State American Revolution Bicentennial Commission by the Washington State Historical Society and the Center for Northwest Folklore, c1978. 124 p. *Wa, WaS, WaSp*

12. Martin, Albro. *James J. Hill and the Opening of the Northwest*. New York: Oxford University Press, 1976. 676 p. ill. *Wa, WaS*

13. Powers, Dorothy. "All of Us: Inland Empire Scots Keep Traditions Alive." *Spokesman-Review*. Community News (16 January 1985): 1, 2.

14. _____. "All of Us: Welsh Keep Spokane Singing and Learning." *Spokesman-Review*. Community News (14 March 1985): 1, 3.

15. _____. "All of Us: British Bring Fortitude and a Double Culture." *Spokesman-Review*. Community News (28 March 1985): 1, 4.

16. Spence, Clark. *British Investments and the American Mining Frontier, 1860-1901*. Ithaca, New York: Published for the American Historical Association [by] Cornell University Press, 1958. 288 p. ill., tables. *Wa*

17. "Wild Old Ways - A Bit of England On San Juan Island." *True West*. Volume 33, Number 4 (March-April 1976): 32-33. ill.

18. Winther, Oscar Osburn. "The British in Oregon Country: a Triptych View." *Pacific Northwest Quarterly*. Volume 58 (1957): 101-112.

19. Winther, Oscar Osburn. "English Migration to the American West, 1865-1900." *Huntington Library Quarterly*. Volume 27 (1956): 159-173.

20. _____. "Promoting the American West in England, 1865-1890." *Journal of Economic History*. Volume 16 (1956): 506-513.

North American

Certain groups of people, many with ancestry that can be traced to the British Isles, have maintained distinctive cultural traditions. Two such groups are the Canadians and peoples from the Upland South.

1. Case, Frederick. "Our Largest Ethnic Minority Is Hard to Find." *Seattle Times*, April 17, 1983.
    On Canadians.

2. Clevinger, Woodrow R. "Southern Appalachian Highlanders in Western Washington." *Pacific Northwest Quarterly*. Volume 33, Number 1 (1942): 3-25.

European American, Nordic

Materials on the Danish, Finnish, Icelandic, Norwegian and Swedish are included in this section. Only four books are included, with the materials being predominantly journal and newpaper articles. The books include Ekstrand's *Notes From a Scandinavian Parlor* which is cultural in content; *Nordic Heritage Northwest* is a beatifully presented pictorial and narrative history; *Norse to the New Northwest* is a history; and Bjork's book is on Norwegian migration to the West. Specialized journals should be noted: *American Swedish Monthly*, The Finnish American Historical Society of the West's series, the *Swedish-American Historical Quarterly* and *Norwegian-American Studies*. The journal and newspaper articles provide a wide range of sources with statewide coverage. The article by Kathleen Burk should also be noted on Pacific Lutheran University's special collection and Walter Johnson's article on the Swedish archives at the University of Washington. Bingham's annotated bibliography is a useful source for further information on Swedish Americans. The Nordic Heritage Museum has a library and photographic archive.

1. "An Album of Norwegian Settlers." *Seattle Times*. Sunday Pictorial (9 November 1975): 2-6.
    Examples of historical photographs depicting early Seattle Norwegians.

2. Alcorn, Rowena L. and Gordon D. Alcorn. "The Nylund Family: Pioneers of Old Ozette." *Pacific Northwest Quarterly*. Volume 53, Number 4 (1962): 151-156.

3. Apsler, Alfred. "Finns of Southwest Washington." *The Sunday Oregonian*. Magazine (28 September 1952): 10-11.

4. Arestad, Sverre. "Bibliography on the Scandinavians of the Pacific Coast." *Pacific Northwest Quarterly*. Volume 36, Number 3 (1945): 269-278.
   Many of the references, including newspapers, are in the Scandinavian languages.

5. _____. "The Norwegians in the Pacific Coast Fisheres." *Pacific Northwest Quarterly*. Volume 34, Number 1 (1943): 3-17.

6. Bingham, Robert D. "Swedish-Americans In Washington State: A Bibliography of Publications." *Swedish Pioneer Historical Quarterly*. Volume 25, Number 2 (1974): 133-140.

7. Bjork, Kenneth O. *West of the Great Divide: Norwegian Migration to the Pacific Coast, 1847 - 1893*. Northfield, Minnesota: Norwegian-American Historical Association, 1958. 671 p. ill. *Wa, WaOE, WaS*

8. Burk, Kathleen. "Scandinavian Immigrant Experience Preserved in Special PLU Collection." *PLU Scene* (December 1985)

9. Carlson, Dale A. "The Swedish Club In Seattle." *Swedish American Historical Quarterly*. Volume 34, Number 4 (1983): 306-311.

10. Dahlie, Jorgen. "Old World Paths in the New: Scandinavians Find Familiar Home in Washington." *Pacific Northwest Quarterly*. Volume 61, Number 2 (1970): 65-71.

11. Duncan, Don. "A Home for Scandinavians." *Seattle Times* (12 September 1982): F1.

12. Ekstrand, Florence. *Notes From a Scandinavian Parlor: An Informal Look at Our Scandinavian Heritage*. Illustrations by Kris Ekstrand Molesworth. Seattle: Welcome Press, 1984. 158 p. *Wa, WaS*

13. Fabbe, Harry F. "Swedish Pioneers of the Pacific Northwest." *American Swedish Monthly*. Volume 24, Number 1 (1957): 26-27.

14. Finnish-American Historical Society of the West. *Finnam Newsletter*. Portland. January, 1974-, Number 1-. Called New Series. *Wa, WaU*

15. _____. *Finnish Emigrant Studies Series*. Portland. 1972-1976? *Wa, WaU*

16. Finnish-American Historical Society of the West. *Pioneer Series*. Portland. July 1977- Volume 10- . Continues *Finnish Emigrant Studies Series. Wa, WaU*

17. Gilje, Shelby and Svein Gilje. "Olympic Scandinavia." *Seattle Post-Intelligencer*. Pictorial Review (9 May 1963): 10.

18. Hale, Frederick. "Danish Immigrant Disillusionment in the Pacific Northwest." *Pacific Northwest Quarterly*. Volume 71, Number 1 (1980): 15-23.

19. Hanley, Patricia J. "Anderson's Landing: Life in the Early Settlements on Hood Canal." *Pacific Northwest Quarterly*. Volume 48, Number 1 (1957): 8-12.

20. Hegstad, Patsy Adams. "Scandinavian Settlement in Seattle, 'Queen City of the Puget Sound.'" *Norwegian-American Studies*. Volume 30 (1985): 55-74.

21. Howell, Erle. "Norwegians Contribute Richly to Growth of Community; Seattle's Many Residents From Norway and Descendants Follow Wide Variety of Constructive Occupations." *Seattle Times*. Magazine Section (16 December 1956): 4.

22. _____. "Seattle Shares Icelandic Culture." *Seattle Times*. Magazine Section (10 June 1956): 7.

23. _____. "Seattle's Danish Residents: Denmark Sent Spirit of Good Citizenship Along With Her People Who Settled Here." *Seattle Times*. Magazine Section (29 September 1957): 5.

24. Johnson, Ruth and Elna Peterson. "The Swedish Women's Chorus of Seattle." *Swedish-American Historical Quarterly*. Volume 34, Number 4 (1983): 294-305.

25. Johnson, Walter. "The Swedish Archives and Harry Fabbe." *Swedish-Historical Quarterly*. Volume 34, Number 4 (1983): 281-293.

26. Larson, Laurence M. "The Norwegian Element in the Northwest." *American Historical Review*. Volume 40, Number 1 (1934): 69-81.

27. Lokken, Dean. "Scandanavian Legacy Endures in Area." *Spokane Chronicle* (23 January 1971)

28. McDonald, Lucile. "Washington's Finnish Settlers: Lodge Committee Seeks Historical Material Regarding Finns Who Came to This State." *Seattle Times*. Magazine Section (13 July 1958): 3.

29. Miller, Richard F. "A Finnish Logging Camp in Washington, 1922-1925." *Pacific Northwest Forum*. Volume 5-6, Number 4-1 (1980-81): 25-30.

30. *Nordic Heritage Northwest.* Text by Nancy Hausauer. Edited by Kristina Veirs. Photography by Scotty Sapiro. Seattle: The Writing Works, 1982. 159 p. *Wa, WaS, WaSp, WaU*

31. *Norse to the New Northwest: A Sesquicentennial Saga.* Editor, Bob H. Hansen. Seattle: The Sesquicentennial, 1975. 48 p. ill. col. *Wa, WaS*

32. Osterberg, Ray. "Scandinavians in the Northwest." *Pacific Northwest Forum.* Volume 5, Number 2 (1980): 11-17.

33. Powers, Dorothy. "All of Us: Finns Came Early to Our City." *Spokesman Review.* Community News (7 March 1985): 1, 2.

34. _____. "All of Us: Sharing Laughter and Faith: Norwegian Legacies Draw Generations Together." *Spokesman-Review.* Community News (6 December 1984): V1, V6.

35. _____. "All of Us: Spokane's Swedish Value Work, Loyalty." *Spokesman-Review.* Community News (27 December 1984): 1, 2.

36. Slind, Marvin G. "Norse to the Palouse: The Selbu Community." *Bunchgrass Historian.* Volume 10, Number 4 (1982): 10-19.

37. Van Arsdol, Ted. "Venersborg - 2. Traces of Swedish Pioneer Origin Vanishing as Community Ties Lost." *The Columbian.* (19 February 1964.) port.

38. Wilson, Elmer. "A Swede's First Logging Camp." *The Swedish-American Historical Quarterly.* Volume 34, Number 4 (1983): 257-280.

European American, Central and Southern

Materials on Basques, Belgians, Dutch, French, Germans, Greeks, Italians, Russian Germans, and Swiss are included in this section. The two Washington American Revolution Bicentennial Commission Ethnic History Series books are by Nicandri on the Italians and Wirsing on the Germans. Two prolific writers on specific European immigration experience are Angelo Pellegrini and Richard Scheuerman. Locati writes about the Italians in Walla Walla County and Theodratus on the Greek community in Tacoma. Most of the other materials are newspaper articles, one scholarly journal article is included. The *Journal of the American Historical Society of Germans From Russia* is important for this eastern Washington community.

1. "An Ancient Tradition from the Pyrenees." *Seattle Times* (1 June 1973): B7. Photo by Josef Scaylea.
   On the Basques.

2. Bartlett, Barry. "Dairy Country-Immigrants Over the Years Have Given Whatcom County's Dairyland a Decidedly Dutch Flavor." *Seattle Times* (17 August 1980): 24. ill.

3. Brandmarker, Alan. "Hutterites Cling to Old Lifestyle." *Wenatchee World* (1 April 1979): 1.

4. Chebuhar, Teresa. "40,000 Strong, The Swiss are Here." *The Seattle Times* (30 September 1978): B1.

5. Douglass, William A. and John Bilbao. *Amerikanuak: Basques in the New World*. Reno: University of Nevada Press, 1975. 519 p. Bibliography: p. 459-490. *Wa, WaOE, WaS*

6. Etulain, Richard W. "Basque Beginnings in the Pacific Northwest." *Idaho Yesterdays*. Volume 18 (Spring), Number 1 (1974): 26-32.

7. Fahey, John. "When the Dutch Owned Spokane." *Pacific Northwest Quarterly*. Volume 72, Number 1 (January 1981): 2-10.

8. "The Farthest With the Fewest." *American West*. Volume 12, Number 4 (July 1975): 4-9, 61-63. Second in a series of articles on the forces and nations that shaped the American West of 1776.
   On the French.

9. "French Breeds." *Walla Walla Union Bulletin* (11 June 1978).

10. Giese, Hans-Otto. "The Germans in Seattle." In: *German American Tricentennial: 1683-1983*. Seattle: German Tricentennial Committee, 1983. *WaU*

11. Hagood, Pat. "Lower Valley's French Tradition Traces Back to Two Families." *Yakima Herald Tribune* (29 April 1970) port.

12. Hedges, James B. *Henry Villard and the Railways of the Northwest*. New York: Russell and Russell, 1967, 1930. 224 p. *Wa, WaOE, WaS, WaU*

13. Hidy, Ralph W., Frank Ernest Hill and Allan Nevins. *Timber and Men: The Weyerhaeuser Story*. New York: Macmillan, 1963. 704 p. *Wa, WaOE, WaS*

14. Howell, Erle. "Belgian Seattleites." *Seattle Times* (2 August 1959): 8.

15. Howell, Erle. "Seattle's French-Americans: Spirit of Lafayette Still Lives in Hearts of Our Citizens From La Belle France." *Seattle Times* (1 July 1956): 4.

16. _____. "Switzerland's Contributions to Seattle." *Seattle Times* (18 January 1959): 1.

17. Jones, Marianna. "Frenchman Farms Family Homestead." *Walla Walla Union Bulletin* (22 February 1976): D1.

18. _____. "Greek Nurseryman Eager to Belong in New Country." *Walla Walla Union Bulletin* (22 February 1976): D3.

19. *Journal of the American Historical Society of Germans From Russia.* Volume 1978- . *WaPS, WaS*

20. Locati, Joe J. *The Horicultural Heritage of Walla Walla County, 1881 - 1977: A Comprehensive Review of Fruit and Vegetable Growing, Shipping and Processing Focused on Walla Walla County - With a Section on the Italian Heritage.* Walla Walla, Wa.: Joe J. Locati, 1978. 281 p. *Wa, WaS, WaSp, WaU*

21. Nicandri, David L. *Italians in Washington: Emigration, 1853-1924.* Tacoma: Washington State Bicentennial Commission, 1978. 71 p. Bibliography pages: 69-71. *Wa, WaS, WaSp, WaU*

22. Pellegrini, Angelo M. *American Dream: An Immigrant's Quest.* San Francisco: Northpoint Press, 1986. 214 p. *Wa, WaS, WaSp*

23. _____. *Americans By Choice.* New York: Macmillan, 1956. 240 p. *Wa, WaS*

24. _____. *Immigrants's Return.* New York: Macmillan, 1951. 269 p. *Wa, WaS*

25. Powers, Dorothy. "All of Us: Italians Built and Fed Spokane." *Spokesman-Review.* Community News (13 December 1984): 1, 7.

26. _____. "All of Us: Spokane Dutch Brought Beauty and Money." *Spokesman-Review.* Community News (17 January 1985): 1, 5.

27. Reddin, John J. "Faces of the City: Greek Fishing Fleet Evokes Fond Memories." *Seattle Times* (15 January 1961): E.

28. Scheuerman, Richard D. "Germans From Russia: Pioneers on the Palouse Frontier." *Bunchgrass Historian.* Volume 11, Number 4 (1983): 4-23.

29. _____. *Pilgrims on the Earth: A German-Russian Chronicle.* 2nd Edition. Fairfield, Washington: Ye Galleon Press, 1976. 165 p. *Wa, WaS, WaSp*

30. Scheuerman, Richard D. and Clifford E. Trafzer. *The Volga Germans: Pioneers of the Northwest*. Moscow, Idaho: University Press of Idaho, 1985. 250 p. *Wa, WaOE, WaS, WaSp*

31. Schlomer, Harm. "Inland Empire Russian Germans." *Pacific Northwesterner* (Fall 1964).

32. Sliter, Vera Evans. "The Russian-Germans of the Palouse." *Spokesman Review*. Magazine Section (7 April 1963).

33. Taylor, Dabney. "Western Basques, People of an Ancient Race: They Herd Sheep, Love a Good Time." *Spokesman-Review* (17 October 1948): 8-9.

34. Theodoratus, Robert J. *A Greek Community in America: Tacoma, Washington*. Sacramento: Sacramento Anthropological Society, Sacramento State College, 1971. 234 p (Sacramento Anthropological Society Paper, 10). *WaChenE, WaPS, WaU*

35. Wirsing, Dale R. *Builders, Brewers and Burghers: Germans of Washington State*. Tacoma: The Washington State American Revolution Bicentennial Commission, 1977. 74p. ill. *Wa, WaS, WaSp*

European American, Eastern and Balkan

Materials on Bulgarians, Croatians, Czechoslovakians, Estonians, Hungarians, Latvians, Lithuanians, Polish, Rumanians, Russians, Serbians, Ukrainians and other Slavic peoples are included in this section. Petrich's and Roje's book on the Yugoslavians is one of the Washington American Revolution Bicentennial Commission Ethnic History Series. The other books in this section are by Green and Van Syckle.

1. Barinoff, Irene. "Seattle's Russian Heritage." *Puget Soundings* (December 1985): 28-30.

2. Buerge, David M. "Russian Seattle." *Seattle Weekly* (30 March 1988): 26-34.

3. Chebuhar, Teresa. "Balkan Immigrants Here Are Few but Enthusiastic." *Seattle Times* (9 December 1978): B1.

4. "Czechoslavakian Family Finds a Home in Spokane." *Seattle Times* (25 December 1983): B7.

5. "Czechs Find New Life In Basin Town." *Seattle Times* (29 December 1969): B6.
   Town located in Adams County.

6. Duncan, Don. "Croatian Patriarch: At 97 (almost), Simon Skalabrin Talks About the Croatian Community in Seattle and How It Grew." *Seattle Times* (13 April 1982): C1.

7. "Estonians Rekindle Dreams." *Seattle Times* (25 February 1980): C1.

8. Feinstein, Alice. "'Coming to America': First Group of Polish Refugees Arrive in Spokane." *Spokane Chronicle* (3 June 1982).

9. Foote, Patricia. "From Prison Camp, to U.S., to Retirement - Quite a Life." *Seattle Times* (20 August 1978): J9. Article on Maria Urbaniak.

10. Green, Roger H., Jr. *South Slav Settlement in Western Washington: Perception and Choice*. San Francisco: R & E Research Associates, 1974. 111 p. *Wa, WaOE, WaS*

11. Howell, Erle. "Many Displaced Latvians Make Seattle Home." *Seattle Times* (10 January 1960): 8.

12. _____. "Seattle Area's Czechoslavakians." *Seattle Times* (31 May 1959): 10.

13. _____. "Seattle's Lithuanians. Their Love of Freedom and Strongly Independent Character Are Factors in the Fine Citizenship Record They Have Maintained." *Seattle Times* (16 April 1961): 11.

14. _____. "Seattle's Lithuanians—Born Residents." *Seattle Times*. Magazine Section (24 April 1961): 11. ill., photos.

15. _____. "Their Ancestral Homeland Lies Behind the Iron Curtain-Our Industrious Ukrainians." *Seattle Times*. Magazine Section (30 October 1960): 4. ill., photos.

16. _____. "Yugoslav Born Enrich State in Many Ways." *Seattle Times* (20 August 1961): 10.

17. Krenmayer, Janine. "Seattle's White Russians Have Rich Cultural Heritage." *Seattle Times*. Magazine Section (25 Feb 1962): 12-13. ill., photos.

18. "The Muleshov Tale : Bulgarian Defectors Adjust to America." *University of Washington Daily*. Volume 95, Number 12 (13 October 1987): 10-11. Portrait of Angel Muleshov.

19. Nappi, Rebecca. "Freedom's Sorrow and Joy." *Spokesman-Review* (22 April 1985): 1, 6. On Rumanian immigrants.

20. Petrich, Mary Ann and Barbara Roje. *The Yugoslav in Washington State: Among the Early Settlers*. Tacoma: Washington State Historical Society, 1984. 92 p. (Washington Sate American Revolution Bicentennial Ethnic History Series) *Wa, WaS, WaSp*

21. Powers, Dorothy. "All of Us: Hungarians Demonstrate the Meaning of Courage." *Spokesman-Review*. Community News (18 April 1985): S1, S3.

22. _____. "All of Us: Latvian Teaches Appreciation of Freedom." *Spokesman-Review*. Community News (11 April 1985): 1, 3.

23. Reddin, John J. "Faces of the City: Fun, Good Eats Are Plentiful at Serbian Wedding Party." *Seattle Times* (27 January 1963)

24. _____. "Faces of the City: Serbian Hall Dedication is Family Affair." *Seattle Times* (15 May 1961): A. ill., photo.

25. Stockley, Tom. "Romance of the Baltic Brings Color to Seattle." *Seattle Times*. Pictorial Magazine (14 July 1968): 24. Photos by Greg Gilbert.

26. "Thankful Very Much: Freedom is 'Like Having Wings' Says Soviet Emigre." *Seattle Times* (22 November 1984): 1. ill., ports.

27. Van Syckle, Edwin. *The River Pioneers-Early Days on Gray's Harbor*. Edited by David James. Seattle: Pacific Search Press, Aberdeen: Friends of the Aberdeen Public Library, 1982. 423p. ill. Bibliography: p. 401-403. *Wa, WaS, WaSp*
    On Yugoslavians.

28. Watts, Alice. "Latvians Pass Torch of Heritage at Shelton Summer Camp." *The Olympian* (1985)

European American, Gypsy

The key publication on the Gypsies in Washington is the Washington American Revolution Bicentennial Commission Ethnic History Series book by Tyrner-Stastny. Seattle Gypsies are discussed in Kaldi's article. Newpaper articles in Spokane and Seattle are also available.

1. Tyrner-Stastny, Gabrielle. *The Gypsy in Northwest America*. Tacoma: The Washington State American Revolution Bicentennial Commission, 1977. 56 p. Bibliography. *Wa, WaS, WaSp, WaU*

2. Kaldi, Leita. "Alternative Education for the ROM." *Explorations in Ethnic Studies*. Volume 6, Number 1 (1983): 21-27.
    Discusses Seattle Gypsy Alternative School established in 1973.

European American, Jewish

One book has been produced by a major publisher, Handlin's *Let Me Hear Your Voice*. Other publications are periodical and newpaper articles or community based histories such as Janton's *History of the Jews in Spokane* and McCann's *A Study of the Jewish Community in the Greater Seattle Area*. Two important community journals are *The Jewish Transcript* and The Washington Sate Jewish Historical Society *Newsletter*. *The Western States Jewish Historical Quarterly* is another important journal. The M.A. thesis by Albert Adatto documents the large Sephardic community in Seattle.

1. Adatto, Albert. *Sephardim and the Seattle Sephardic Community*. [M.A. Thesis (History)] [Seattle.]: University of Washington, 1939. 264 leaves. *WaU*

2. Angel, Marc D. "Notes On the Early History of Seattle's Sephardic Community." *Western States Jewish Historical Quarterly*. Volume 7, Number 1 (1874): 22-30.

3. Droker, Howard. "A Coat of Many Colors: A History of Seattle's Jewish Community." *Portage*. Volume 4, Number 2 (1983): 4-9.

4. Fisher, Patricia. "Resettled Jews: Emigrants Will Remember Only Best of Russia." *Seattle Times* (30 July 1978): J2.

5. Glatzer, Robert. "On Being a Jew in Spokane." *The Falls* (25 April 2, 8): 2, 8.

6. Handlin, Mimi E. and Marilyn Smith Layton. *Let Me Hear Your Voice: Portraits of Aging Immigrant Jews*. Photographs by Rochelle Casserd. Seattle: University of Washington Press, 1983. 110 p. ill., photos. *WaOE, WaU*

7. Janton, Moses N. *History of the Jews in Spokane, Washington, From the Early Days Until the Present*. Spokane, Washington: 1926. Photocopy of the original. 16 leaves. *Wa, WaSp*

8. *The Jewish Transcript*. Seattle. January 24-March 4, 1927, Jan 1928- Volume 1- . Jewish Federation and Council of Greater Seattle. *WaU*

9. Kramer, William M. and Stern, Norton B. "The Beginnings of the Organized Jewish Community of Tacoma, Washington." *Western States Jewish Historical Quarterly*. Volume 17, Number 1 (1985): 48-51.

10. McCann, James. *A Study of the Jewish Community in the Greater Seattle Area*. With the assistance of Debra Friedman. Seattle: Jewish Federation of Greater Seattle, 1979. 84 p. *Wa, WaS*

11. Stern, Norton B. "Marcus Oppenheimer of Marcus, Washington." *Western States Jewish Historical Quarterly.* Volume 15, Number 4 (1983): 334-337.

12. Washington State Jewish Historical Society. *Newsletter.* Volume- .

13. Winn, Karyl. "The Seattle Jewish Community." *Pacific Northwest Quarterly.* Volume 70, Number 2 (1979): 69-74.

African American

There are three bibliographies to use as sources for further research. Abajian's bibliography covers the West while Davis's and Mills's and Pryor's bibliographies focus on sources for the history of Blacks in Washington. There are a number of histories covering the Blacks in the West and the Pacific Northwest that include Washington history. These are: Anderson's *Black Pioneers of the Northwest, 1800-1918*, Katz's *The Black West* and Quintard Taylor's articles and dissertation. Historian Esther Mumford writes specifically on Black communities in Washington. The early Black pioneers, George Washington Bush and George Washington, are covered in Franklin, Heikel, Karolewitz, and Smith. The history of Blacks in specific locations in Washington include Bowker, *Bremerton Celebrates. . .* , and Powers. Cayton and Moore have written personal histories of experiences in Washington. Campbell and Stern's articles cover the coal mining experiences of Blacks.

Oral history is very important in developing community histories, and is the basis for the book *Voices From Black Family Albums,* produced as a part of the All My Somedays project in Tacoma. In addition to the Tacoma Public Library, other sources for oral histories are the Washington State Archives' Oral/Aural History Program, Washington State University Library, Eastern Washington University, and the University of Washington Manuscripts Division. Community newspapers are *The Medium, The Facts,* and *Northwest Dispatch.* Located in archive collections, Horace Cayton's *The Seattle Republican* (1894-1915) and *Cayton's Weekly* (1916-1921) were important historical newspapers.

The civil rights era is documented in Droker's article and in the report *Race and Violence in Washington State: Report of the Commission on the Causes and Prevention of Civil Disorder.* Artistic expression includes work by Charles Johnson and Colleen McElroy, and the visual art and life of Jacob Lawrence is thoroughly documented in Wheat's book. The gospel singers of Seattle are another important means of community expression covered in Pierce's article.

Total Experience Gospel Choir.
Seattle, 1986
Photo by Pete Kuhns
Courtesy of *The Seattle Weekly*

1. Abajian, James. *Blacks and Their Contribution to the American West: A Bibliography and Union List of Library Holdings Through 1970*. Boston: G.K. Hall, 1974. 487 p. *Wa, WaOE, WaS, WaSp*

2. Anderson, Martha E. A. *Black Pioneers of the Northwest, 1800-1918*. Portland, Oregon: Pioneer Publishing Co., 1980. 228 p. ill. Bibliography: p. 223-224. *Wa, WaS, WaU*

3. Bowker, Gordon. "A Town Divided: Pasco, Wash. is Full of Tumbleweeds and Trouble." *Seattle Magazine*. Volume 75 (June 1970): 32-39.

4. *Bremerton Celebrates Over 100 Years . . . : A Story Untold*. Kitsap County Black History Committee, 1985. 25 p. ill. *Wa*

5. Campbell, Robert A. "Blacks and the Coal Mines of Western Washington, 1888-1896." *Pacific Northwest Quarterly*. Volume 73, Number 4 (October 1982): 146-155.

6. Cayton, Horace R., Jr. *Long Old Road*. 1st Edition. New York: Trident Press, 1965. 402 p. *Wa, WaS*

7. _____. *Long Old Road*. 2nd Edition. Seattle: University of Washington Press, 1970. 402 p. *WaOE*

8. Davis, Lenwood G. "History of Blacks in Washington State: Sources for History of Blacks in Washington State." *Western Journal of Black Studies*. Volume 2, Number 1 (Spring 1978): 60+. ill., bibl.

9. Droker, Howard A. "Seattle Race Relations During the Second World War." *Pacific Northwest Quarterly*. Volume 67 (October 1976): 163-174.

10. *The Facts*. Seattle: Alzene Pub. Co. Volume 1, Number 1- July 5, 1962- . Weekly. *Wa, WaU*
    "The Northwest's largest Black owned publication."
    Title varies.

11. Franklin, Joseph. "Black Pioneers: George Washington and George Washington Bush." *Pacific Northwest Forum*. Volume 1, Number 4 (Fall 1976): 19-27. ports.

12. Heikel, Iris White. *The Wind-Breaker: George Washington Bush: Black Pioneer of the Northwest*. 1st Edition. Vantage Press, 1980. 211 p. *Wa*

13. Johnson, Charles Richard. *Being and Race: Black Writing Since 1970*. Bloomington: Indiana University Press, 1988. *Wa, WaOE, WaS*

14. Karolevitz, Bob. "George Washington: Northwest City Builder." *Negro Digest*. Volume 12 (September 1963): 70-75.

15. Katz, William Loren. *The Black West*. New York: Doubleday, 1971. *Wa, WaS, WaSp*

16. McElroy, Colleen J. *Bone Flames: Poems*. Middletown, Connecticut: Wesleyan University Press, 1987. *WaOE, WaS*

17. _____. *Jesus and Fat Tuesday and Other Stories*. Berkeley: Creative Arts Book, 1987. *WaOE, WaS*

18. *The Medium* (Seattle). January 21, 1970-1983. Volume 1- , Number 1- . Weekly. Continued by *Seattle Medium*, 1984- .

19. Mills, Hazel E. and Nancy B. Pryor. *The Negro in the State of Washington, 1788-1969: A Bibliography of Published Works and of Unpublished Source Materials on the Negro in the Evergreen State*. Revised Edition. Olympia, Washington: Washington State Library, 1970. 21 p. *Wa, WaOE, WaS, WaSp*

20. Moore, Ernest. *The Coal Miner Who Came West*. In collaboration with Gloria Phelps. Ernest Moore, 1982. 77 p. *Wa*

21. Mumford, Esther Hall. *Black Women of Washington*. Seattle: Ananse Press, (in progress) 1989.

22. _____. *Seattle's Black Victorians, 1852-1901*. Seattle: Ananse Press, 1980. *Wa, WaOE, WaS, WaSp*

23. Mumford, Esther Hall. Editor. *Seven Stars and Orion/Reflections of the Past*. Seattle: Ananse Press, 1986. 103 p. *Wa, WaOE, WaS, WaSp*

24. *Northwest Dispatch*. Volume- 1982- Tacoma. weekly.

25. Northwood, Lawrence K. and Ernest A. Barth. *Urban Desegregation: Negro Pioneers and Their White Neighbors*. Seattle: University of Washington Press, 1965. *Wa, WaOE, WaS*

26. Pierce, Kingston. "Amazing Grace: The Gospel According to Seattle's Black Churches." *Washington: The Evergreen State Magazine*. Volume 4, Number 6 (Mar/April 1988): 40-45.

27. Powers, Dorothy. "All of Us: Spokane Blacks Helped Build City in Many Ways." *Spokesman-Review*. Community News (7 February 1985): 1, 2.

28. *Race and Violence in Washington State: Report of the Commission on the Causes and Prevention of Civil Disorder*. Olympia: Commission on the Causes and Prevention of Civil Disorder, 1969. *Wa, WaS WaSp*

29. Smith, Herndon. Comp. *Centralia, the First Fifty Years, 1845-1900.* Centralia, Washington: 1942-. *Wa, WaOE, WaS*

     Section on George Washington, the founder of Centralia, p. 192-233.

30. Stern, Mark. "Black Strikebreakers In the Coal Fields: King County, Washington: 1891." *Journal of Ethnic Studies.* Volume 5, Number 3 (1977): 60-70.

31. Taylor, Quintard Jr. "The Emergence of Black Communities in the Pacific Northwest, 1865 - 1910." *Journal of Negro History.* Volume 64, Number 4 (1979): 342-354.

32. _____. *A History of Blacks in the Pacific Northwest: 1788-1970.* [Ph. D. Dissertation (History)] University of Minnesota, 1977. *Wa, WaU*

33. _____. "Migration of Blacks and Resulting Discriminatory Practices in Washington State Between 1940 and 1950." *Western Journal of Black Studies.* Volume 2, Number 1 (Mar 1978): 65-71.

34. *Voices From Black Family Albums.* Tacoma: All My Somedays, 1982. 55 p. ill. ports. *Wa*

35. *The Western Journal of Black Studies.* Pullman: Washington State University Press. March, 1977- Volume 1, Number 1- . *Wa, WaPS, WaU*

36. Wheat, Ellen Harkins. *Jacob Lawrence, American Painter.* With a contribution by Patricia Hills. Seattle: Seattle Art Museum, 1986. 235 p. ill. col. Bibliography: p. 225-231. Wa, *WaOE, WaS, WaSp*

African American, Recent Arrivals

General newspaper articles are the only source of information on recently arrived Africans and only on Ethiopians. Ethiopians are also included in the multi-ethnic source *A Cultural Guide: Our Changing Ethnic Community.*

1. Langie, Carolene. "Ethiopians, Grateful to Seattle, Appeal Again." *Seattle Times* (16 February 1988): B3.

2. Powers, Dorothy. "All of Us: Ethiopians Add a New Culture to Spokane." *Spokesman-Review.* Community News (25 April 1985): 1,3.

Middle Eastern

The only format for publications on Middle Eastern communities in Washington is general newpaper feature articles. An overview of the communities can be found in the multi-ethnic source, *Contact*, which also lists organizations.

1. Howell, Erle. "America to Them Signifies Freedom." *Seattle Times* (8 September 1960): 2.

2. Reddin, John J. "Faces of the City: Lebanese News Began With Shoes and the Tabits." *Seattle Times* (31 October 1965): 27.

3. Saba, Behrouz. "For Most of Us, Iran Means Turmoil, Pain. But For Iranians in Exile, It Is the Home and Family They May Never See Again." *Seattle Times* (11 November 1981): C1.

4. Tarzan, Deloris. "Yearning for Home; Iranians in Seattle Carry the Burdens of Homesickness, Worry and America's Anger." *Seattle Times* (11 November 1981): C1.

5. Wolcott, John. "Muslims in the Northwest." *The Progress* (16 January 1986): 12-13.

Asian/Pacific American, General

General sources covering all Asian/Pacific Americans are included in this section, with separate sections on specific communities to follow. The bibliography, *Asians in the Northwest,* is an important research source as is the demographic profile in the two issues of *Countdown*. Contemporary issues are reported in *Ten Years Later*. Washington State is included in Knoll's *Becoming American*. The Burkes' history and Chin and Bacho's article document Seattle's Asian/Pacific American communities. The *International Examiner*, which just celebrated fifteen years of publication, is the journal of Seattle/King County's Asian communities, but Sumida's article covers eastern Washington as well.

The Asian/Pacific American communities have a rich heritage of cultural expression in all of the arts. This heritage is beautifully presented in *Turning Shadows Into Light*. The recently published "Blue Funnel Line" issue of *Seattle Review* and the earlier anthology of poetry, *Breaking Silence*, include literary work. A very recent anthology of Asian American women writers and visual artists, *The Forbidden Stitch*, includes Washington writers and artists.

There are many more sources of information on the unique and diverse community histories of each individual Asian/Pacific American group.

Bon Odori.
Seattle, 1988
Photo by Julie Myeda

1. *Asians in the Northwest: An Annotated Bibliography.* By Joan Yoshitomi, et al. Sponsored by the University of Washington Asian American Studies Research Group and the Asian American Studies Program at the University of Washington. Seattle: Northwest Asian American Studies Research Group, 1978. 92 p. 10 leaves. *Wa, WaEC, WaOE, WaS*

2. "Blue Funnel Line." *Seattle Review.* Guest Editor, Shawn Wong. Volume 11, Number 1 (Spring/Summer 1988). Special Asian American issue including Washington authors, Peter Bacho and Stephen Sumida.

3. *Breaking Silence: An Anthology of Contemporary Asian American Poets.* 1st Edition. Edited by Joseph Bruchac. Greenfield Center, New York: Greenfield Review Press, 1983. 295 p. ill. *WaOE, WaS, WaSp*

4. Burke, Edward and Elizabeth Burke. *Seattle's Other History: Our Asian-American Heritage.* Seattle: Profanity Hill Press, 1979. 40 p. *Wa, WaS*

5. Chin, Doug, and Peter Bacho. "The International District: History of an Urban, Ethnic Neighborhood in Seattle." *International Examiner* (October 1985): 12.

6. *Countdown: A Demographic Profile of Asian and Pacific Islanders in Washington State.* Written by Roger Tang. Seattle: Washington State Commission on Asian American Affairs, 1982. 28 p. Bibliography: p. 28. *Wa, WaOE, WaU*

7. *Countdown: A Detailed Demographic Profile of Asian and Pacific Islanders in the State of Washington,* Volume 2. Compiled by Roger W. Tang. Seattle: Washington State Commission on Asian American Affairs, 1987. 49 p. tables. *WaOE, WaU*

8. *Forbidden Stitch: an Asian American Women's Anthology.* Corvallis, Oregon: Calyx Books, 1988. 271 p. ill. Also published as Volume 11 Numbers 2 and 3 of *Calyx, a Journal of Art and Literature by Women. WaOE*

9. *International Examiner,* Seattle. 1974- Volume 1- . *Wa, WaU*

10. Knoll, Tricia. *Becoming Americans: Asian Sojourners, Immigrants and Refugees in the Western United States.* Portland, Oregon: Coast to Coast Books, 1982. 356 p. Bibliography: p. 327-335. *Wa, WaOE, WaS, WaSpSF*

11. Sumida, Stephen H. "State of the Art; Discovering the Historical Legacies of Asian American Pioneers in Eastern Washington." *International Examiner* (21 May 1986): p. 6, 7.

12. *Ten Years Later: A Public Hearing on the Issues Impacting Washington State's Asian Pacific Americans in the 1980's, November 20, 1982, King County Council Chambers: Report to the Governor.* The Washington State Commission on Asian American Affairs, 1983. 141 p. *Wa, WaU*

14. *Turning Shadows Into Light: Art and Culture of the Northwest's Early Asian/Pacific Community*. Edited by Mayumi Tsutakawa and Alan Chong Lau. Art Direction and Design by Victor Kubo. Seattle: Young Pine Press, 1982. 99 p. ill., photos. *Wa, WaOE, WaS, WaSp*

Asian/Pacific American, Chinese

Art and Doug Chin have been the key chroniclers of the history of the Chinese in Washington State and Seattle. Early history is documented in Hildebrand's *Straw Hats, Sandals and Steel*, one of the Washington State American Revolution Bicentennial Commission Ethnic History Series publications. *The Annals of the Chinese Historical Society* include a number of essays on Washington State history. Feichter's M.A. thesis covers eastern Washington State history with Wilbert's article being specific to Whitman County and *The Pacific Northwesterner* article is on "Upper Columbia Chinese Placering." Wong's and Wynne's histories cover all of the Pacific Northwest. The anti-Chinese outbreaks in 1885-1886 are covered by Halseth, Hildebrand and Karlin as well as in many general Washington State histories.

The community newspaper is *The Seattle Chinese Post*. The general newspaper articles cover information on Spokane (Powers) and the Taiwanese in *The Seattle Times* (1980).

The article on James Wong Howe, noted cinematographer, in the *Yardbird Reader*, Volume 3 and Alan Chong Lau's *Songs For Jadina: Poems* document some of the cultural expression of the Chinese community. *Turning Shadows into Light*, in the general Asian Pacific American sources, includes other writers.

1. Chin, Art. *Golden Tassels: A History of the Chinese in Washington, 1857-1977*. Seattle: Art Chin, 1977. 121 p. *Wa, WaS, WaSp*

2. Chin, Doug and Art Chin. "The Legacy of Washington State's Early Chinese Pioneers." *International Examiner*. Volume 14, Number 5 (4 March 1987): 9-15.

3. _____. *Uphill: The Settlement and Diffusion of the Chinese in Seattle Washington*. Seattle: Shorey Book Store, 1973. 70 p. *Wa, WaS, WaSKC*

4. Chinese Historical Society of the Pacific Northwest. *The Annals of the . . . .* 1984. *WaS*

5. Feichter, Nancy Koehler. *The Chinese in the Inland Empire During the Nineteenth Century.* [M.A. Thesis] Pullman: Washington State University, 1958. 153 leaves. *Wa, WaPS, WaU.*

6. Halseth, James A. and Bruce A. Glasrud. "Anti-Chinese Movements in Washington, 1885-1886: A Reconsideration." In: *Northwest Mosaic: Minority Conflicts in Pacific Northwest History.* Edited by James A. Halseth and Bruce A. Glasrud. 1st Edition. Boulder, Colorado: Pruett Publishing Co., 1977. pp. 116-139. *Wa, WaOE, WaS, WaSp*

7. Hildebrand, Lorraine Barker. *Sinophobia: The Expulsion of the Chinese from Tacoma and Seattle, Washington Territory, 1885, 1886: An Annotated, Illustrated Bibliography.* Nashville: Fisk University Library, 1976. 90 leaves. ill. *WaS*

8. _____. *Straw Hats, Sandals and Steel: The Chinese in Washington State.* Tacoma: The Washington State Historical Society, 1985, 1977. 97 p. (Washington State American Revolution Bicentennial Commission Ethnic History Series) *Wa, WaOE, WaSp, WaU*

9. "James Wong Howe . . . as Told to Frank Chin." In: *Yardbird Reader, Volume 3.* Guest Editors: Shawn Wong and Frank Chin. Berkeley, California: Yardbird Publishing Inc., 1974. 294 p. *WaS*

10. Karlin, Jules Alexander. "The Anti-Chinese Outbreaks in Tacoma, 1885-1886." *Pacific Northwest Quarterly.* Volume 39 Number 2 (April 1948): 103-130.

11. Lau, Alan Chong. *Songs for Jadina: Poems.* Greenfield Center, New York: Greenfield Review Press, 1980. *WaU*

12. Powers, Dorothy. "All of Us: Chinese Respect Age and Instruct Youth." *Spokesman-Review.* Community News (29 November 1984): 1, 2.

13. "Revised Law to Allow More Immigrants from Taiwan, China." *Seattle Times* (8 January 1980): B2.

14. "Upper Columbia Chinese Placering." *Pacific Northwesterner* (Winter 1959): 6-11.

15. Wilbert, William F. "The Chinese in Whitman County, 1870-1910." *Bunchgrass Historian.* Volume 10 Number 1 (1982): 10-25.

16. Wong, Karen C. *Chinese History in the Pacific Northwest.* Seattle: Karen C. Wong, 1972. 137 p. *Wa, WaS, WaPS*

17. Wynne, Robert Edward. *Reaction to the Chinese in the Pacific Northwest and British Columbia, 1850 to 1910.* New York: Arno Press, 1978. 511 p. Bibliography: p. 500-511. (The Asian Experience in North America: Chinese and Japanese) *WaU*
    Originally a Ph.D. dissertation, University of Washington, 1964

Asian/Pacific American, Filipino

The most important publication on the Filipino community is Fred Cordova's *Filipinos: Forgotten Asian Americans, 1763-1963* which is national in scope and includes Washington State. Fred and Dorothy Cordova's work in starting the Filipino American Historical Society and Dorothy's work with the Demonstration Project for Asian Americans have contributed further to the documention of the Filipino history in the U. S. and Washington State. Other histories, predominantly pictorial, are the Filipino-American Intercommunity Council of the Pacific Northwest's . . . *Commemorative Yearbook* and the book on Rizal Park. Women's history is documented by Dorothy Cordova's essay and the article on Filipino war brides in the *International Examiner*. Oral history material is available through the Washington State Archives Oral/Aural History Program. *Alaskeros*, the brochure accompanying an exhibit of photographs by John Stamets, documents the history of the elderly cannery workers. The histories of specific locations in the state are by Nomura and Powers as well as the special edition of the *Wapato Newsletter*.

The community newsletter is *Bayanihan Tribune*. Many historical community newspapers are located in the University of Washington Library.

Turning Shadows Into Light in the general section on Asian/Pacific Americans documents Filipino musicians and the important writing of Carlos Bulosan. Bulosan's autobiography *America Is In the Heart* and his poetry are major literary works.

1. *Alaskeros: A Documentary Exhibit on Pioneer Filipino Cannery Workers.* [Exhibit Brochure]. Project Director and Photographer: John Stamets. Text by Peter Bacho. Advisors: Dorothy Cordova and Trinidad Rojo. Edited by Ron Chew. Seattle: IBU/ILWU Region 37, [1988]. 8 p. *WaOE (Vertical Files)*

2. *Bayanihan Tribune.* Seattle. October 25, 1974- Volume 1-. *WaU*

3. Bulosan, Carlos. *America Is in the Heart: A Personal History.* Introduction by Carey McWilliams. Seattle: University of Washington Press, 1973, 1943. 327 p. *Wa, WaOE, WaS*

4. Bulosan, Carlos. *If You Want To Know What We Are: a Carlos Bulosan Reader-*. Originally edited by E. San Juan Jr. Introduction by Leigh Bristol-Kagan. [Minneapolis, Minnesota]: West End Press, 1983. 80 p. *WaS*

5. "Carlos Bulosan." *Amerasia Journal*. Special Edition. Volume 6, Number 1 (May 1979).

6. Cordova, Dorothy Laigo. "Pinays-Filipinas in America." In: *Gathering Ground: New Writing and Art by Northwest Women of Color*. Edited by Jo Cochran, J. T. Stewart and Mayumi Tsutakawa. Seattle: The Seal Press, 1984. pp. 113-122. *Wa, WaOE, WaS*

7. Cordova, Fred. *Filipinos: Forgotten Asian Americans, 1763-1963: A Pictorial Essay/1763-Circa-1963*. Edited by Dorothy Laigo Cordova. Dubuque, Iowa: Kendall/Hunt , 1983. 235 p. ill., photos. *Wa, WaOE, WaS*

8. Evangelista, Susan. *Carlos Bulosan and His Poetry: A Biography and Anthology*. Seattle: University of Washington Press, 1985. 178 p. *Wa, WaOE*

9. *Filipino-American Intercommunity Council of the Pacific Northwest: 1952-1982 Commemorative Yearbook: 30 Years*. 1982. ill. *WaU*

10. "The First Filipino Marriages." *International Examiner* (November 1979): 7.

11. Nomura, Gail M. "Within the Law: The Establishment of Filipino Leasing Rights on the Yakima Indian Reservation." *Amerasia Journal*. Volume 13, Number 1 (1987): 99-117.

12. Powers, Dorothy. "All of Us: Filipinos Came, Studied and Contributed." *Spokesman-Review*. Community News (21 March 1985): 1, 2.

13. *Rizal Park, Symbol of Filipino Identity: Glimpses of "Pinoy" Life in the Pacific Northwest*. Edited by D. V. Corsilles. Seattle: Magiting Corp., 1983. 280 p. ill. *WaOE, WaU*

14. *Wapato Newsletter, Special Edition*. March 22, 1952 Sponsored by the Filipino Community of Yakima Valley on the Grand Opening of its Hall. Wapato, 1952. 89 p. *WaS, WaU*

Asian/Pacific American, Japanese

Mayumi Tstutakawa's *Kanreki: The 60th Anniversary History of the Japanese-American Society of the State of Washington, 1923-1983* is a statewide history of this particular organization. There are a number of histories of specific communities including Miyamoto's and Yanagisako's on Seattle, Powers, Wilbert and Gallacci's on Spokane, *A Pictorial Album of the History of the Japanese of the White*

River Valley and *Profile, Yakima Valley Japanese Community, 1973*. Radermaker's Ph.D. disssertation and Nishinoiri's M.A. thesis document the farming communities, and Murayama's article documents the railroad workers. Women's history is covered by Nomura and "Amerika Nodeshiko." Histories that are national in scope and include information on Washington communities are Kazuo Ito and Wilson and Hosokawa.

The internment is well documented in Daniels, Davidson and Weglyn with the issue being brought to the present in *Japanese America: Contemporary Perspectives on Internment,* and Hohri's *Repairing America.*

The contemporary times of the Spokane community are covered in Felgenhauer's article. The national Japanese American Citizens League newspaper, *Pacific Citizen*, includes articles on Washington State.

John Okada's *No No Boy* is a major novel on the post internment period. Another major literary work is Monica Sone's autobiography, *Nisei Daughter*. Other literary works are Lonny Kaneko's *Coming Home From Camp*, Momoko Iko's play, *The Gold Watch* in *Aiiieeeee!*, and James Masao Mitsui's *After the Long Train: Poems. Turning Shadows Into Light* in the general Asian American section documents early photographers, artists and includes poets.

1. "Amerika Nodeshiko: Japanese Immigrant Women in the U. S., 1900-1924." *Pacific Historical Review* (May 1980).

2. Daniels, Roger. *Concentration Camps; North American Japanese in the United States and Canada During World War II*. Malabar, Forida: R.E. Krieger, 1981. 226 p. Bibliography: p. 201-206. *Wa, WaOE, WaSp, WaU*

3. Davidson, Sue. "Aki Kato Kurose: Portrait of an Activist." *Frontiers*. Volume 7, Number. 1 (1983): 91-97.

4. Felgenhauer, Neil. "Times Change for Japanese-Americans." *Spokane Chronicle* (23 February 1973): 20.

5. Hohri, William Minoru. *Repairing America: An Account of the Movement for Japanese-American Redress*. Foreword by John Toland. Pullman: Washington State University Press, 1988, 1984. 247 p. Bibliography: p. 88-169. *Wa, WaOE, WaPs, WaS, WaU*

6. Iko, Momoko. "Act 1 of *The Gold Watch*." In: *Aiiieeeee! An Anthology of Asian American Writers*. Edited by Frank Chin, Lawson Fusao Inada, Jeffrey Paul Chin and Show Hsu Wang. Washington, D.C.: Howard University Press: 1983. c1974. 200 p. *Wa, WaOE, WaS, WaSp*

7. Ito, Kazuo. [*Hokubei Hyakunenzakura*. English.] *Issei; a History of Japanese Immigrants in North America*. Translated by Shinichiro Nakamura and Jean S. Gerard. Japanese Community Service, 1973. 1016 p. ill. *Wa, WaS*

8. *Japanese America: Contemporary Perspectives on Internment*. Edited by Karen Seriguchi and Frank Abe. Proceedings of Conferences held January-March 1980 in the State of Washington. Sponsored by the American Friends Service Committee and Combined Asian American Resources Project Inc. [1980]. 56 p. *WaS*

9. Kaneko, Lonny. *Coming Home From Camp*. = *[Kanpu Kara Uchi e Kaerse]*. Limited Edition. Waldron Island, Washington: Brooding Heron Press, 1986. 10 leaves. *Wa, WaSKC*

10. Mitsui, James Masao. *After the Long Train: Poems*. Minneapolis, Minnesota: The Bieler Press, 1986. 39 p. *WaS, WaU*

11. Miyamoto, Shotaro Frank. "An Immigrant Community in America." In: *East Across the Pacific: Historical and Sociological Studies of Japanese Immigration and Assimilation*. Edited by Hilary Conroy and T. Scott Miyakawa. Santa Barbara, California: ABC-CLIO Press, 1972. 322 p. Bibliography: p. 217-243. *Wa, WaS*

12. _____. *Social Solidarity Among the Japanese in Seattle*. Seattle: University of Washington Press, 1984. 74 p. Bibliography: p. 73-74. *Wa, WaEC, WaOE, WaSp*

13. Murayama, Yuzo. "Contractors, Collusions, and Competition: Japanese Immigrant Railroad Laborers in the Pacific Northwest, 1898-1911." *Explorations in Economic History* Volume 21, Number 3 (1984): 290-305.

14. Nishinoiri, John Isao. *Japanese Farms in Washington*. [M.A. Thesis] Seattle: University of Washington, 1926. 2 Vols. ill. maps. tables. *WaU*.

15. Nomura, Gail M. "Tsugiki, A Grafting: A History of a Japanese Pioneer Women in Washington State." In: *Women of the Pacific Northwest*. Edited by Karen J. Blair. Seattle: University of Washington Press, 1988. 259 p. *Wa, WaOE*

16. Okada, John. *No-No Boy*. Seattle: University of Washington Press, 1977, 1956. 260 p. *Wa, WaOE, WaS, WaU*

17. *Pacific Citizen*. Volume -. Japanese American Citizen League. Weekly. Continues *Nikkei Shimin*. November 1929- . *WaU*

18. *A Pictorial Album of the History of the Japanese of the White River Valley*. Edited and Photography by Koji Norikane. [Auburn, Washington]: White River Valley Chapter of the Japanese American Citizens League, 1986. 73 p. ill. Bibliography: p. 73. *WaSKC, WaU*

19. Powers, Dorothy. "All of Us: Japanese Have Enriched Spokane Culture." *Spokesman-Review*. Community News (15 November 1984): 1, 3.

20. *Profile, Yakima Valley Japanese Community, 1973*. Edited by Kara Kondo. Yakima, Washington: Yakima Valley Japanese Community, 1974. 42 p. ill., photos. *Wa*

21. Radermaker, John Adrian. *The Ecological Position of the Japanese Farmer in the State of Washington*. [Ph.D Disertation] Seattle: Univerity of Washington, 1939. 377 leaves. ports., maps. Bibliography. *WaU*.

22. Sone, Monica Itoi. *Nisei Daughter*. Introduction by Frank Miyamoto. Seattle: University of Washington Press, 1979, 1953. 238 p. *Wa, WaOE, WaS, WaSp*

23. Tsutakawa, Mayumi. *Kanreki: The 60th Anniversary History of the Japanese-American Society of the State of Washington, 1923-1983*. Designed by David Kageyama. Seattle: Japanese American Society of the State of Washington, 1983. 19 p. ill., ports. *WaU*

24. Weglyn, Michi Nishiura. *Years of Infamy: The Untold Story of America's Concentration Camps*. New York: Morrow 1976. 351 p. ill., photos. Bibliography: p. 331-341. *Wa, WaOE, WaS, WaSp*

25. Wilbert, Deborah and Ann Gallacci. *A History of the Formation of the Japanese American Community in Spokane, Washington, 1890-1941*. 1982. 128 leaves. maps. *WaPS*

26. Wilson, Robert Arden and Bill Hosokawa. *East to America: a History of the Japanese in the United States*. 1st Edition. New York: Morrow, 1980. 351p. ill. *Wa, WaOE, WaS, WaSp*

27. Yanagisako, Sylvia Junko. *Transforming the Past: Tradition and Kinship Among Japanese Americans*. Palo Alto: Stanford University Press, 1985. 287 p. *WaOE, WaS, WaSp*

Asian/Pacific American, Korean

Newspaper articles and journal articles comprise the only published documentation on the Korean community in Washington State. Mochizuki's article is on a major photographer, Johsel Namkung. Other information may be found in general Asian/Pacific American sources.

1. Bryant, Hilda. "The Northwest's New Immigrants; Samoans, Koreans and Chinese Carve Out Their Niche in American Life." *Seattle Post-Intelligencer* (13 December 1981): B1.

2. "Korean Women Pioneers of the Pacific Northwest." *Oregon Historical Quarterly*. Volume 79, Number 1 (Spring 1978): 51-60.

3. Mochizuki, Ken. "'People Have the Gift of Looking, But Not Everybody Has the Gift of Seeing.'" *International Examiner* Volume 13, Number 7 (1 Apr 1986): 6.

4. Moody, Fred. "Seattle's Koreans." *The Weekly* (12 - 18 March 1986): 33-35.

5. Powers, Dorothy. "Spokane Enriched by Koreans." *Spokesman-Review* (4 October 1987).

Asian/Pacific American, Hawaiian

All of the material cited in this section is historical. There are general newpaper articles on Hawaiian American events, but they do not give a full picture of the culture of the community. Other information may be found in general Asian/Pacific American sources.

1. Duncan, Janice K. *Minority Without a Champion; Kanakas on the Pacific Coast, 1788-1850*. Portland: Oregon Historical Society, 1972. 24 p. ill., footnotes. Bibliography. *Wa, WaS, WaU*

2. Hussey, John A. *The History of Fort Vancouver and Its Physical Structure*. [Tacoma]: Washington State Historical Society, 1975. 256 p. ill. *Wa, WaOE, WaS, WaSp*
   "Published in cooperation with the National Park Service, United States Department of the Interior."

3. Naughton, E. Momilani. *Hawaiians in the Fur Trade: Cultural Influence on the Northwest Coast, 1811-1875*. [M.A. Thesis] Bellingham: Western Washington University, 1983. 102 leaves. Bibliography: leaves 93-102. *WaU*

Asian/Pacific American, East Indian

Four sources cover the East Indian community specifically in Washington; two are historical (Das and Hallberg) and two contemporary (the *International Examiner* article and articles by Gerheim and Rhodes).

1. Das, Rajani Kanta. *Hindustani Workers on the Pacific Coast*. Berlin: W. de Gruyter and Co., 1923. 126 p. *WaPS, WaU*

2. "The Dilemma of the Asian Indian." *International Examiner*. Volume 16, Number 4 (November 1977): 9.

3. Gerheim, Earl. "Comeback: India Family Endures Trials in New World." *Spokesman-Review* (7 March 1979).

4. Hallberg, Gerald N. "Bellingham, Washington's Anti-Hindu Riot." *Journal of the West* Volume 12 (1973): 163-175.

5. Rhodes, Elizabeth. "Local Minority Preserves Cultural Ties to India; Well-Adapted to Living in the U.S., Area's Indian Residents Are Often Professionals." *Seattle Times* (24 January 1985): E1, 8.

Asian/Pacific American, Recent Arrivals

Information available on Asian/Pacific American recent arrivals is contained predominantly in newspaper articles. One book (Vuong) is national in scope, while one journal article is on the Samoans in the Seattle area (Kotchek), and a report written about the Indochinese was produced by the Washington State Commission on Asian American Affairs. Cultural expression is covered in Chinn and Tsutakawa's article in *Gathering Ground* and in the Spokane *Spokesman-Review* article. Recent arrivals are also included in the general Asian/Pacific American source *A Cultural Guide: Our Changing Ethnic Community*.

1. Bryant, Hilda. "The Northwest's New Immigrants; Samoans, Koreans and Chinese Carve Out Their Niche in American Life." *Seattle Post-Intelligencer* (13 December 1981): B1.

2. Camden, Jim. "The Odyssey of the Hmong: Refugees Beset by Culture Shock." *Spokesman-Review* (4 April 1982): D1, 5.

3. Case, Frederick. "A New Year in a New Home." *Seattle Times* (7 February 1983): D1-2.
   An article on traditions of Seattle's most recent Asian immigrants - the Laotians.

4. Chin, Sue and Mayumi Tsutakawa. "Mien and Hmong Women's Textile Work." In: *Gathering Ground: New Writing and Art by Northwest Women of Color*. Edited by Jo Cochran, J. T. Stewart and Mayumi Tsutakawa. Seattle: The Seal Press, 1984. pp. 146-150. *Wa, WaOE, WaS*

5. "Customs of Her Native Thailand Still Matter to This 'New' American." *Spokesman-Review*. Community News (16 May 1985): 1, 2.

6. Frisino, Joe. "New Start in New Land: Move from Burma 'Took Courage'." *Seattle Post-Intelligencer* (22 October 1977): A5.

7. "Indochina Refugees: A Rich Contribution." *Seattle Times* (1 November 1975): A8.

8. Jensen, Janet. "Vietnamese in Spokane Today." *Spokesman-Review*. Sunday Magazine (28 August 1977): 6-11.

9. Johnson, Julie. "Brambles to Beans - Laotians Putting Down Roots in a New Land." *Seattle Times* (12 March 1981): A1.

10. Kotchek, Lydia, and Ruth Dougherty. "Ethnic Visibility and Adaptive Strategies: Samoans in the Seattle Area." *The Journal of Ethnic Studies*. Volume 4, Number 1 (1977): 29-38.

11. Lalonde, James E. "Passage to Washington; as Cambodians' Year of the Tiger Dawns, This State's Fastest-Growing Refugee Group Struggles to Adapt to a New World." *Seattle Times* (13 April 1986): K1.

12. Moody, Fred. "The Seattle-ization of the Hmong." *The Weekly* (2-8 May 1984): 30-37.

13. Nelson, Robert T. "Asian Refugees Get Singed in Melting Pot: The Need for Housing, Jobs Creates Tensions in Tacoma." *Seattle Times* (2 November 1986): B2.

14. Powers, Dorothy. "All of Us: Afghan Families Offer Examples of Courage." *Spokesman-Review*. Community News (2 May 1985): 1, 2.

15. Rinearson, Peter. "Seattle's Chams Find Freedom But Jobs Are Scarce." *Seattle Times* (2 November 1982): B2.

16. Simon, Jim. "The Samoan Way: Preserving Old Traditions in a New Land Hasn't Come Without Cost to a Community." *Seattle Times* (28 February 1988): E1-3.

17. Tuiasosopo, P. David. "Plight of Samoan Islanders Who Have Come to Seattle." *Seattle Times* (1 December 1984): A19.

18. Vuong, Gia Thuy. *Getting to Know the Vietnamese and Their Culture*. New York: Ungar, 1976. Wa, WaOE, WaS, WaSp

19. Washington State Commission on Asian American Affairs. *A Report on a Conference of Delegates from Indochinese Associations in Washington State*. Seattle: Washington State Commission on Asian American Affairs, [1977]. 20 p. *Wa*

Hispano American

Doña Juanita Barrón and her granddaughter, Juanita. Seattle, 1984
Photo by Bob Haft
Chicano Archives,
The Evergreen State College Library

This section includes material on Chicanos, Mexican immigrants, and people from Central and South America. A separate section is given to the recent arrivals which includes more newspaper articles. My bibliography reveals more materials than I have listed here. Erasmo Gamboa is the historian of the Hispanos in Washington and the Northwest, as the author of a number of articles based on his M.A. thesis and Ph.D. dissertation research and as a native of Washington. Bruce Johansen and Roberto Maestas have published a brief history of the Latino community and a major book, *El Pueblo: The Gallegos Family's American Journey, 1503-1980*. Carlos Gil's monograph *The Many Faces of the Mexican American: An*

243

Essay Concerning Chicano Character is general in scope. Richard Slatta has also done scholarly work on the Chicanos and Latinos in the Pacific Northwest. The *Chicano and Latino Artists in the Pacific Northwest* exhibition catalog documents the history and culture of Washington Chicanos and Latinos in addition to presenting the work of visual artists. A special issue of *Metamorfosis* also documents the artists. *La Voz* is the community news journal and contains feature articles on the Chicano and Latino communities.

1. *Chicano and Latino Artists in the Pacific Northwest*. Edited by Sid White. Essays by Lauro Flores, Erasmo Gamboa, Pat Matheny-White, Sid White and Tomás Ybarra-Frausto. Olympia, Washington: The Evergreen State College, 1984. 48 p. ill., photos. Bibliography: p. 48. *WaOE, WaS, WaSpSF*
   Exhibiting Artists: Cecilia Alvaréz, Alfredo Arreguín, Arturo Artoréz, Paul Berger, Eduardo Calderón, José E. Orantes, José Reynoso, José Luís Rodriguez, Rubén Trejo.

2. Gamboa, Erasmo. "Braceros in the Pacific Northwest: Laborers in the Domestic Front, 1942-1947." *Pacific Historical Review*. Volume 2, Number 3 (August 1982).

3. _____. "Mexican Labor in the Pacific Northwest, 1943-1947, A Photographic Essay." *Pacific Northwest Quarterly*. Volume 73, Number 4 (October 1982): 175-181. Reprinted in *La Voz: The News Magazine of the Concilio for the Spanish Speaking of Seattle*, November 1983.

4. _____. "Mexican Migration Into Washington State: A History, 1940-1950." *Pacific Northwest Quarterly*. Volume 72, Number 3 (July 1981): 121-131.

5. _____. "The Other Northwesterners: The Chicanos." *Metamorfosis; Northwest Chicano Magazine of Art and Literature*. Volume 4/5, Number 2/1 (1982-1983): 8-11.

6. Gil, Carlos B. *The Many Faces of the Mexican American: An Essay Concerning Chicano Character*. Seattle: Centro de Estudios Chicanos, University of Washington, 1982. 31 p. (Working Paper Series Number 1) *WaOE, WaU*

7. Hessburg, John. "Hispanics Add Growing Latin Accent to State." *Seattle Post-Intelligencer* (19 November 1984): A1, A9. (Washington's Hispanic Imprint, part 1).

8. Johansen, Bruce E. and Roberto F. Maestas. *The Creation of Washington's Latino Community, 1935 - 1980*. Seattle: El Centro de la Raza, 1981. 12 p. *Wa, WaS, WaSp*

9. Johansen, Bruce E. and Roberto F. Maestas. *El Pueblo: The Gallegos Family's American Journey, 1503-1980.* New York: Monthly Review Press, 1983. 205 p. *Wa, WaOE, WaS*

10. Matheny-White, Patricia. *Bibliography of Chicano/Latino Art and Culture in the Pacific Northwest.* Olympia: The Evergreen State College Library, 1982. 60 p. *Wa, WaOE, WaS*

11. *Metamorfosis: Northwest Chicano Magazine of Art and Literature.* Seattle: Centro de Estudios Chicanos, University of Washington. Volume - , Number - . *WaOE, WaU*

12. Powers, Dorothy. "All of Us: Hispanics Fastest Growing Minority in Washington." *Spokesman-Review.* Community News (14 February 1985): 1, 2.

13. Slatta, Richard W. "Chicanos in the Pacific Northwest: A Demographic and Socioeconomic Portrait." *Pacific Northwest Quarterly.* Volume 70, Number 4 (1979): 155-162.

14. Slatta, Richard W. and Maxine Atkinson. "The 'Spanish Origin' Population of Oregon and Washington: A Demographic Profile, 1980." *Pacific Northwest Quarterly.* Volume 75, Number 3 (1984): 108-116.

15. *La Voz; The News Magazine of the Concilio for the Spanish Speaking.* Seattle: The Concilio. February 1979- Volume 1-. Monthly. *Wa, WaOE, WaU*

16. White, Sid and Patricia Matheny-White. "Chicano/Latino Art and Artists: A Regional Overview." *Metamorfosis; Northwest Chicano Magazine of Art and Literature.* Volume 4 Number 2 and Volume 5, Number 1 (1982/1983): 12-24. Reprinted in: Quirarte, Jacinto, *Chicano Art History; a Book of Selected Readings.* San Antonio: Research Center for the Arts and Humanities, The University of Texas at San Antonio, 1984. *WaU*

Hispano American, Recent Arrivals

1. Belanger, Herb. "Cuban Refugees: Some Went as Far as Seattle." *Seattle Times* (8 March 1980): B1.

2. "A Brighter World: Ambitious Couple From Colombia Has Found a New Life in El Norte." *Seattle Times* (29 November 1984): D1.

3. "Chileans in Seattle: Six Exiles Tell Their Painful Stories." *Seattle Times* (13 November 1984): A6.

4. "Increasing Number of El Salvadorans 'Taking Underground Railroad' to State." *Seattle Post-Intelligencer* (24 April 1983): F1.

5. Murphy, Michael. "Living in the Shadows." *Spokane Chronicle* (29 August 1983): 26, 21.

Mrs. Lippie Marks shows
daughters and grandchild
the art of sewing beautiful
fabrics.
Spokane Gypsy commu-
nity, 1972.
Courtesy of *Spokesman-
Review*

INDEX

About the Authors

Carlos B. Gil is an Associate Professor of History at the University of Washington. He came from Los Angeles to Washington in 1957 to study at Seattle University. He received his Ph.D. in history at the University of California, Los Angeles in 1975. He has spent six years in Latin America serving in the U.S. Foreign Service. Dr. Gil's areas of teaching, research and publication are in Latin American history including Mexican history.

Pat Matheny-White is a faculty librarian in the arts and humanities at The Evergreen State College. She was raised in Minnesota and came to Washington in 1970 to serve on the planning staff for The Evergreen State College Library. She has produced major bibliographies and co-authored essays in conjunction with a Chicano/ Latino Art and Culture project from 1982 to 1984, and continues to do research and teaching in multicultural studies.

Esther Hall Mumford is an independent scholar and a founding member of the Black Heritage Society of Washington State. Raised in a northern Louisiana, Ms. Mumford came to Seattle in 1961, where she continues to reside. During the 1970s she was an interviewer for the Washington State Archive Oral/Aural History Program. She has produced numerous exhibits and published two books on Washington's African American community, and is currently working on a third book.

Gail M. Nomura is the Director of the Asian/Pacific American Studies Program at Washington State University and also holds joint appointments in the Department of Comparative American Cultures and the Department of History. She was raised and educated in Hawaii, receiving her Ph. D in History at the University of Hawaii, Manoa, in 1978. Dr. Nomura has written extensively on Washington Asian/Pacific American communities and produced an exhibition on the Japanese American community in Yakima prior to World War II.

Richard D. Scheuerman is administrative assistant for Endicott-St. John Cooperative Schools in Endicott, Washington. He was born and raised in the Palouse country of eastern Washington. He is currently completing his doctoral studies in the field of Education at Gonzaga University. He has published numerous articles and a book on the Volga Germans, based in part on research in London and the Soviet Union in 1976. He also has published on other European immigrants to Washington and on Washington's Native Americans in eastern Washington.

S. E. Solberg is an independent scholar who has been associated with the Department of Asian Studies at the University of Washington in the 1970s and 1980s. He was raised in Montana and came to Seattle in the 1950s to complete his graduate studies at the University of Washington. He received his Ph. D. in comparative literature from the University of Washington in 1971. Dr. Solberg resided in Asia for six years and is an authority on contemporary Korean literature. He has published primarily on American ethnic literature, specializing in Asian American literature.

Clifford E.Trafzer is chair of the Department of American Indian Studies at San Diego State University. A Wyandot originally from Arizona, he was a member of the Washington State University Native American Studies faculty between 1977 and 1982. He received his Ph.D. in American History, with an emphasis on American Indians, from Oklahoma State University in 1973. Dr. Trafzer has done extensive research and has published widely on the Indians on the Northwest Plateau, and is presently completing books on the Yakimas and Chinooks.

Sid White is a member of the Arts and Humanities faculty and Gallery Curator at The Evergreen State College and also serves as Director of Exhibit Touring Services of Washington State. He was born in Michigan and has resided in various parts of the world. He came to Washington in 1970 from Oregon to serve as a member of the planning faculty at The Evergreen State College. He has produced a number of arts and humanities exhibits and has edited and authored articles and publications focusing on cultural diversity.